Alastair Sawday's

SPECIAL
PLACES TO STAY
IN BRITAIN

Alastair Sawday's

SPECIAL
PLACES TO STAY
IN BRITAIN

*"There is nothing which has yet been contrived
by man by which so much happiness is produced
as by a good tavern or inn"... (or B&B) .*
Dr Johnson to Lord Chesterfield

ASP
Alastair Sawday Publishing

ACKNOWLEDGEMENTS

For five long months Richard St George ploughed a lonely furrow through the vast, and sometimes hostile, B&B and hotel field. Those who hadn't heard of us were suspicious; those who had were enthusiastic. Then Simon Greenwood was plucked from London to complete the project.

For two hectic months Simon leaned on the indefatigable Nicia, our star inspector, and a growing team of enthusiasts. Sheila and Maureen held us together, invoicing, packing books and doing more than any accounts department should. Dave Kelly rescued us from a flood of paper, Ruth added intelligence to the computer; Maria's late nights got us to deadlines; Emily came to practise her writing skills... and did more. Ann Cooke-Yarborough yet again returned to edit, drive us, co-ordinate and write... with all her customary flair and with the loving support of Brendan Flanagan.

Many others made this book possible, not least the team at *Country Living* magazine: Susy Smith (Editor), Brian Whittaker (Publisher), Henrietta Holder (Features Editor), Emma Dally (Editorial Director of Book Publishing). They have been patient and supportive.

Series Editor : Alastair Sawday
Production Management : Ann Cooke-Yarborough
Project Managers : Richard St George and Simon Greenwood
Editors : Ann Cooke-Yarborough and Simon Greenwood
Sub-Editors : Nicia Carter-Johnson, Ruth Coleman, Suzanne Wolyzinska, Emily Walmsley
Administration : Sheila Clifton, Maureen Humphries, Dave Kelly
Research/Inspections : Wendy Arnold, Gail Atkinson, Angela Baker, Maria Campbell, Kaaren Demorest, Tony Gloster, Annabel Greenwood, Stewart Hamilton, Ione Harris, Catherine Heaton, Juliet Jeffrey, Teresa Levonian Cole, Sarah McKean, Auriol Marson, Eliza Meredith, Michael Millbourn, Lachie Rattray, Lindsay Rebbeck, Catherine Rees, Jane Ryder, Eleanor Salter, Caroline Walmsley, Emily Walmsley, Judy Wright
Data Processing Consultants : Verdine Bradshaw, Andy Waterer, Sam Duby
Accounts : Sheila Clifton and Maureen Humphries
Design : Springboard Design, Bristol
Cover Illustration : Celia Witchard
Photographs : Trudi Bide, Dave Clifton, Quentin Craven, Nicia Carter-Johnson
Maps : *Maps in Minutes* RH Publications, Sam Duby
Typesetting, Data Conversion & Repro : Avonset, Bath
Printing : The Bath Press, Bath
UK Distribution : Portfolio, London
USA Distribution : St. Martin's Press, Inc., 175 Fifth Avenue, NY 10010.

Many thanks are due to Bella, Eliza and the others at Alastair Sawday's Tours for their help, above all to my friend Annie Shillito. I owe much to René Atkinson, Stephen Alexander, David Mabey, Clive Litchfield and others for ideas... and to all those readers of my other guides who wrote in with their own suggestions. I hope I have left nobody out and apologise if I have.

Lastly, thank you Em, Rowan, Toby and Auriol for your support and love.
Alastair Sawday

INTRODUCTION

You know the scene: the pubs are closed, light hangs limply from the lamp-posts, illuminating the detritus of a provincial town or village, and you have nowhere to sleep.

The only hotel in town has been taken over by Forte. There is a guesthouse called Lime Villa - to which an S shoud be prefixed and which lurks behind a tight belt of young conifers. The pub has a room but it is over the bar. All that remains is the Crest Hotel... or is it a Novotel, or Stakis, or whatever... 3 miles away and on the by-pass, 'meeting the growing demand for faster access and customer-focussed corporate hospitality'?

You contemplate driving through the night to get home for breakfast. Then you remember the dog-eared copy of *Special Places to Stay in Britain* that George stuffed in the front pocket as you drove away.

Half an hour later your feet are on the fender by a blazing fire, a hot chocolate in your lap and the children snugly asleep upstairs. Your hosts rose magnificently to the occasion.*

Breakfast the next day bears no resemblance to anything you have at home: real porridge, butcher's sausages and bacon, garden tomatoes, homemade bread, and as much good coffee as your system can manage. Views over the lawn and beyond to the Malvern Hills. Silence... broken only by birds and bleating sheep.

We have found hundreds of the sort of places I describe (honestly!). Many of them are bed and breakfast homes; some are hotels and a few are pubs. They are real refuges from the homogeneity of the 1990's. Not all of them will be perfect; but I hope that the text will give you all you need to make your own choice.

* I'm not encouraging late night visits to B&B owners!

WHERE TO SLEEP?

We all know that tourism is taking over from travel. We know, too, that in this New International Order corporations take over from communities and we are consumers before we are people.

When you want to lay your head down you are faced with a depressing choice. Four major groups own about 650 hotels between them. About 4,000 of the biggest hotels in the country are owned by groups and consortia, with over a quarter of a million beds... very roughly half the British hotel total.

The Bed and Breakfast scene is almost as depressing. More and more once-individual houses are being homogenised by the Tourist Boards, eager to establish 'standards'. So you may soon travel from John O'Groats to

Land's End in a familiar cocoon of neat modern bedrooms equipped with trouser-presses, tea and coffee-making kit and UHT milk in irritating little packets.

BUT THERE IS HOPE. That is one reason why this book is being published... to celebrate the efforts by hundreds of people in B&B's and hotels to 'do their own thing'.

THE GOOD HOTEL GUIDE AND THE *WHICH?* GUIDES

As a latecomer I must salute the efforts of other editors who have for many years celebrated individuality and character in hotels and B&Bs. Prominent among them are the *Which?* book names and the superb *Good Hotel Guide* edited by Hilary Rubinstein, a book of real integrity and an inspiration to me. His views on chain hotels, the creeping accommodation monoculture and decline in standards I share wholeheartedly. For almost 20 years he has championed honest, small family-run hotels, those who discourage smoking and encourage women travellers. He has slated overcharging, tipping, pretentiousness and poor value. I hope that in a small way my own book adds another strong voice to his choir.

COUNTRY LIVING MAGAZINE

We are delighted to be working with *Country Living magazine* on this book. We share a great many values and ideas and are a natural pair, passionate about the countryside, crafts, good taste, fine buildings, gardens and the best aspects of country living. They have for many years sought out unusual and interesting places to stay all over Britain and have even published their own *Book of Escapes,* full of bright ideas. Their regular *Escapes* section still ploughs its own furrow, taking readers to the most attractive places.

So we feature many small hotels and B&B's that have been written up by *Country Living magazine.* However, any errors of judgement and inconsistencies are almost certainly ours.

OUR OTHER BOOKS.

In 1994 we first published our *Guide to French Bed and Breakfast* and have sold nearly 30,000, presumably to people who are also in quiet revolt against the corporate culture. We then published *Special Paris Hotels,* a collection that rescues some Paris hotels from the reputation of being cold, unfriendly and rotten value.

In Spain more hotels are homogenised than in most countries. So we published *Special Places to Stay in Spain,* a delightful gathering of unusual and interesting places to sleep: inns, palaces, monasteries, townhouses and simple B&Bs... some in the cities, some very remote, some very grand. They were chosen because they are all special in some way.

WRITING THIS BOOK.

Writing lively prose about over 400 people's houses or hotels is not easy. However, we have tried to tell you what the places look and FEEL like. We feel that a touch of levity is justified when we are really serious, just as brevity is fine when fulsome. I trust that we have got the balance right more often than we have got it wrong. We have tried to avoid giving you information that is available elsewhere, whether in the individual picture our symbols or in general books about Britain. We have also avoided mention of things that don't add to the 'specialness' of a place, such as TV and coffee-making kits.

ABOUT THIS BOOK.

We have a fresh approach to selecting places to stay. Our inspectors are asked to include only the houses or hotels that they LIKE. So the grandest hotels are rejected if the owners are pretentious or frosty. If the house is in poor taste or dirty it is excluded, although 'marginal' places may be accepted if the owners, the village or the countryside are special. So, we have no rigid set of rules; we give you the places WE like and hope you make the right choice for YOU.

What we look for are: character, interesting and lovely buildings, entertaining and nice people, freedom from noise and ugliness... and something special. We try to exclude hotels owned by large companies but one or two have slipped through the net.

The text... and how to read it. We say as much as we can with the symbols but you should read the text carefully for the hidden meaning. You should be able to tell why we like the place, whether it be grand or humble, luxurious or simple, exquisite or just endearingly eccentric. As we only have places we like you will not find much criticism in the text. So don't be surprised by the taste (there are one or two oddly decorated places) if we have described it!

Paying to be included. Researching and publishing a full-colour guide is expensive, so every owner has paid to be in the book, hotel owners more than B&B owners. We make no apology for this and are utterly clear that we do NOT include houses just because they can pay. That would be counter-productive and there is simply no need for it. We have excluded many places, however keen they were to pay.

Inspections. Nearly every place has been fully inspected. If not we tell you, by wrapping a circle around the number at the bottom of the page. If we didn't inspect it was either because we couldn't get there (to the isles of North Uist, Sark and Shetland, for example) or because the entry was last minute. But in every case the hotel or house has been recommended to us. We then follow up with long phone calls and brow-furrowed study of the brochures and photographs, menus and other papers.

VAT. Prices generally include VAT. However, I was surprised by a VAT bill recently when at a B&B. It would be wise to check when you are booking/arriving.

HOW TO USE B&Bs

It is always wise to book ahead and sensible to get there before supper time.
One of the perks for B&B owners is that they can shut down to deal with, say, a family crisis. So you should not be upset if your prospective hosts are away or unavailable when you ring to book.

Children. Attitudes vary wildly and we have tried to let you know. It is best to phone ahead and ask if your liberally-educated 6-year-old twins will be welcome. Some places will never let them over the threshold, others will sweep them in, others might have them if... Please find out what the 'if' is if it is not in the text.

INTRODUCTION

Tipping. I join the ranks of the guide editors who have condemned tipping over the years. Its logic is escapable; why do we not tip school teachers, vicars and shop assistants? It is a device either to hide the real cost of dining out and sleeping or to exploit staff. So, screw up your courage and use me as an excuse for not tipping if you wish (I refer to hotels; there is no tipping in B&B's).

Smoking. This is a minefield, so our symbol just tells you that a house is totally non-smoking. Otherwise ask you hosts about it; they may allow it in the bedrooms or the woodshed. However, common courtesy tells us not to smoke in bedrooms that may be occupied by non-smokers after we leave.

Animals. The symbol tells you if your dog will be welcome IN the house. Some owners only welcome dogs which sleep in the car but will allow them in some rooms in the house during the day. Check ahead.

TIPS FOR RAIL USERS.

I hope that our maps help you to get about by train. Many of the hosts will arrange bicycles for you and pick you up from the train station, sometimes charging for it and sometimes not. You might also ask your hosts how to get there by bus.

LASTLY... A WORD ABOUT ORGANIC FOOD.

I have made it easy for organic farmers and producers to join us and have used the organic symbol for garden produce where there is a lot of it. But there are many other houses and hotels in this book that serve their own-grown organic food, a welcome trend. I am a committed supporter of the organic movement and will welcome advice on how to promote it through the next edition of this book.

THE WRITING.

If there is any of the writing that you find upsetting (owners), inaccurate or plain irritating (readers) remember, please, that it could be worse.

"He writes the worst English that I have ever encountered. It reminds me of a string of wet sponges; of tattered washing on the line; it reminds me of stale bean soup, of college yells, of dogs barking idiotically through endless nights. It is so bad that a sort of grandeur creeps into it. It drags itself out of the dark abysm of pish, and crawls insanely up to the topmost pinnacle of posh. It is rumble and bumble. It is flap and doodle. It is balder and dash." H.L.Menken.

A WORD FROM *Country Living*

As Britain's best-selling country lifestyle magazine, *Country Living* has long championed small rural businesses. Many bed and breakfasts, whether small cottages or manor houses, are just that: family-run enterprises, which bring valuable income to country communities. In addition, they give those that do not live in rural regions the opportunity to visit and be treated to the very best of British countryside - pastures, hedgerows and woodlands, cliffs, beaches and river valleys - and man's mark upon it, in ancient hill fort or market town. It is this living landscape that we at *Country Living* celebrate every month in our pages.

When, early last summer, Alastair Sawday came to visit us at *Country Living* and presented us with his highly successful French and Spanish guide books, we quickly recognised that his philosophy on what makes a special place to stay was similar to ours. For the eleven years since *Country Living* magazine began, we have endeavoured to judge standards of British bed and breakfasts, hotels, pubs and country cottages without the straitjacket of criteria adopted by others. We have awarded marks for rooms with stunning views not full-length mirrors, for modest posies of fresh garden flowers not colour televisions, for breakfasts featuring home-made, local or organic produce, not for whether you can order it from your bedroom.

So, too, has Alastair Sawday, and we therefore decided to support his new book: *Special Places to Stay in Britain*. Although the following 424 suggestions for bed and breakfasts, small hotels, pubs and inns and country cottages across the country have all been chosen by his own inspection team, we have every confidence in recommending them to you and in the quality and honesty of the information given. When you read each entry, you will know exactly what to expect to find, if, as we hope, you decide to visit.

Susy Smith
Editor
Country Living magazine

Explanations of symbols

 Working farm

 Children are positively welcomed but cots are not necessarily available. The text gives restrictions where relevant.

 You can garage your own bike here or hire one locally.

 Good country walks in the area/Walkers welcome.

 Pets welcome to sleep in the house as long as they are properly trained. There may be a supplement to pay.

 Vegetarians catered for with advance warning.

 Some, but not necessarily all, ingredients are organically grown.

 Indicates basic ground-floor access but not full facilities for handicapped guests.

 Swimming is possible on the premises or nearby, in a pool, a lake, a river or the sea.

 No smoking anywhere in the house.

 Inspected properties

 Uninspected properties

DISCLAIMER

We make no claims to pure objectivity in judging our special places to stay. They are here because we *like* them. Our opinions and tastes are ours alone and this book is a statement of them; we cross our fingers and hope that you will share them.

We have done our utmost to get our facts right but apologise unreservedly for any mistakes that may have crept in. Sometimes, too, prices shift, usually upwards, and 'things' change. We would be grateful to be told of any errors or changes, however small.

Alastair Sawday has asserted his right to be identified as the author of this work.

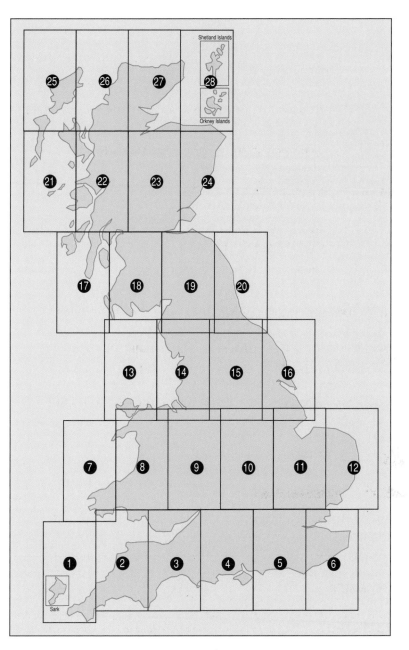

General Map

CONTENTS

CONTENTS

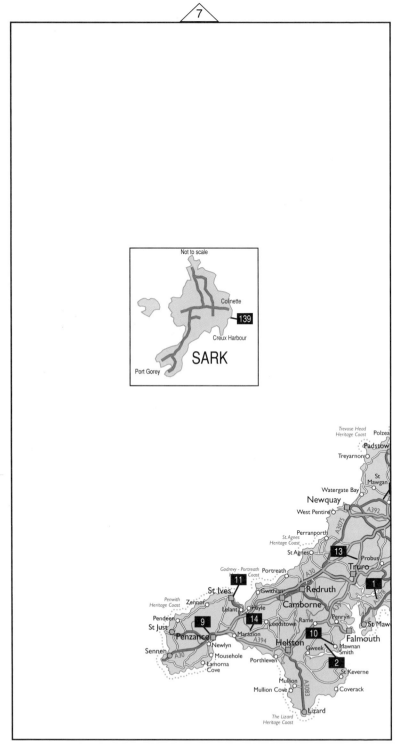

Not to scale

Colinette

139

Creux Harbour

SARK

Port Gorey

Trevose Head
Heritage Coast
Polzea
Padstow
Treyarnon
St
Mawgan
Watergate Bay
Newquay
A392
West Pentire
A3075
Perranporth
St.Agnes
Heritage Coast
St Agnes
13
Probus
Truro
Godrevy - Portreath
Coast
Portreath
11
St Ives
Gwithian
Redruth
1
Penwith
Heritage Coast
Zennor
Lelant
Hayle
Camborne
A30
Pendeen
9
Leedstown
Rame
Penryn
St Maw
St Just
14
Penzance
Marazion
A394
Helston
10
Falmouth
Newlyn
Gweek
Mawnan
Smith
Sennen
A30
Mousehole
Porthleven
2
Lamorna
Cove
St Keverne
Mullion
A3083
Coverack
Mullion Cove
Lizard
The Lizard
Heritage Coast

Map scale: 14.3 miles to 1 inch

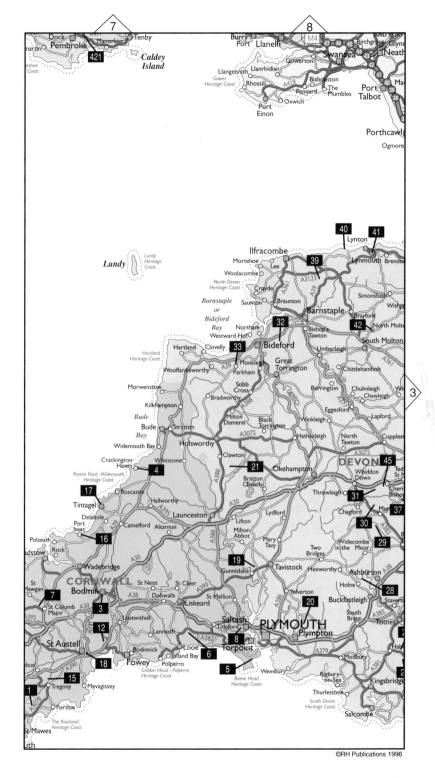

2

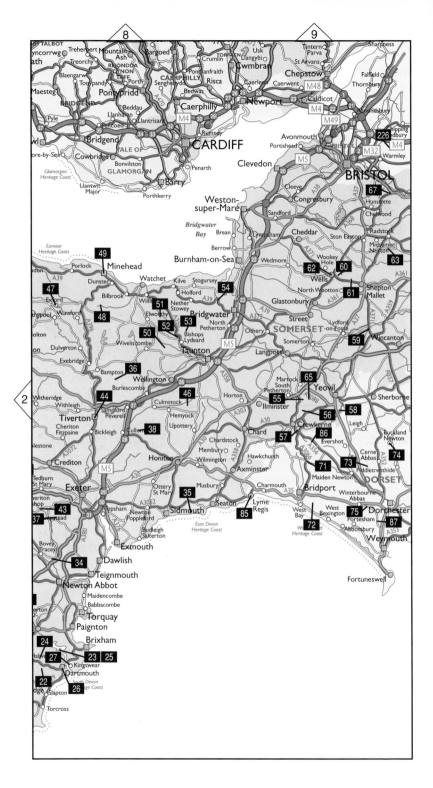

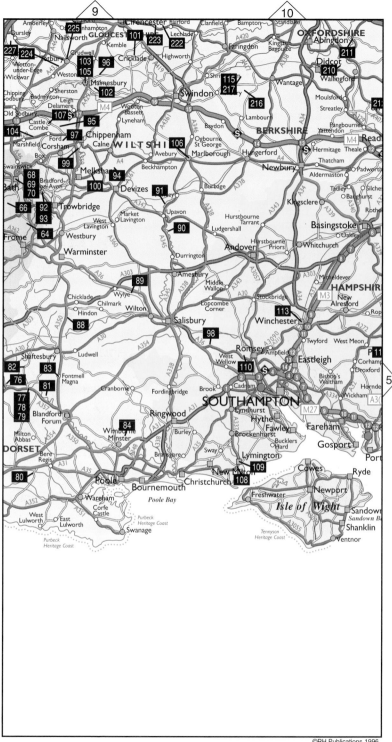

4

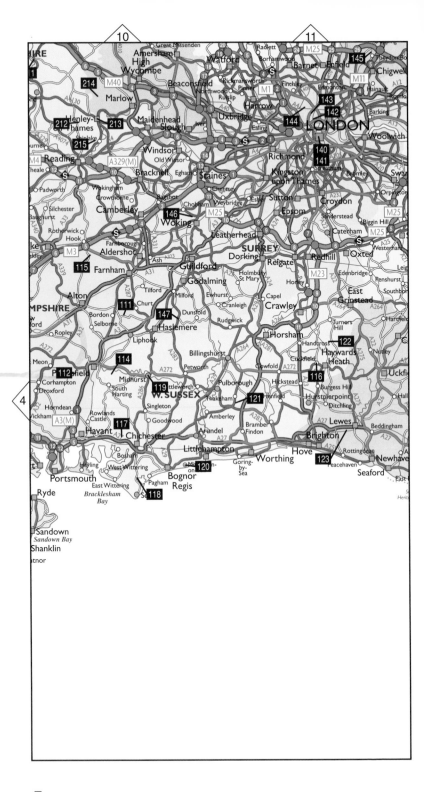

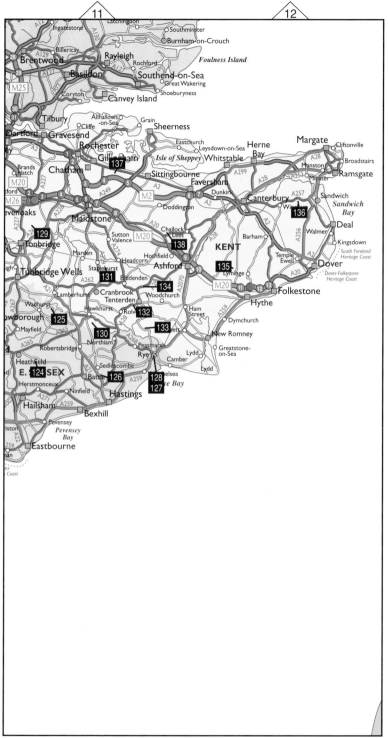

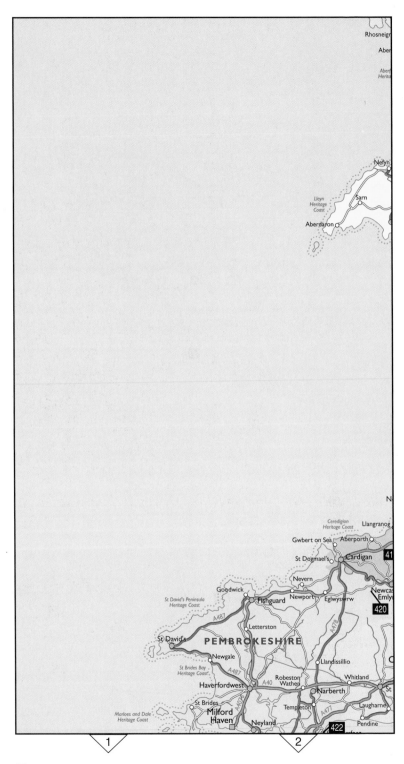

Rhosneigr

Aber

Aber
Herit

Nefyn

*Lleyn
Heritage
Coast*

Sarn

Aberdaron

N

*Ceredigion
Heritage Coast* Llangranog

Gwbert on Sea Aberporth

St Dogmael's Cardigan **41**

Nevern

Newca
Emly

Goodwick

*St David's Peninsula
Heritage Coast* Fishguard Newport Eglwyswrw

420

A487

Letterston

St David's **PEMBROKESHIRE**

Newgale

*St Brides Bay
Heritage Coast* A487 Llandissilio

Robeston
Wathen Whitland

Haverfordwest A40

St Brides Narberth St

Templeton Laugharne

*Marloes and Dale
Heritage Coast* Milford
Haven Neyland **422** Pendine

1 2

7

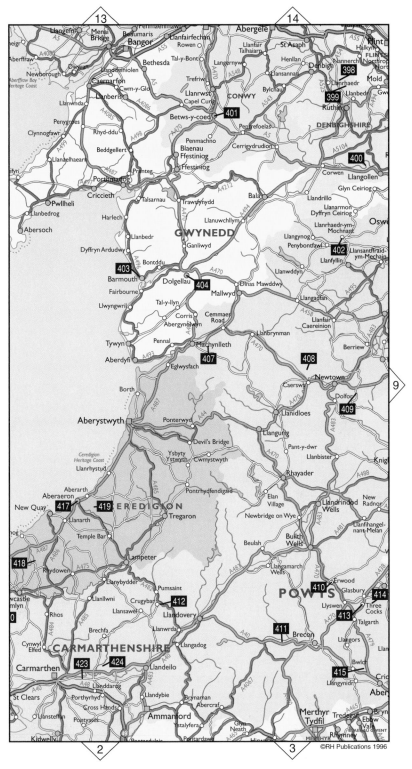

8

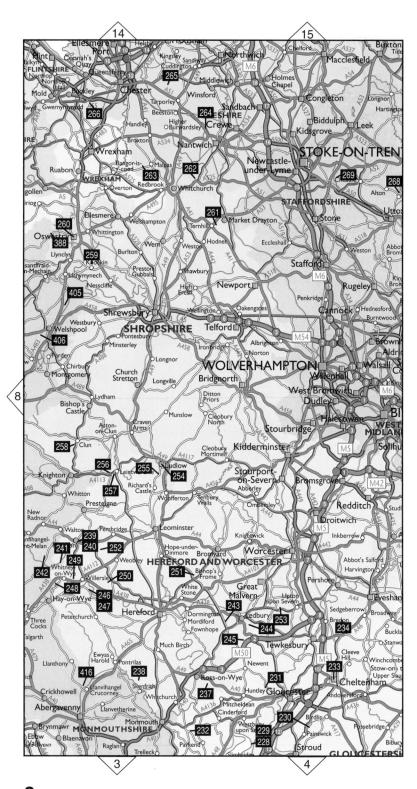

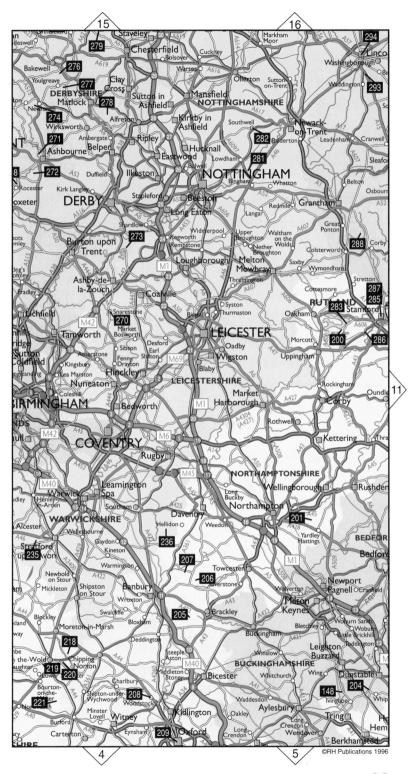

©RH Publications 1996

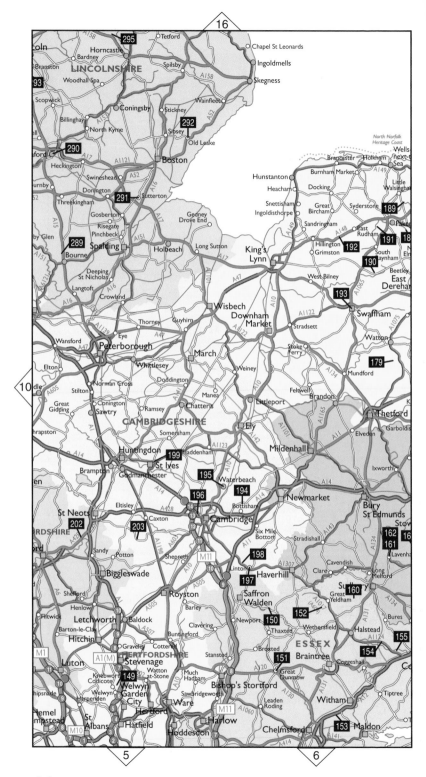

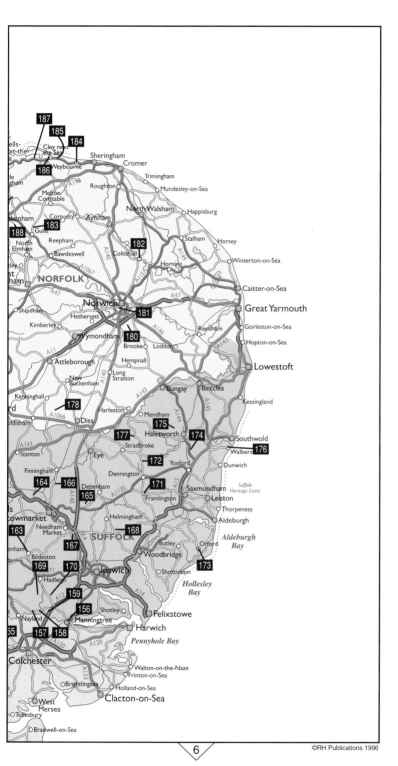

©RH Publications 1996

12

13 .

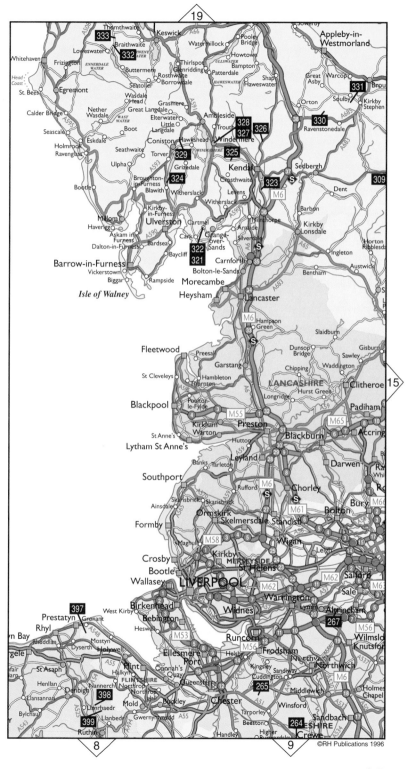

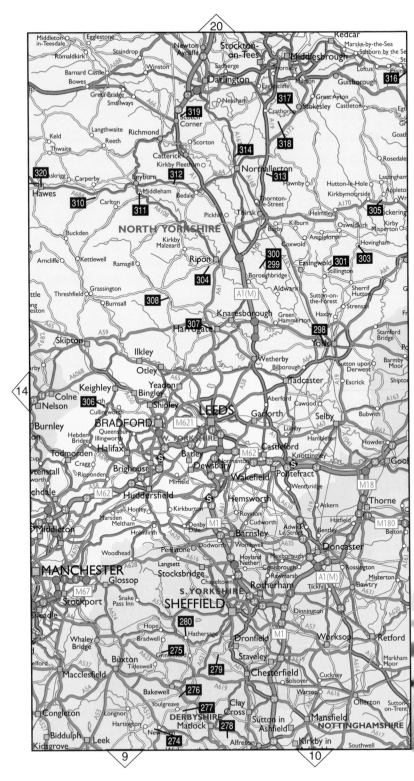

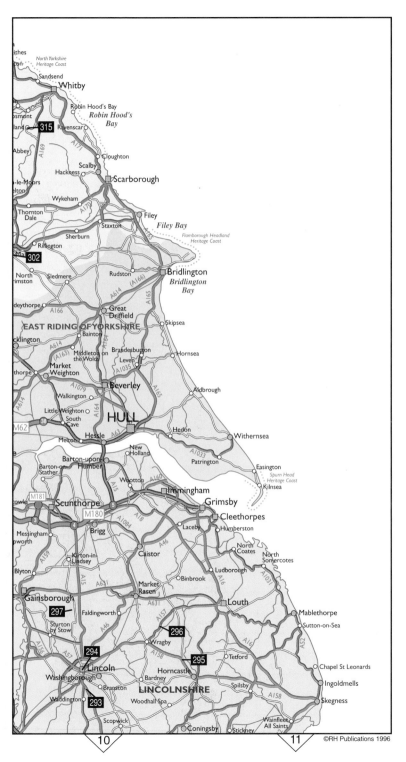

©RH Publications 1996

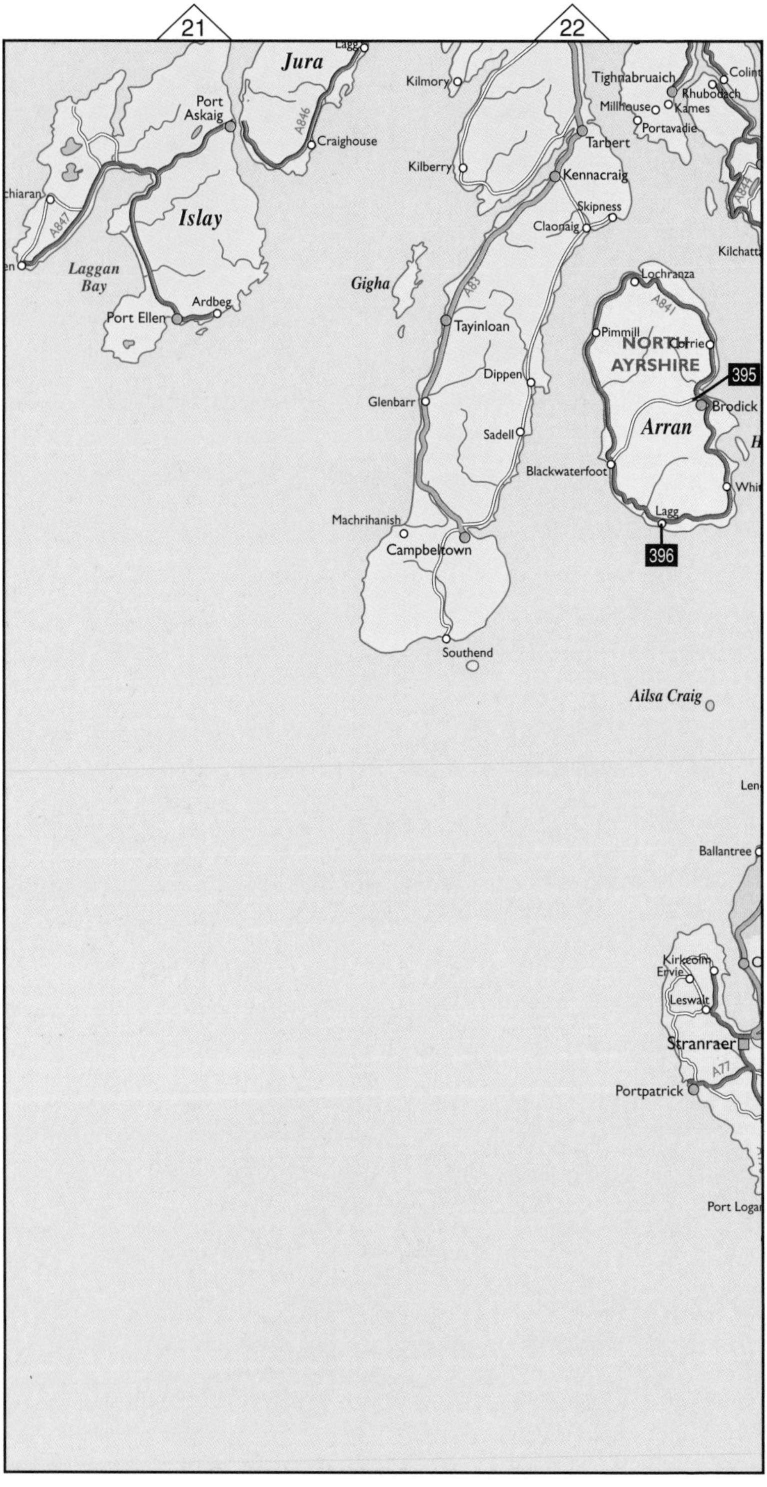
21
22
Jura
Lagg
Kilmory
Port Askaig
A846
Craighouse
Kilberry
Tighnabruaich
Millhouse
Kames
Rhubodach
Colint
Portavadie
Tarbert
Kennacraig
chiaran
A847
Islay
Skipness
Claonaig
en
Laggan Bay
Gigha
Lochranza
A841
Ardbeg
Port Ellen
A83
Tayinloan
Pimmill
NORTH AYRSHIRE
Corrie
Dippen
395
Glenbarr
Brodick
Arran
Sadell
Blackwaterfoot
Whit
Lagg
396
Machrihanish
Campbeltown
Southend
Ailsa Craig
Kilchatt
Len
Ballantree
Kirkcolm
Ervie
Leswalt
Stranraer
A77
Portpatrick
Port Logan

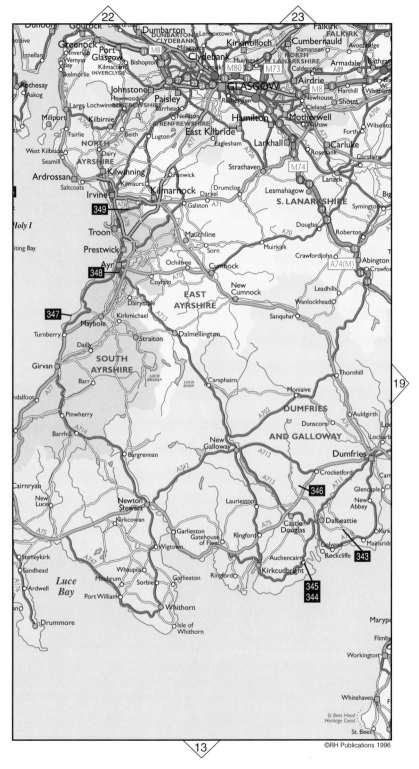

©RH Publications 1996

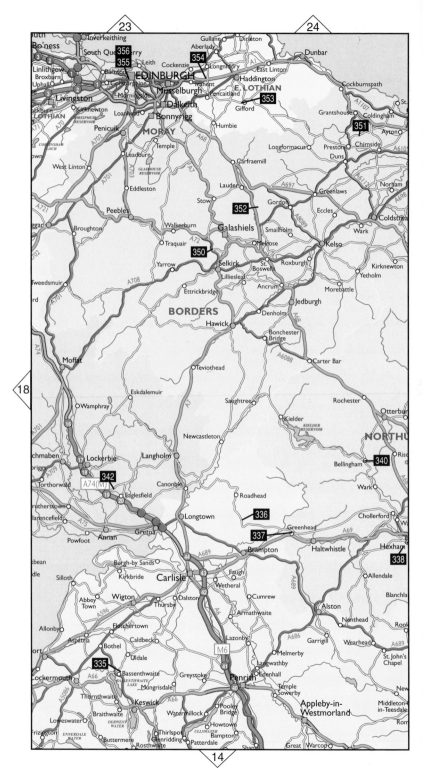

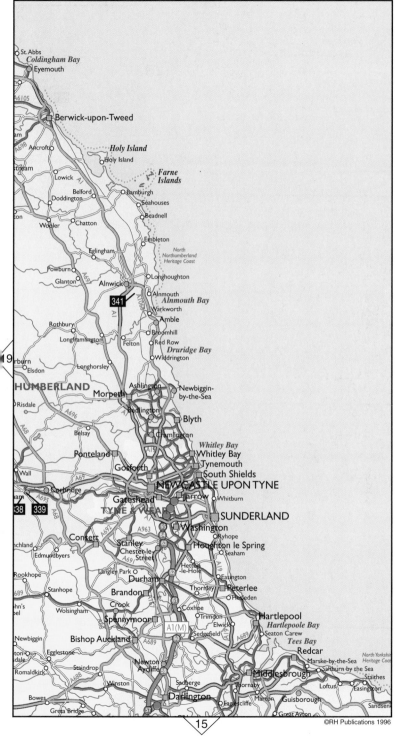

St.Abbs
Coldingham Bay
Eyemouth
A6105
am
Berwick-upon-Tweed
A698
Ancroft
A1
tream
Holy Island
Holy Island
Lowick
A1
Farne Islands
Belford
Doddington
Bamburgh
ton
Seahouses
Wooler
Chatton
Beadnell
Embleton
Eglingham
North Northumberland Heritage Coast
Powburn
A691
Longhoughton
Glanton
Alnwick
341
Alnmouth
Alnmouth Bay
Warkworth
Rothbury
A1
Amble
Longframlington
Felton
Broomhill
Red Row
Druridge Bay
Widdrington
rburn
Elsdon
Longhorsley
9
Risdale
HUMBERLAND
Ashington
Morpeth
Newbiggin-by-the-Sea
A696
Bedlington
Belsay
Blyth
Cramlington
Ponteland
A19
Whitley Bay
Whitley Bay
Gosforth
Tynemouth
Wall
A69
South Shields
Corbridge
A695
NEWCASTLE UPON TYNE
am
338 **339**
A68
Gateshead
Jarrow
Whitburn
TYNE & WEAR
SUNDERLAND
Consett
A691
Washington
A963
65
Stanley
Chester-le-Street
63
Houghton le Spring
Ryhope
Seaham
uchland
A69
Langley Park
Hetton-le-Hole
62
A19
Easington
Edmundbyers
Durham
Rookhope
Stanhope
Brandon
Thornley
Peterlee
Hesleden
689
hn's
el
Wolsingham
Crook
Coxhoe
Trimdon
Hartlepool
Spennymoor
Hartlepoole Bay
Newbiggin
Bishop Auckland
A1(M)
Elwick
Seaton Carew
60
Sedgefield
A689
Tees Bay
ton-
dale
Egglestone
A689
Redcar
Staindrop
Newton Aycliffe
59
North Yorkshire Heritage Coast
Romaldkirk
A688
Marske-by-the-Sea
Saltburn by the Sea
Winston
Sadberge
Middlesbrough
Staithes
Bowes
Thornaby
Loftus
Easington
Darlington
Marton
Guisborough
Greta Bridge
57
Eaglescliffe
Great Ayton
Sandsen

©RH Publications 1996

20

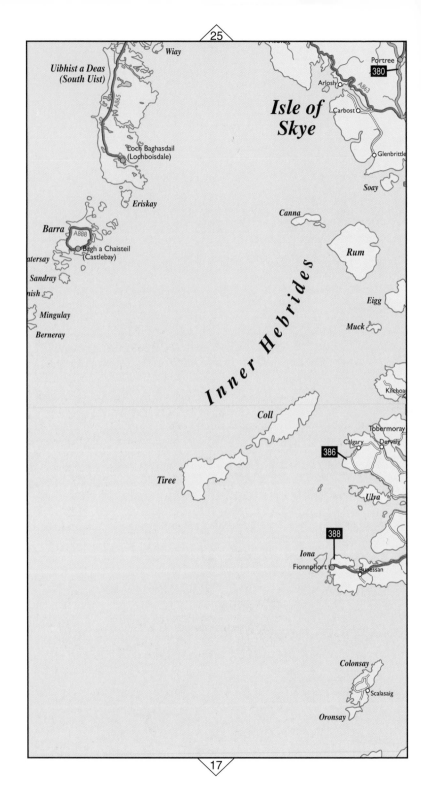

Wiay

Uibhist a Deas
(South Uist)

*Isle of
Skye*

Portree
380

Arlosh

Carbost

Loch Baghasdail
(Lochboisdale)

Glenbrittle

Soay

Eriskay

Canna

Barra
A888

Bagh a Chaisteil
(Castlebay)

Rum

atersay

Sandray

nish

Eigg

Mingulay

Muck

Berneray

I n n e r   H e b r i d e s

Kilchoa

Coll

Tobermoray

Calgary   Dervaig

386

Tiree

Ulya

388

Iona
Fionnphort   Bunessan

Colonsay

Scalasaig

Oronsay

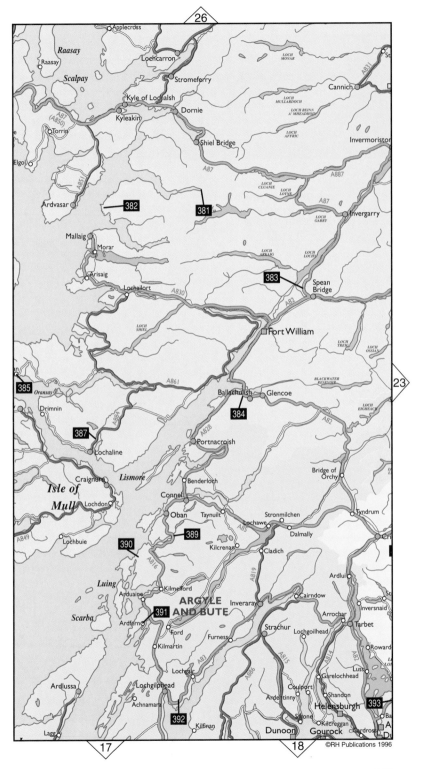

Raasay

Applecross

Raasay

Scalpay

Lochcarron

Stromeferry

LOCH
MONAR

Cannich

D

St

Kyle of Lochalsh

A87
(A850)

Dornie

Kyleakin

LOCH
MULLARDOCH

LOCH BEINN
A' MHEADHOIN

Torrin

Shiel Bridge

LOCH
AFFRIC

Invermoriston

Elgol

A851

A87

A887

382

381

LOCH
CLUANIE

LOCH
LOYNE

A87

Ardvasar

LOCH
GARRY

Invergarry

Mallaig

Morar

LOCH
ARKAIG

LOCH
LOCHY

Arisaig

Lochailort

A830

383

Spean
Bridge

A82

LOCH
SHIEL

Fort William

LOCH
TREIG

LOCH
OSSIAN

A861

23

385

Oransay

Drimnin

BLACKWATER
RESEVOIR

Ballachulish

Glencoe

A82

LOCH
EIGHEACH

A884

A828

384

387

Lochaline

Portnacroish

Craignure

Lismore

Benderloch

Bridge of
Orchy

Isle of
Mull

Lochdon

Connel

A849

Lochbuie

Oban

Taynuilt

Stronmilchen

Tyndrum

A85

Lochawe

Dalmally

Cri

389

Kilcrenan

Cladich

390

A816

Luing

Kilmelford

A819

Ardlui

St

Arduaine

Cairndow

Inversnaid

Scarba

ARGYLE
AND BUTE

391

Inveraray

Arrochar

Tarbet

Ardfern

Ford

Furness

Strachur

Lochgoilhead

Roward

A814

Kilmartin

A83

A815

Garelochhead

Luss

LO

Ardlussa

Lochgair

A886

Coulport

Shandon

393

Lochgilphead

Ardentinny

Helensburgh

Ba

Achnamara

392

Kilfinan

Sutone

Kilcreggan

A

Lagg

Dunoon

Gourock

Cardross

D

©RH Publications 1996

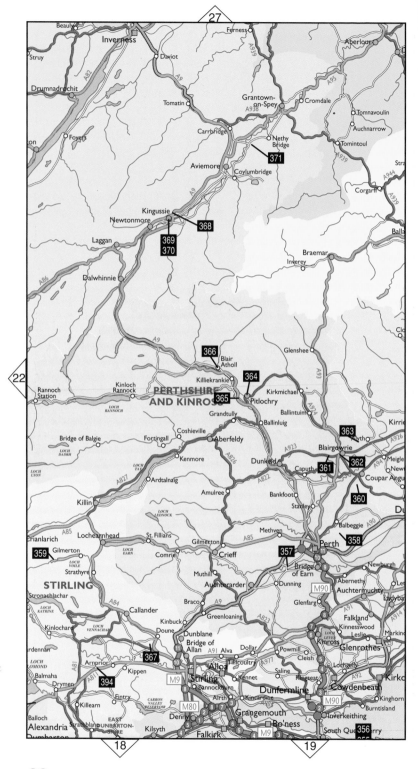

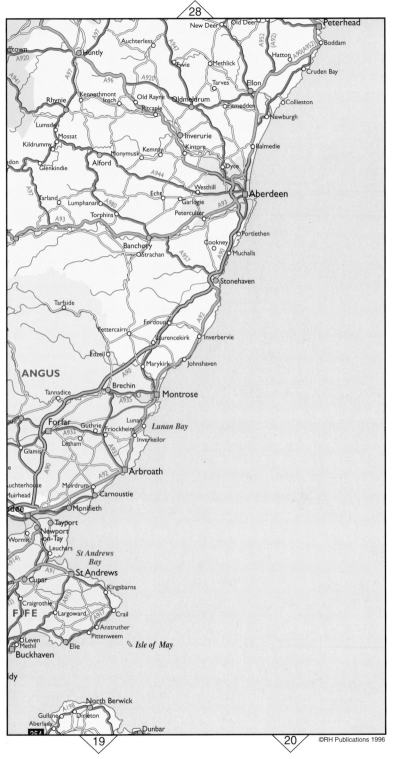

Peterhead
New Deer Old Deer
Boddam
fftown   Auchterless   Hatton   Cruden Bay
Huntly   Fyvie   Methlick
A920   Tarves   Ellon   Collieston
A96   A920   Old Rayne   Pitmedden   Newburgh
Rhynie   Kennethmont   Oldmeldrum
Insch   Pitcaple
Lumsden   Balmedie
Mossat   Kemnay   Inverurie
Kildrummy   Monymusk   Kintore
Glenkindie   Alford   Dyce
A944
Tarland   Lumphanan   Echt   Westhill   Aberdeen
A980   Garlogie
Torphins   Peterculter
A93   Portlethen
Banchory   Cookney
Strachan   Muchalls
A957   A90
Stonehaven
Tarfside
Fordoun
Fettercairn   A92
Laurencekirk   Inverbervie
Edzell
ANGUS   Marykirk   Johnshaven
A90
Tannadice   Brechin
Forfar   Guthrie   Lunan
A935   Montrose
A932   Friockheim
Letham   Inverkeilor   Lunan Bay
Glamis
A92   Arbroath
uchterhouse   Muirdrum
Muirhead   Carnoustie
dee   Monifieth
Tayport
Wormit   Newport-on-Tay
Leuchars   St Andrews
914)   A91   Bay
Cupar   St Andrews
A915   Kingsbarns
Craigrothie
FIFE   Largoward   Crail
A917
Anstruther
Leven   Pittenweem
Methil   Elie   Isle of May
Buckhaven
dy
North Berwick
A198
Gullane   Dirleton
Aberlady   Dunbar

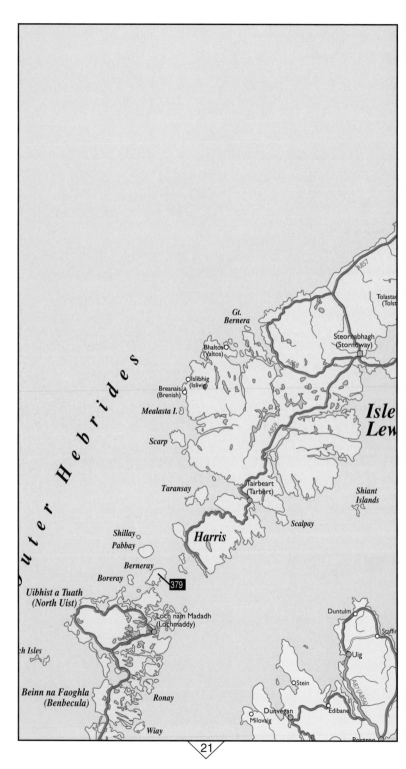

25

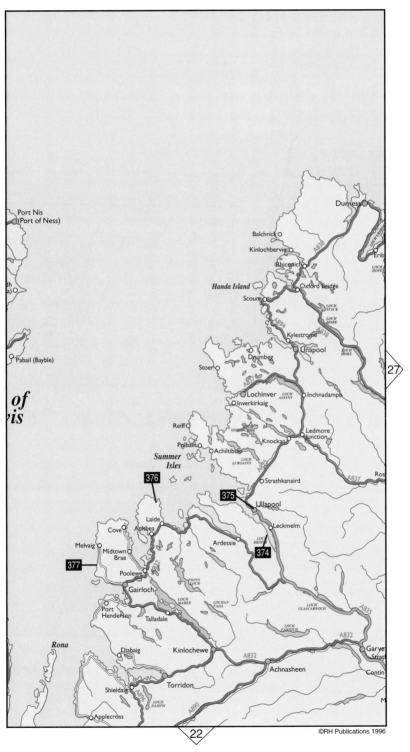

Port Nis
(Port of Ness)

Pabail (Bayble)

of
vis

Rona

Durness

Balchrick

Kinlochbervie

Rhiconich

Handa Island

Oxford Bridge

Scourie

Kylestrome

Unapool

Drumbeg

Stoer

Lochinver

Inverkirkaig

Inchnadamph

Reiff

Polbain

Achiltibure

Knockan

Ledmore
Junction

Summer
Isles

376

Strathkanaird

375

Ullapool

Laide

Cove

Aultbea

Leckmelm

Melvaig

Midtown
Brae

Ardessie

374

377

Poolewe

Gairloch

Port
Henderson

Talladale

Diabaig

Kinlochewe

Garve

Achnasheen

Shieldaig

Torridon

Applecross

Erib

27

22

©RH Publications 1996

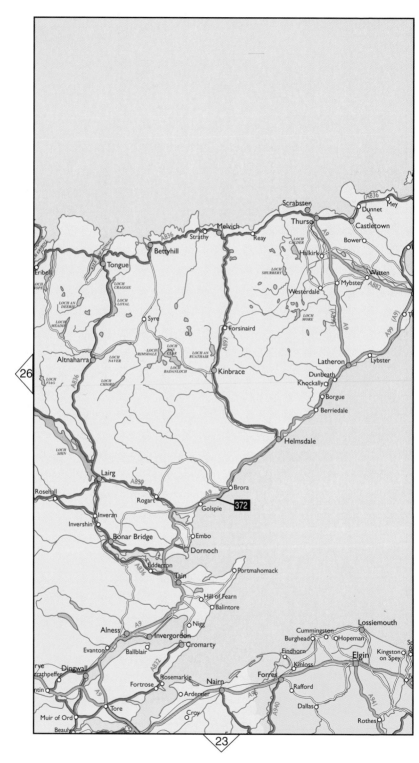

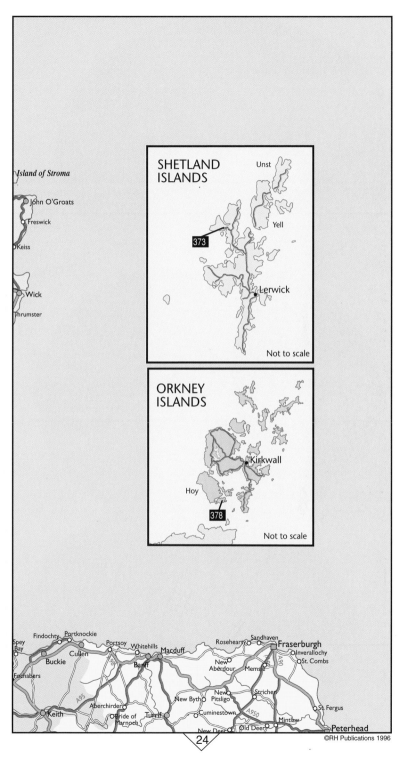

Island of Stroma

John O'Groats

Freswick

Keiss

Wick

Thrumster

SHETLAND ISLANDS

Unst

Yell

373

Lerwick

Not to scale

ORKNEY ISLANDS

Kirkwall

Hoy

378

Not to scale

Findochty Portknockie
Spey Bay
Cullen
Portsoy Whitehills Macduff
Roseherty Sandhaven
Fraserburgh
Buckie
Banff
New Aberdour Memsie
Inverallochy
St. Combs
Fochabers
New Byth New Pitsligo Strichen
St. Fergus
Keith
Aberchirder
Bride of Marnoch Turriff
Cuminestown
Mintlaw
New Deer Old Deer
Peterhead

24

©RH Publications 1996

28

The South West

A lovely Queen Anne manor house with the elegance and warmth of old-time country-house hospitality. Afternoon tea if you arrive in time. No packed lunches but great hampers; no simple suppers but candlelit dinner parties in the panelled dining room then coffee in the drawing room under the eye of Admiral Sir Arthur Kemp, reputed to haunt Crugsillick. He was responsible for the magnificent plaster ceiling moulded by his French Napoleonic prisoners. The bedrooms are stylish and comfortable. Coastal path ¾ mile away.

Rooms: 1 twin with en suite shower, 1 twin/double en suite bathroom, 1 double with private bathroom.

Price: £40-£44 p.p. doubles/twins; £60 single.

Breakfast: Included – full English/continental.

Meals: Dinner £20, by arrangement. Lunch hamper on request.

Closed: New Year.

Take A390 from St Austell, left on B2387 to Tregony. A3078 through Ruan High Lanes. Sharp first left towards Veryan, right after180 metres.

Map Ref No: 2

Oliver & Rosemary Barstow
Crugsillick Manor
Ruan High Lanes
Nr. St. Mawes, Truro
Cornwall TR2 5LJ
Tel: 01872-501214
Fax: 01872-501214 + 01872-501228

The mediæval farmhouse was 'modernised' in the 16th century. The U-shaped granite house is entered through a picturesque courtyard and is surrounded by walled gardens. Our inspector loved it: higgledy-piggledy lived-in feel, warm woods, warm kitchen, lots of antiques, dark oak, open fireplace, granite-walled candle-lit dining room... all in perfect taste. The Fords are easy hosts; he is keen on sailing and she on cooking (homemade bread, preserves and garden produce).

Rooms: 1 twin with private bathroom, 2 doubles en suite.

Price: £19-£25 p.p.

Breakfast: Included – full English/continental.

Meals: Dinner £17 p.p.

Closed: Christmas.

A working 200-acre dairy farm with all the smells and atmosphere... even parading ducks; an historic farmstead, only 300 yards from the National Trust's Lanhydrock House. Pat is easy-going and enthusiastic about travelling, a keen walker and cyclist. The house is as genuine as she is: dark pine panelling throughout, wooden floors, very much a farming home. Good honest food, too: homemade honey, free-range eggs. Pat can organise a complete holiday for you.

Rooms: 2 twin en suite, one 4-poster with en suite shower & separate wc.

Price: £21 p.p.

Breakfast: Included – full English/continental.

Meals: Not available.

Closed: Christmas – New Year.

From Truro, take Falmouth Rd (A39). At Hillhead roundabout follow sign to Constantine. 0.5 miles after High Cross Garage turn left to Port Navas. House is opposite the granite mushrooms.

Map Ref No: 1

Mrs Judy Ford
Treviades Barton
High Cross
Constantine
Cornwall TR11 5RG
Tel: 01326-340524
Fax: 01326-340524

A38/A30 to Bodmin town centre. At mini-roundabout turn left onto B3269 towards Lostwithiel for 2.5 miles to 2nd mini-roundabout. Right at sign to Lanivet. Farm is 100m down lane on right.

Map Ref No: 2

Pat Smith
Treffry Farmhouse
Lanhydrock
Bodmin
Cornwall PL30 5AF
Tel: 01208-74405
Fax: 01208-74405

A Domesday-listed manor house held by the half-brother of William the Conqueror, the loveliest for 20 miles and in 25 acres of farmland. But it is an easy house. I'll describe a bedroom: plain walls, curtains and green carpet, painted white wardrobes, cast-iron lights and arched wooden door, window seat, flagstoned bay windows with views of the courtyard and garden. The sitting room makes you want to take your shoes and socks off and curl up; and the 'honesty' bar adds zest to the nightly dinner parties.

Rooms: 4 twin/doubles en suite, 1 twin/double with private bathroom.

Price: £30 p.p. doubles, £35 single.

Breakfast: Included – full English.

Meals: Dinner £10-£15 p.p.

Closed: Christmas Day.

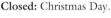

Bring your own music... there's a boudoir grand to be played as well as a music centre you can use. Ann is fun and a natural entertainer, the sort of person who happily giggles. Our inspector loved every minute of her stay. Wonderfully comfortable house with touches of luxury and matchless views over Plymouth Sound. It is at the top of a steep hill overlooking a charming village of 600 souls. To cap it all Ann is a wholefood cook and serves homemade dishes where she can.

Rooms: 1 twin/double en suite, 1 twin en suite, 1 double en suite.

Price: £20-£22.50 p.p. doubles.

Breakfast: Included – full English.

Meals: Dinner £20 p.p., supper £9 p.p.

Closed: Never!

From Wainhouse Corner on A39, follow sign to Crackington Haven. At beach turn inland for 1 mile and left into Church Park Road and then first right into lane.

Map Ref No: 2

Mrs Muriel Knight
Manor Farm
Crackington Haven
Bude
Cornwall EX23 0JW
Tel: 01840-230304

B3247 towards Mount Edgcumbe. Go down hill to right, left fork on bend into Kingsand village. Second left then left again. House is fourth on left with yellow door.

Map Ref No: 2

Ann Heasman
Cliff House
Devonport Hill
Kingsand
Cornwall PL10 1NJ
Tel: 01752-823110

THE SOUTH WEST

Alex was a photographic journalist and Sally a cook before they took on this 10-bedroomed Indian hill station bungalow, soon winning the title 'Best Guesthouse in the West'. They have poured themselves into the task and remain chatty and entertaining. There is dark oak with open fires, grandfather chairs and some lovely furniture. Separate tables in the dining room... as in a hotel... but all is beautifully done and candles are lit. There are also separate cottages (one is a converted games room, the other has 3 rooms, all en suite).

Rooms: 3 twins, 3 doubles, 3 family rooms – all en suite.

Price: From £23-£30 p.p. 25% discount for children over 5 and under 14 sharing with 2 adults.

Breakfast: Included – full English/continental.

Meals: Dinner £14 p.p.

Closed: 1 November – 28 February.

Your children will love the Vietnamese pot-bellied pigs, the goats and the large dogs. You will appreciate the traditional farmhouse hospitality and the quiet nights in this solid old house. You can enjoy carriage rides and even learn to harness and drive a horse and carriage. This is rural England at its best, cosy but certainly not twee, with a certain elegance (four-posters, big bathrooms, good china), kind and welcoming hosts and really good English food at the beginning and end of the day.

Rooms: 2 doubles, 1 family room, all en suite.

Price: £22-£24 p.p.

Breakfast: Included – full English.

Meals: Dinner £12 p.p.

Closed: Never!

House is on B3253 1 mile west of Hessenford, 3.5 miles east of Looe, just south of Widegates village.

Map Ref No: 2

Alexander & Sally Low
Combe Farm
Widegates
Looe
Cornwall PL13 1QN
Tel: 01503-240223
Fax: 01503-240895

Take A3059 west to Newquay. In 0.5 miles follow signs to Tregaswith. Farm is second on right.

Map Ref No: 2

John & Jacqui Elsom
Tregaswith Farmhouse
Tregaswith
Near Newquay
Cornwall TR8 4HY
Tel: 01637-881181
Fax: 01637-881181

A rare and intriguing house to stay in, Erth Barton is a Grade II listed 13th-century farmhouse overlooking Plymouth Sound. It is a maze of rooms full of art and paintings, the drawing room is vast as is its fireplace, the atmosphere is alive, homely, informal and fun. Guy is eccentric, funny, keeps horses and farms 6000 acres. 'Fantastic views, fantastic host' said our inspector. Well-behaved children only.

Rooms: 1 twin with separate private bathroom, 2 doubles both en suite.

Price: £32 p.p.

Breakfast: Included – full English/continental.

Meals: Dinner £17.50

Closed: Never!

Quietly removed from "touristy" Cornwall, Tremearne is a large, rambling family house where every bit of upholstery is not painstakingly designed to match another, old toys lie around for new children to play with and the large lovingly-lined wardrobe is not an antique. Sally is funny, vivacious, easy and obviously enjoys the arts and entertaining. The walled rose garden smells divine, the kitchen garden provides for her farmhouse suppers. She is a wonderful person to meet and she loves children.

Rooms: 1 twin, 1 double, both en suite; 2 cottage suites for 2-4 people.

Price: £17.50-£20 p.p. doubles, £25 p.p. cottage suite. Under 5s £5, 10-16 years £10.

Breakfast: Included – full English/continental.

Meals: Dinner £12.50 p.p. Children £6.

Closed: 1 November – 1 March. Cottage suites available all year,

Take A38 from Plymouth & cross Tamar Bridge. Through by-pass tunnel over roundabout. On top of next hill left to Trematon; through village to Elmgate, right by white cottage with letterbox. House is signed.

Map Ref No: 2

Mr Guy Bentinck
Erth Barton
Saltash
Cornwall
PL12 4QY
Tel: 01752-842127
Fax: 01752-842127

Leave A30 bypass towards Land's End at Heamoor roundabout. Go through village to crossroads and right down Joseph's Lane. Bone Valley is first left. Continue along valley until you see very high granite wall with green door.

Map Ref No: 1

Sally Adams
Tremearne
Bone Valley
Penzance
Cornwall TR20 8UJ
Tel: 01736-64576
Fax: 01736-50957

Tidy gardeners avaunt! The 10 acres at Carwinion are a natural unmanicured Victorian valley garden with a superb collection of bamboos, ferns and other sub-tropical plants. The large rambling manor house has the faded grandeur and collections of oddities (magnifying glasses, pens, propelling pencils) that successive generations never get rid of. The charmingly ecccentric Anthony will introduce you to his ancestors, his antiques, his fine old bedrooms – and produce a magnificent breakfast each morning.

Rooms: 3 doubles, all with private bathrooms.

Price: £25 p.p.

Breakfast: Included – full English/continental.

Meals: Dinner £12-£18 p.p.

Closed: Never!

A position to die for: on the wild side, the cliff's edge faces the live blue bay while a secluded garden with a path to the beach offers chaises longues for the lazy; on the civilised side, St. Ives itself with all the finer delights that this ancient-and-modern village has to offer. The Shearns have been running their guest house for years and still enjoy their visitors. She has a reputation as an excellent cook, the rooms are simply, comfortably furnished, the views are nothing less than spectacular.

Rooms: 2 twin/triples en suite; 3 doubles en suite; 2 doubles and 2 singles sharing 2 bathrooms.

Price: Suites: £33-£40 p.p., others £27-£37 p.p.

Breakfast: Included – full English/continental.

Meals: Dinner £15.50 p.p.

Closed: Mid-October – mid-March.

Follow signs off A394 (going south) to Mabe & Mawnan Smith (4 miles). Fork left at Red Lion. 460 metres up hill on right is gate marked Carwinion.

Map Ref No: 1

Mr & Mrs Anthony Rogers
Carwinion
Near Falmouth
Cornwall
TR11 5JA
Tel: 01326-250258

From A30 take A3074 & continue through Lelant and Carbis Bay. Entering St. Ives along Trelyon Avenue, Blue Hayes is prominent on right.

Map Ref No: 1

Jan & John Shearn
Blue Hayes
Trelyon Avenue
St. Ives
Cornwall TR26 2ND
Tel: 01736-797129

A solid yet elegant 16th-century manor house, generous in size and full of light, Nanscawen sits in five lush acres in the wooded Luxulyan valley. The Martins have imbibed the environing sense of quiet seclusion; their gentle welcome and non-intrusive manner prove it is so. But their hospitality is lavish in modern luxuries such as hot tub, swimming pool, ruffled towels and exotic bathtime goodies. And moreover... smoked salmon for breakfast. Children over 12 welcome.

Rooms: 1 twin, 2 doubles, all en suite. (1 four-poster.)

Price: £34-£39 p.p.

Breakfast: Included – full English/continental.

Meals: No, but locally available.

Closed: Christmas & Boxing Day.

A winding lane with lovely old Cornish hedges leads to Arrallas (the name means 'silver court' in old Cornish dialect) which sits peacefully looking down its own special sheltered valley. The surrounding woodlands teem with wild life and flowers. In this listed farmhouse, previously used as a sporting lodge, you will find the civilisation of plush rooms and fine English food. Barbara is the fourth generation of her family to welcome guests – she does it well.

Rooms: 1 twin, 2 doubles, all en suite.

Price: £19-£21 p.p.

Breakfast: Included – full English.

Meals: Dinner £11.50 p.p.

Closed: 1 November – 31 January.

A390 south towards St. Austell. In St. Blazey take right immed. after railway. House is 0.75 miles on right.

Map Ref No: 2

Keith & Janet Martin
Nanscawen House
Prideaux Road
St. Blazey
Cornwall PL24 2SR
Tel: 01726-814488
Fax: 01726-814488

Follow A30 south past Newquay exit. Take second exit after McDonalds on right to Chapel Town & Summercourt. Turn right. Arrallas is signed from opposite clock garage.

Map Ref No: 2

Ian & Barbara Holt
Arrallas
Ladock
Nr. Truro
Cornwall TR2 4NP
Tel: 01872-510379
Fax: 01872-510200

Windswept walks are within easy reach; seabird acrobatics will dazzle; magical Prussia Cove will enchant you. Return spellbound to a house full of wood, warmth and fun. Log fires, candlelit suppers of sinful seduction and romantic bedrooms (4-posters, lace-edged linen, Celtic quilts) lead you to deep sleep. The flower-laden garden greets you on your way to an early-morning dip in the heated pool. Mrs White sparkles with life and intelligence and loves having people to stay, especially for her superb-value winter breaks.

Rooms: 1 twin, two 4-posters, all en suite; 1 luxury self-catering studio for 2.

Price: £22.50-£30 p.p., single supp. of £5. Studio £150-£400 per week according to season.

Breakfast: Included – full English/continental.

Meals: Dinner £17.50 p.p. Children under 12 £12.50 p.p.

Closed: Christmas.

A cocktail of outdoor treats: Roseland Peninsula, the River Fal and the 14th-century church of St. Crida nearby, a 5-acre landscaped garden, a walled herbaceous garden and a trickle stream feeding several ponds. With its broad-leafed trees and wooded hills this is more like Sussex than Cornwall. Lally has won awards as a hostess and no wonder – a lovely and elegant house, every comfort and, by all accounts, a rare gift for making you feel at home.

Rooms: 3 twin/doubles all with private bathrooms.

Price: £25-£30 p.p.

Breakfast: Included – full English/continental.

Meals: Locally available.

Closed: Christmas & New Year.

2 miles east of Marazion on B3280 look for sign leading down Trewhella Lane. Keep going to Ennys.

Map Ref No: 1

Mr & Mrs John White
Ennys
St. Hilary
Penzance
Cornwall TR20 9BZ
Tel: 01736-740262

Take A390 to Grampound. Just beyond the clock tower turn left into Creed Lane. After 1 mile turn left at grass triangle opposite Creed church. House is behind second white gate on the left.

Map Ref No: 2

Lally & William Croggon
Creed House
Creed
Grampound, Truro
Cornwall TR2 4SL
Tel: 01872-530372

All ages will love this quirky Victorian establishment. Kids explore the mazes and follies in the famously eccentric gardens, David Crawford introduces his pets: Henrietta Hen and Lobby Lobster! The Tregenna Tavern, in the grounds, has darts, pool, table football and video games. The freshest ever lobster and crab are served in the conservatory-like dining room. Cornish Cream Teas and a weekly summer B-B-Q are also provided, so you will need those spectacular coastal walks.

Rooms: 11 doubles, all with private bathrooms. 1 converted coach house suitable for family.

Price: £22-£25 p.p. doubles, £27.50-£31.25 p.p. singles. 3-night break £48 p.p.

Breakfast: Included – full English/continental.

Meals: Lunch. Dinner £12 p.p., or in hotel Tavern.

Closed: Never!

It may take time to reach Trebrea Lodge but it's worth the effort. The Bray family owned the property for nearly 600 years and successive generations have enlarged and improved the house. Today's owners have created a romantic and stylish environment – brocaded bedspreads, oil paintings, tapestries. Also elegant food, served in the oak-panelled dining room. The 'be at home' maxim is exemplified by the welcoming snug sitting room with open fire and honesty bar.

Rooms: 3 twins, all with en suite shower; 4 doubles, all with en suite bathrooms.

Price: £32-£42 p.p. doubles, £52.50-£57.50 single.

Breakfast: Included – full English.

Meals: Dinner £19.50 p.p.

Closed: January

From Trelights village follow clear sign-posting to hotel.

Map Ref No: 2

David & Dorothy Crawford
Long Cross Hotel & Victorian Gardens
Trelights
Port Isaac
Cornwall PL29 3TF
Tel: 01208-880243

From Tintagel, turn into Trenale Lane beside R.C. church. Once in Trenale village, turn towards Trewarmett. Hotel is almost immediately on left.

Map Ref No: 2

John Charlick & Sean Devlin
Trebrea Lodge
Trenale
Tintagel
Cornwall PL34 0HR
Tel: 01840-770410
Fax: 01840-770092

A place to fall in love with – or at! Mary and Andrew no longer have a chef and manager – they relish having 'hands on'. Mary is head chef, Andrew does breakfast, meets and greets, all with style. 7 bedrooms in the Manor, 2 in the garden cottage. Everything is here to delight; spa or jacuzzi baths, exercise room, heated swimming pools, croquet, snooker, even two practice golf holes. No need to be sport mad, though: the gardens are rich and informal and you can explore the old mining buildings within.

Rooms: 2 twins en suite, 4 twin/doubles en suite, 2 singles en suite, 2 suites.

Price: £55-£70 p.p. doubles, £65-£75 single.

Breakfast: Included – full English/continental.

Meals: Dinner £20 p.p. residents, £22.50 p.p. non-residents. Light lunch also available for residents.

Closed: 31 October – 31 March.

A beautiful family house in 4 acres of grounds, the Horn of Plenty is first and foremost a restaurant. The house is a flowery nest, both elegant and homely, visibly much-loved, designed to welcome and envelop you. The bedrooms in the converted coach house are functional and unfussy. All have balconies overlooking the garden, the mood-changing Tamar Valley and bleak Bodmin Moor beyond. Be tempted to walk as well as to eat! A friendly unassuming family awaits your return.

Rooms: 7 twin/doubles, all en suite.

Price: £41.50-£49 p.p. twin/doubles, £63-£78 single.

Breakfast: Included – full English/continental.

Meals: Dinner £28.50 p.p. Lunch £10.50-£17.50 p.p.

Closed: Christmas & Boxing Day.

2 miles east of St. Austell off A390. Turn up road signposted Tregrehan (almost opposite St. Austell garden centre). House is 150m on left.

Map Ref No: 2

Andrew & Mary Flint
Boscundle Manor
Tregrehan
St. Austell
Cornwall PL25 3RL
Tel: 01726-813557
Fax: 01726-814997

Go south to Gulworthy on the A390. Pass church and school on left and take next right signed. If you reach the river you have gone too far!

Map Ref No: 2

Elaine & Ian Gatehouse
The Horn of Plenty
Gulworthy
Tavistock
Devon PL19 8JD
Tel: 01822-832528
Fax: 01822-832528

Bob and Frances gained a sense of relaxed hospitality, some fine handmade quilts and an eye for decorative detail while living in America. In proper country style the pine furniture is old pine and the loo seats are wooden. The English tradition reaches the Edwardian dining hall where mouthwatering meals include local salmon, game and garden veg. Guests have a private sitting room (luxury!) and there is a terrace where you may watch the doves and savour the peace. Children over 14 welcome.

Rooms: 2 twins and 1 single, all with en suite bath and shower.

Price: £28 p.p.

Breakfast: Included – full English.

Meals: Dinner £18 p.p. by arrangement only. Also available locally.

Closed: Christmas.

A lovely converted mill in the heart of hidden Devon where you can walk, ride, sail to your heart's content. The Archers' intention is that their guests find the peace they seek, be relieved of all tension and enjoy the natural and man-made treasures of this delectable part of the country. To this end, they offer you glasses of wine in their large, homely kitchen, envelop you in human warmth, guide you towards the lesser-known 'sights'... and even talk to you in Cantonese if need be. Children and pets by arrangement.

Rooms: 1 double en suite (also with sitting room).

Price: £22 p.p., infants free, 7 years & under £2.50.

Breakfast: Included – full English/continental.

Meals: Dinner £10 p.p.

Closed: Christmas & New Year.

Take B3416 off A38 and follow signs to Hemerdon. Pass Miner's Arms pub and telephone box. Continue past cottages on right. 300 metres down lane first right, then gate on right over cattle grid.

Map Ref No: 2

Mr & Mrs Bob Tagert
The Barn, Windwhistle Farm
Hemerdon
Plymouth
Devon PL7 5BU
Tel: 01752-347016
Fax: 01752-335670

Turn north off A30 at Stowford Cross. Follow signs to Roadford Lake, go to Ashwater. Renson Farm is 1 mile north of Ashwater just by Thorney Cross. Mill entrance is inside farm driveway.

Map Ref No: 2

Geoffrey & Sonia Archer
Renson Mill
Ashwater
Devon
EX21 5ER
Tel: 01409-211665
Fax: 01409-211665

Wadstray, a solid, English, finely-gardened (sub-tropical) early Georgian country house, has atmosphere. Flagstones and a grandfather clock in the hall, open fires in the dining room and in the gentlemanly library that is all dark colours and antiques. The bedrooms have balconies or canopied beds or sea views. Your friendly hosts have created a house of taste and comfort. There is a lovely walled garden and the self-catering Orangery has its own secret patio-with-ruin.

Rooms: 2 twins, 1 double... both en suite; 2 self-catering apartments suitable for 2 adults each.

Price: £25 p.p. Single £35.

Breakfast: Included – full English.

Meals: Available nearby.

Closed: Christmas Day & Boxing Day.

Quintessential Devon congregates at the Linhay – tiny lanes with high hedges, the smell of fresh coffee and homemade rolls, and clotted cream. A captivating waft from the kitchen greeets you as you step inside Clare Shaw's brilliant home. She has brought a rare warmth to this Victorian converted barn. Only two rooms to stay in, but absolutely top marks for style: one rather Mexican with rugs and terracotta, the other romantic with Swedish sleigh beds. Over the hills and the sea is not far away....

Rooms: 1 twin with private bathroom, 1 double en suite, 1 single.

Price: £20-£25 p.p.

Breakfast: Included – full English/continental.

Meals: Dinner £15 p.p. Available on request.

Closed: 1 December – 31 January.

House is on A3122 Dartmouth/Totnes road, 0.5 miles from the Dittisham turn and the Sportsman's. But don't go into Blackawton village. 1 mile from Dartmouth Golf & Country Club.

Map Ref No: 3

Philip & Merilyn Smith
Wadstray House
Wadstray
Blackawton
Devon TQ9 7DE
Tel: 01803-712539

Take A3122 towards Dartmouth. Turn left at The Sportsman's signed to Dittisham. After 2 miles Bozomzeal is signed on right. Linhay is second drive on left.

Map Ref No: 3

Clare Shaw
The Linhay
Bozomzeal
Dittisham, Dartmouth
Devon TQ6 0JJ
Tel: 01803-722457
Fax: 01803-722503

The house is in the Domesday Book but this 3rd generation of Coopers have unleashed their arty, bohemian taste to create an impressionistic ancient-and-modern interior that is ungrandly elegant, warmly welcoming and unobtrusively luxurious. They are intelligent, informal, green-leaning farmers who produce horses, poultry and organic veg. Their house is lovely, the outdoor pool is heated, some rooms have sea views and Jason runs courses in coppicing and woodwork.

Rooms: 2 doubles en suite with king size beds; 1 twin & 1 double with en suite bath; 1 double/single private bath & jacuzzi.

Price: £40-£70 p.p. £5 per child in same room as adult(s).

Breakfast: Included – full English/contintental.

Meals: Dinner £25 p.p., lunch/picnic: £8.50 p.p.

Closed: Never!

Don't come if you are stuffy. But I challenge anyone with an open mind and sense of fun to fail to enjoy Fingals. Is it a home or is it a hotel? Beautiful and stuffed with all the bits and pieces to make you happy and comfortable (inside pool, jacuzzi, sauna, wonderful grass tennis court, library, superbly comfortable rooms etc.) it throbs with the vitality and enthusiasm of both Richard and Sheila. Conversation, good food and wine flow loosely round the family dinner table and throughout the house. A smashing place... and there's even a stream flowing through the garden.

Rooms: 1 family/twin/double, 1 twin, 7 doubles all en suite & self-catering barn with 1 twin, 1 double and 1 bathroom.

Price: £30-£47.50 p.p.

Breakfast: Included – full English.

Meals: Dinner £25 p.p.

Closed: 2 January – 21 March.

Follow A3122 to Forces Tavern and then turn left. Take first right to Tideford then right at Tideford and then left over cattle grid.

Map Ref No: 3

Diana Cooper
Higher Tideford
Cornworthy
Totnes
Devon TQ9 7HL
Tel: 01803-712387
Fax: 01803-712388

Take A381 south from Totnes up hill then left to Cornworthy/Ashprington. Turn right at ruin to Dittisham. Descend steep hill. Hotel is signed on right after bridge.

Map Ref No: 3

Richard Johnston
Fingals at Old Coombe Manor Farm
Dittisham
Dartmouth
Devon TQ6 0JA
Tel: 01803-722398
Fax: 01803-722401

A National Trust house that you can sleep in is a rare treat. And, moreover, it was built in 1926 by a pupil of Lutyens for the D'Oyly Carte family; the local stone is tenderly yellow-grey, as soft as the touch of the air here. The sub-tropical gardens alone are worth the trip. The interior is furnished in proper period style – well-behaved children and manicured dogs only – and the Howes are proud of the house and its history. Brian cooks, including your breakfast breads and jams.

A stunning little Regency townhouse set up on a hill overlooking the sights and sound of the famous naval town of Dartmouth. It is full of light, with elegant but homely rooms, a romantic first-floor balcony wrapped in vines and a walled garden. Richard Turner loves to cook and also may play the pianola in the drawing room to amuse you. Right in the heart of town, but village-quiet at night. All the assets of a hotel but with the intimacy of a private house.

Rooms: 2 twin/doubles en suite; 2 doubles: 1 en suite, 1 with private bathroom.

Price: £25-£40 p.p.

Breakfast: Included – full English/continental.

Meals: Dinner by prior arrangement, £22.50-£30 p.p.

Closed: 1 November – 1 March.

Rooms: 5 twin/doubles, all with private bathrooms; 1 self-contained flat with 2 bedrooms.

Price: £28.50-£35 p.p. double, £35 single.

Breakfast: Included – full English.

Meals: Dinner £20 p.p. Available on request.

Closed: Christmas Day & New Year's Day.

In Dartmouth town centre turn left in front of the NatWest bank onto Victoria Road. House is up the hill on the right hand side.

Map Ref No: 3

Richard Turner
Ford House
44 Victoria Road,
Dartmouth
Devon TQ6 9DX
Tel: 01803-834047
Fax: 01803-834047

At T-junction on A380 outside Torquay, right towards Brixham/ Dartmouth on A3022. Between 2 Esso garages right to Dartmouth/ Kingswear. Follow NT signs for Coleton Fishacre.

Map Ref No: 3

Brian & Susan Howe
Coleton Fishacre House
Kingswear
Dartmouth
Devon TQ6 0EQ
Tel: 01803-752683
Fax: 01803-752683

"Very special people and a lovely place to stay in the middle of nowhere," says our inspector. The Hendersons' 17th-century longhouse has a gorgeous cobbled yard, a bridge across to the island (shades of Monet), goats and their enchanting kids. They produce their own moorland water, all their fruit and vegetables and make cheese. The rooms are simply country-style, the attitude very 'green' (hedge-laying, stone wall-mending, humane lamb-rearing) and the conversation fascinating.

Rooms: 2 twins, 2 singles, all with hand-basins and sharing 1 bathroom.

Price: £16-£16.50 p.p. twins, £15.50 singles. Children under 2 free, under 5 half price in parents' room.

Breakfast: Included – full English/continental.

Meals: Evening meal £10 p.p. Available occasionally or locally.

Closed: Christmas.

Stay for just one night, or rent the house from Mrs. E. for the summer when she aways to bonny Scotland. The house is small, cosy, unpretentious and fits around you like a well-worn glove. Mrs. E. is welcoming and plies you with tea and well-travelled companionship. The valleys of the Teign river are a marvellous part of Devon. You should do a lot of walking with your binoculars around your neck to catch the birds – your hostess will name places to go and paths to follow.

Rooms: 1 twin/double with private bath, 1 single with private bath.

Price: £19 p.p.

Breakfast: Included – full English/continental.

Meals: Dinner available on request.

Closed: Mid-March – mid-November.

Leave A38 at second Ashburton turning, follow signs for Dartmeet. After 2 miles fork left to Holne. Pass church, after 175 metres, turn then left for Michelcombe. Left again at foot of hill, house is 175 metres ahead.

Map Ref No: 2

John & Judy Henderson
Dodbrooke Farm
Michelcombe
Holne
Devon TQ13 7SP
Tel: 01364-631461

From Bovey Tracey follow signs to Manaton/Becky Falls. From Kestor Inn in Manaton follow signs to Moretonhampstead for 3.3 miles. Lane to house is second on left after Heatree Cross.

Map Ref No: 2

John & Christina Everett
Vogwell Cottage
Manaton
Newton Abbott
Devon TQ13 9XD
Tel: 01647-221302

THE SOUTH WEST

Old, old, old – for feel and for real! It shows few traces of its 13th-century origins but the house is listed, there are pieces of oak and granite everywhere and the Merchants have added their own antiques and old photographs to create bushels of atmosphere. Bedrooms offer more wooden furniture, patchwork quilts, simple decoration and calm views. Come down to enjoy a Devon farmhouse dinner with home-grown meat and vegetables in the pretty little dining room.

Rooms: 1 twin, 2 doubles, all with en suite shower.

Price: £20-£21 p.p.

Breakfast: Included – full English.

Meals: Dinner £12 p.p.

Closed: Never!

The high Georgian ceilings and windows absorb the bohemian bustle of an active artistic family and spread the gentle Devon light. Stephen is an architect, Lucinda upholsters antiques, they have pictures all over their walls, a talking parrot, a dog called Murphy. Each lovely guestroom has its own personality. It is all genuine, alive, intelligent and utterly welcoming. A wonderful place for art-lovers and seekers of peace and great views.

Rooms: 1 twin, 2 doubles: 1 en suite bath, 1 shared bath/shower.

Price: £18 p.p. en suite, £15 p.p. double, £22.50 single.

Breakfast: Included – full English/vegetarian.

Meals: Dinner £12.50 – also locally available.

Closed: Christmas.

Take A382 from Bovey Tracey. After Moretonhampstead, look for signs to Farm.

Map Ref No: 2

Trudie Merchant
Great Sloncombe Farm
Moretonhampstead
Devon
TQ13 8QF
Tel: 01647-440595

Leave A30 between Exeter and Okehampton at Cheriton Bishop exit. Go through Crockernwell; immediate left to Drewsteignton. Cross village square, turn left, house is on right after 50m.

Map Ref No: 2

Lucinda & Stephen Emanuel
The Old Rectory
Drewsteignton
Exeter
Devon EX6 6QT
Tel: 01647-281269
Fax: 01647-281269

Gill has all the enthusiasm of the beginner, having only just bought this 30-acre beef farm with her husband. As an interior designer, however, she is off to a cracking start... ably supported by 3 acres of lovely gardens (with walled kitchen garden) and a lake. There are southerly views over open countryside and the Grade II listed Georgian house has all you expect: big hall, library, dining room and sitting-room. The bedrooms are going to be superb, by all accounts.

Rooms: One 4-poster en suite bathroom, 1 twin en suite shower/bathroom .

Price: £30-£35 p.p. doubles, £40 single.

Breakfast: Included – full English/continental.

Meals: Available locally.

Closed: Never!

The Langtons are warm, grandmotherly (sorry Jack!) types – their smiles are utterly genuine, they really are pleased to see you. Elizabeth David adepts, they love cooking and care greatly about using organic ingredients; everything is homemade. The same attention to detail is apparent in the fresh bright guestrooms where fruit, mints and sherry await you. Climb all over the cobbled streets of typical Clovelly, then come back exhausted to be spoilt.

Rooms: 2 twin/doubles: 1 en suite, 1 with adjacent private shower room; 1 double en suite.

Price: £35-£39 p.p. doubles, £50-£55 singles.

Breakfast: Included – full English/continental.

Meals: Dinner £23 p.p.

Closed: November – 28 February, but please enquire.

M5 junction 27 Barnstaple exit. At r'bout turn to Bideford. At second r'bout left to Newton Tracey. After about 2.5 miles right towards Horwood. After 0.25 miles house sign & 2 white entrance pillars on left over cattlegrid.

Map Ref No: 2

Gill Barriball
Horwood House
Horwood,
Nr. Bideford
Devon EX39 4PD
Tel: 01271-858231

Leave the A39 at Horn's Cross beyond Bideford. Follow signs for Parkham. Take first left into Rectory Lane after church on right. Old Rectory is just around next corner after Rectory on left.

Map Ref No: 2

Jean & Jack Langton
The Old Rectory
Parkham
Bideford
North Devon EX39 5PL
Tel: 01237-451443

Up a long pasture-lined drive, Culver Combe, a solid square house set in rolling lamb-dotted green between Dartmoor and the sea, has a delicious garden and a large lake. Mrs Rooth is passionate about other people's gardens too, welcomes garden lovers especially and will advise on local delights, including golf on the site of a former tin mine. Her two rooms, one smaller than the other, are simple but comfortable; her house bustles with laughter and life. She clearly loves entertaining.

Rooms: 1 twin, 1 double, both with shared bathroom.

Price: £20 p.p.

Breakfast: Included – full English/continental.

Meals: Not available.

Closed: Christmas and Easter.

Three cheers! A hotel designed and run with families in mind. Everything is aimed at keeping the sprogs giggling, entertained and safe while their long-suffering parents rest, eat good food and swap offspring horror stories. The two-bedroom/bathroom set-up works well and there is a kitchen and laundry room for everyone's use. No flash decorations here, but then there are those sticky little fingers.... Grown-ups can take refuge in their own sitting room. Food is for all ages and, whenever possible, additive-free.

Rooms: 6 suites each with two bedrooms & en suite bathroom, 4 units each with two bedrooms and a bathroom.

Price: £43 per unit, £61 per suite, based on 2 adults & 2 children under 12. From £38 twin/double.

Breakfast: Included – full English/continental.

Meals: Dinner £13.75 p.p. & high tea for children free if dinner taken, or £3.50.

Closed: Never!

Turn off A38, going south to Chudleigh Knighton. Turn right just before village, and right at white thatched cottage. House is signed.

Map Ref No: 3

Chris & Gina Rooth
Culver Combe
Chudleigh
Newton Abbot
Devon TQ13 0EL
Tel: 01626-853204

From A3052 take the Branscombe Cross turning towards Bulstone. The Bulstone Hotel is 0.75 miles further along on the left.

Map Ref No: 3

Judith & Kevin Monaghan
The Bulstone Hotel
Higher Bulstone
Branscombe
Devon EX12 3BL
Tel: 01297-680446
Fax: 01297-680446

Unusual, remote, relaxed and hugely entertaining. Few conventional frills but a lot of unconventional ones: an 'honesty' bar, a relaxed young staff who don't hover, Victorian baths and some real fireplaces in the bathrooms, perhaps a piano (or two) in the bedroom, memorable communal dinners and the easiest-going owners in England. Toss logs on the fire, choose your own records, play snooker – but don't look for hotel service. This is much more fun. One of our favourite hotels, unpretentious yet stately... and not for the stuffy.

Rooms: 11 twin/doubles, 3 family rooms, all en suite.

Price: From £65-£70 p.p. doubles; from £60-£90 single.

Breakfast: Included – full English/continental/health food.

Meals: Dinner £35 p.p.

Closed: Never!

Definitely for lovers of The Great Outdoors; an impressive 18th-century stone farmhouse hiding in the Teign valley. The converted barn has mighty bedrooms with stunning views, unplastered stone walls and exposed beams, true to the original building. Extra comfortable with character and more treats than is standard. Unfussy, delicious food with dashes of exotica using bounty from the home farm. 170 acres on which to walk, fish, relish flora and fauna. Also clay pigeon shooting and, back home, snooker.

Rooms: 1 twin en suite, 4 doubles en suite.

Price: £25-£30 p.p. doubles, £35-£45 single.

Breakfast: Included – full English.

Meals: Dinner available on request.

Closed: Never!

From M5 Junction 27, turn sharp right on bridge in Sampford Peverell. Continue 2 miles to Uplowman and then for 4 miles to Huntsham.

Map Ref No: 3

Mogens & Andrea Bolwig
Huntsham Court
Huntsham
Nr. Bampton
Devon EX16 7NA
Tel: 01398-361365
Fax: 01398-361456

A38 exit at Chudleigh Knighton. Turn right; right again to Teign Valley. After 5 miles right at crossroads into Ashton. Before post office sharply left. After 2 miles house signed on left.

Map Ref No: 3

Maria Cochrane & Angela & Colin Edwards
Great Leigh Guesthouse
Doddiscombsleigh
Nr. Exeter, Devon EX6 7RF
Tel: 01647-253008
Fax: 01647-252058

You fish? This is the place for you. A homely cottage free of television and with well-furnished, good-bedded, patchwork-quilted bedrooms, bountiful breakfasts cooked on the Aga (fresh tomatoes baked with parsley, rhubarb and yoghurt, homemade marmalade...), linen table napkins and a vast lake in the midst of the rolling peace of the Devon hills. You can hire rods here or play tennis, but swimming is not recommended.

Rooms: 1 twin, 1 double, both with en suite bath & shower; 2 singles sharing bath, shower & wc.

Price: £22.50 p.p. doubles, £21 singles.

Breakfast: Included – full English/continental.

Meals: Not available.

Closed: Never!

A rural idyll; not a sound, but a meadowed, wooded valley falling away to a distant view of Arlington Court. Sheep, cows, dogs, cats, old slate-roofed barns, a pond... all is here. The immensely friendly Tom and Erica overhauled the house and added a wing, all with rare sympathy. The kitchen/dining room is an oak-beamed design masterpiece. So, too, are the bedrooms: mod cons hidden in attractive wooden cupboards, every imaginable extra. As appealing as it is luxurious.

Rooms: 3 doubles, all with bath and/or shower en suite.

Price: £35 p.p. doubles, £50 single.

Breakfast: Included – full English.

Meals: Dinner by arrangement.

Closed: Never!

A373 east towards Honiton and follow signs for Kentisbeare. Right after post office in village, and after about 200m right again and cross ford to Millhayes.

Map Ref No: 3

Mrs Jackie Howe
Millhayes
Kentisbeare
Cullompton
Devon EX15 2AF
Tel: 01884-266412
Fax: 01884-266412

From Barnstaple on A39. Second left after Shirwell, signed to Upcott; up hill for 1.5 miles. Follow sign to Churchill. Farm next on right.

Map Ref No: 2

Tom & Erica McClenaghan
Ashelford Farm
East Down
Nr. Barnstaple
North Devon EX31 4LU
Tel: 01271-850469
Fax: 01271-850862

This is an astonishingly lovely part of the Exmoor National Park, recently designated one of three remaining 'tranquil' areas in England. The hotel is a remarkable place, run with a light touch by two interesting people who are only recently hoteliers. The bedrooms are full of charm and character, all with extraordinary views over the sea. The sitting room is full of books, to be devoured by the blazing log fire after some of the loveliest walks in Devon. To top it all the food is sublime... fresh, elegant and imaginative.

Rooms: 12 : 2 twins; 1 family suite (1 double, 1 twin, shared bathroom); the rest all doubles, all en suite.

Price: £25-£33 p.p.

Breakfast: Included – full English.

Meals: 4-course dinner, £18.50 p.p.; à la carte steak menu from £12; bar meals for lunch.

Closed: January, November, December; February weekdays.

Snug in the tiny harbour, boats rise and fall with the tide only yards from the bedroom windows. Hugo has wrought a small miracle, squeezing luxury and a wonderful dining room into a tiny head-ducking building. Hugo effervesces, the sea-breeze sweeps clean your addled brain, the superb food gilds the lily, the walks up the wooded valley or along the coast are as lovely as any in the country and the village is tourist-stuffed yet magical. I hate to use the word 'picturesque'....

Rooms: 2 twin, 12 double, 1 single, 1 cottage suite, all en suite.

Price: £39.50-£55 p.p. doubles, £49.50 p.p. single.

Breakfast: Included – full English.

Meals: Dinner from £25 p.p.

Closed: Never!

From Barbrook on A39 to Matinhoe Cross, right to Woody Bay, signed 3 miles to hotel.

Map Ref No: 2

Colette & Martin Petch
Woody Bay Hotel
Woody Bay
Devon
EX31 4QX
Tel: 01598-763264
Fax: 01598-763563

From A39 turn into town centre and follow sign to harbour. Hotel overlooks harbour at the end on left.

Map Ref No: 2

Hugo Jeune
The Rising Sun Hotel
Harbourside
Lynmouth
North Devon EX35 6EQ
Tel: 01598-753223
Fax: 01598-753480

They are a fun-loving, intelligent couple and their very English house has a cosmopolitan atmosphere. After admiring the heart-lifting views from house and garden, the amazing rustic swimming pool overgrown with roses, the very unusual Charles I blackrock overmantle above the drawing room fireplace and the omnipresent ancestors you will be happy to recover from your emotions in a comfortable and relatively simple room for the night.

Rooms: 1 twin, 1 double, both en suite with shower and/or bath.

Price: £30 p.p. doubles, £40 single.

Breakfast: Included – full English.

Meals: Dinner £20 p.p.

Closed: 31 October – 1 March.

Long, low, thatched, stone-chimneyed – it is utterly traditional, yet built in 1934. This is the 2nd longest single-ridged thatched roof in England, the granite chimneys are 45ft high, the wide-open interior design is Richard's grandmother's. Altogether an unusual house with a quiet informal air and its own herb farm. Richard is a Savoy-trained cook, they both love entertaining and the place enfolds you in the quiet of Dartmoor. There is space for all, both indoors and out.

Rooms: 1 twin, 2 doubles, all with en suite bath.

Price: £30 p.p. double/twin, £37.50 p.p. single.

Breakfast: Included – full English/continental, even breakfast in bed.

Meals: Dinner £25 p.p. on request.

Closed: Never!

Take A361 towards South Molton, follow signs for North Molton. From here go up hill to square. With church on left, take drive beside old school buildings. Court Hall is just round bend.

Map Ref No: 2

Charles & Sally Worthington
Court Hall
North Molton
South Molton
Devon EX36 3HP
Tel: 01598-740224

Take B3212 from Exeter, then second turn to Christow on left. Go over humpback bridge, up the hill and look for signs.

Map Ref No: 3

Richard & Lynne Hutt
Rock House
Dunsford
Exeter
Devon EX6 7EP
Tel: 01647-252514

Wisteria drips from the eaves of this 13th-century Devon longhouse. These are country folk, utterly without pretension, who open their oak-beamed, inglenooked, spiral-staircased house and their big hearts to people looking for a quiet retreat among the rolling hills. Ruth has a huge St. Bernard called Jessica, a fine collection of teaspoons and a natural sense of hospitality. Her bedrooms are simply pastel with lovely views of fields, hills and her almond tree.

Only 900 years old and still humming with life: there's a goat in love with a goose, a pony in the rambling gardens, dogs, cats, guinea fowl, rabbits, foxes and Sally-Anne. She is an eccentric, arty, slightly zany, adventurous and utterly lovable person. The house: higgledy-piggledy, sloping floors, huge flagstone fireplace, odd modern art, antiques, exposed beams, low doors and thoroughly lived in. Not a road in sight, perfect quiet and sweeping views.

Rooms: 1 twin/double/family en suite; 2 doubles with shared bathroom.

Rooms: 1 twin, 1 double, both with shared bathroom.

Price: £16-£19 p.p.

Price: £18-£20 p.p. doubles, £25 single.

Breakfast: Included – full English.

Breakfast: Included – full English/continental.

Meals: Dinner £8.50 p.p.

Meals: Available nearby.

Closed: Christmas.

Closed: Christmas & New Year.

From M5 junction 27 take A361 to Tiverton. Just before town, take B3391. Right at 3rd roundabout, straight over at 4th, left at 5th and follow sign to Collipriest (approx.1.5 miles). House is last on right.

A30 to Okehampton. After 10 miles left exit into Cheriton Bishop, second left between 2 cottages. Go down and up hill. Road turns sharp left. Go down lane, farm signed.

Map Ref No: 3

Map Ref No: 2

Ruth Hill King
Little Hollwell
Collipriest
Tiverton
Devon EX16 4PT
Tel: 01884-257590
Fax: 01884-257590

Sally-Anne Carter-Johnson
Higher Eggbeer Farm
Cheriton Bishop
Nr. Exeter
Devon EX6 6JQ
Tel: 01647-24427

The Blackdown Hills is an area of Outstanding Natural Beauty, so go while Pear Tree Cottage is still such wonderful value. The Parrys describe it as a happy house and love sharing it. There is nothing grand about it, no memorable frills; the rooms are smallish and the decor simple. But the beds are comfortable, the views wonderful, the Parrys laid-back and utterly genuine, the garden is part of the National Garden Scheme and the arboretum is of their own planting.

Rooms: 1 family suite with 2/3/4 beds en suite bath & wc; 1 double and 1 single sharing adjacent bath & separate wc.

Price: By room: £45 family suite, £26 double, £20 single.

Breakfast: Included – full English.

Meals: Dinner £8 p.p. for 2 courses, £9 for 3 courses.

Closed: Perhaps Christmas Day.

The West Country

From Taunton head south on B3170. Turn west for Churchinford. Follow finger posts for Stapley. Alternative routes via Wellington Hemyock or Upottery for eastbound travellers from West Country.

Map Ref No: 3

Pam Parry
Pear Tree Cottage
Stapley, Churchstanton
Taunton
Somerset TA3 7QA
Tel: 01823-601224
Fax: 01823-601224

A rambling, old, characterful (even down to the towel rails) pink house, garden-sheltered and tree-protected, Edgcott is a haven on the blasted heath. George Oakes painted those striking Strawberry Hill Gothic murals the full length of the sitting/dining room. Mrs Lamble is a lovely gentle hostess, a dedicated gourmet who cooks with her own garden vegetables. She's also an Exmoor enthusiast – rides, walks, village visits galore will be suggested. And you may play the family piano.

Rooms: 1 twin with sep. bathroom, 1 twin/double en suite; 1 double sharing bathroom with twin.

Price: £19 – £22 p.p.

Breakfast: Included.

Meals: Dinner £12 p.p.

Closed: Never!

Recharge your batteries in a heady mixture of luxury and rural isolation deep in the Exmoor National Park. Old Stowey is a 16th-century farmhouse in its own sheltered and wooded valley (but not far from some good pubs). Much of the house has been little altered for 30 years or so but it is comfortable and attractive. Log fires and a wood-burning stove, fresh vegetables and game in season, glorious countryside and stabling for any horse you happen to have with you.

Rooms: 3 twins, 1 double, all with en suite shower or bath.

Price: From £27 p.p.

Breakfast: Included – full English.

Meals: Dinner from £12 p.p.

Closed: Never!

Take A358 from Taunton, then left on B3224 to Raleighs Cross, Wheddon Cross and Exford. In Exford take Porlock road. Edgcott is 0.25 miles from village.

Map Ref No: 3

Gillian Lamble
Edgcott House
Exford
Somerset
TA24 7QG
Tel: 01643-831495

From Minehead A396 to Timberscombe. At the Lion Inn left to Luxborough. After about 2 miles, left at cross roads – entrance is 75 metres on right.

Map Ref No: 3

Phil & Robin Watson
Old Stowey Farm
Wheddon Cross
Minehead
Somerset TA24 7BT
Tel: 01643-841268
Fax: 01643-841268

The picture-book Priory – 'Old' it is, 12th-century old – leans against its church, has a rustic gate, a walled garden, flowers everywhere. Indoors, the old oak tables, flagstones, panelled doors, books and higgledy-piggledy corridors sing 'there'll always be an England'. But a perfect English house in a sweet Somerset village needs a touch of pepper. Cosmopolitan Jane has a red sitting room and some Mexican-style hand-painted wardrobes. House and hostess are at once friendly, elegant and homely.

Rooms: 1 twin with en suite shower; one 4-poster en suite bathroom; 1 twin with en suite bath.

Price: £22.50-£25 p.p.

Breakfast: Included – full English/continental/home baked health food.

Meals: No, but locally available.

Closed: Christmas.

Meet the Wolversons: they'll enjoy meeting you. A friendly, well-travelled, intelligent couple, they have recently bought this comfortable village house with its fine terraced garden and croquet lawn. The generous rooms with period mouldings are decorated in gentle pale colours and furnished with colourful rugs on sea-grass matting and lots of cushions. There are cats and dogs, fine linens and lace, books and plants and masses of atmosphere.

Rooms: 1 family/double sharing bathroom, sep. shower & wc with 1 other double.

Price: £19.50 p.p. doubles, £25 single.

Breakfast: Included – full English/continental.

Meals: Excellent home cooking available locally.

Closed: Christmas & New Year.

Turn off A39 into village of Dunster, right at Blue sign 'unsuitable for goods vehicles'. Follow until church. House is adjoined.

Map Ref No: 3

Jane Forshaw
The Old Priory
Dunster
Somerset
TA24 6RY
Tel: 01643-821540

From M5 exit 25, follow the signs to A358/Minehead. Left to Halse. Rock House is in the middle of the village, signed, 100 metres from pub.

Map Ref No: 3

Christopher & Deborah Wolverson
Rock House
Halse
Nr. Taunton
Somerset TA4 3AF
Tel: 01823-432956
Fax: 01823-432956

The hamlet is tiny, tucked into a hidden valley; the house inside is as warm as the pink stone outside, a 17th-century farmhouse full of antiques. There are two sitting rooms, both with open fires, books, magazines and pictures. The dining room is elegant, the bedrooms big and comfortable (hill views) and the furnishings are a 'delight to the eye'. There are lots of thoughtful touches, such as torches. Breakfast is a flagstone-floored orgy of fresh eggs, butcher's sausages and bacon and homemade marmalade.

Rooms: 1 twin en suite bath; 1 twin and 1 double sharing bath & sep. wc.

Price: £28 p.p. en suite/single, £25 p.p. double, £14 p.p. children 0-4.

Breakfast: Included – full English.

Meals: Excellent pubs nearby.

Closed: Christmas.

Tucked away in a minute hamlet on the edge of the Quantocks this barn conversion beside the family house with its log fires has masses of character as well as proper facilities. There are slanting ceilings, beams, a wooden staircase, space and light everywhere. There are antiques mixed with more recent pine beds. Phillida and Nick love gardening and are passionate about the countryside and its traditions. A very warm and happy welcome awaits you.

Rooms: 1 twin with private bathroom, 1 double en suite, 2 self-catering cottages sleeping 2-4 people.

Price: £22-£25 p.p. doubles, £32-£35 single.

Breakfast: Included – full English.

Meals: Dinner £15-£20 p.p. Available on request.

Closed: Never!

From Taunton take A358. Left onto B3224 to Monksilver etc. After 4.5 miles right to Higher & Lower Vexford & Willet; through Willet, past a pink gate-lodge, right at T-junction to Higher Vexford.

Map Ref No: 3

Nigel & Finny Muers-Raby
Higher Vexford House
Higher Vexford
Lydeard St. Lawrence
Somerset TA4 3QF
Tel: 01984-656267
Fax: 01984-656707

Take A358 NW past Bishops Lydeard and under 2 railway bridges. After 1 mile turn left signed Trebles Holford. Follow No Through Road to end. Redlands House is on right.

Map Ref No: 3

Mrs Phillida Hughes
Redlands House
Trebles Holford
Combe Florey
Somerset TA4 3HA
Tel: 01823-433159

In 1993 Charles and Jane Ritchie fled London and headed for Somerset's lovely Quantock Hills to renovate this exquisite 17th-century stone farmhouse. Their philosophy is simple – why should visitors be any less comfortable on holiday than they are at home? Thus their place is deliciously welcoming, with very pretty, fresh and spacious rooms looking over the cobbled courtyard and garden beyond. Breakfast may include home-baked bread and cold ham and you will probably feel so at home that you will want to stay for dinner.

Rooms: 1 twin, 1 double with shared bathroom; 1 double with en suite shower & wc.

Price: £17-19.50 p.p. £2.50 single supplement.

Breakfast: Included – full English/continental.

Meals: Dinner £15 p.p., by prior arrangement.

Closed: Never!

Familiar with garderobes, piscinas and solars? If not, visit this remarkable Grade 1 listed 15th-century farmhouse and be enlightened. Explore the West Bedroom with massive-timbered walls, a ceiling open to the beamed roof and a four-poster bed; the oak panelled Gallery Bedroom with recently uncovered secret stairway. Feel baronial while seated for breakfast beside the Great Hall's massive fireplace at the 16f oak table. Minimum disturbance to fabric and flavour (except suitable washing facilities), maximum atmosphere.

Rooms: 1 family room with en suite shower; 3 doubles all with en suite shower &/or bath.

Price: £18-£24 p.p. doubles, £20-£25 p.p. singles.

Breakfast: Included – full English/continental.

Meals: Dinner available locally.

Closed: Never!

Leave M5 at junction 25. A358 towards Minehead. Leave A358 at West Bagborough turning. Follow through village for 1.5 miles. Farmhouse third on left past pub.

Map Ref No: 3

Charles & Jane Ritchie
Bashfords Farmhouse
West Bagborough
Taunton
Somerset TA4 3EF
Tel: 01823-432015
Fax: 01823-432520

From Bridgwater A39 W around Cannington. After second roundabout, follow signs to Minehead. Take first left after Dairy Crest creamery. Farm is first house on the right.

Map Ref No: 3

Mrs Ann Dyer
Blackmore Farm
Cannington
Bridgwater
Somerset TA5 2NE
Tel: 01278-653442
Fax: 01278-653442

Lying in the shadow of an Iron-Age hill fort the village is a stone-and-thatch delight. Courtfield is a typical 18th-century gent's residence with beautiful gardens and tennis court where Richard, great-great grandson of the famous John, paints and Valerie cooks. Decorated with his paintings, good furniture and bits of fine art the house is not a museum but a home and the welcoming Constables are genuinely interested in meeting people. First guests get the nearest bathroom! Children over 8 welcome.

Rooms: 1 twin,1 double, each with own sep. bathroom & wc.

Price: £20-£25 p.p.

Breakfast: Included – full English/health food.

Meals: Dinner £12.50 p.p.

Closed: Christmas.

"My wife and I were put in the cottage: we were tempted to take root," wrote our inspector. Flagstones, coir carpet, prints, plain colours and white walls... and only the kitchen garden between us and the swimming pool in its own walled garden. The main house is also a find: glorious comfort without any pretence, and sheer prettiness. Breakfasts are memorable (own bread) and exquisitely served and if Charmian and Guy are available you will enjoy talking to them. Interesting and worthwhile people and the best of B&Bs. The cottage can be rented separately.

Rooms: 2 twins (1 en suite, 1 with private bathroom); 1 double with private bathroom.

Price: £27.50 p.p. doubles, £35 single.

Breakfast: Included – full English/continental.

Meals: Dinner £22 p.p. by prior arrangement. Packed lunch available.

Closed: Never!

Leave A303, to take A356 south towards Crewkerne. Second left to Norton-sub-Hamdon. House in centre of village at foot of Church Lane.

Map Ref No: 3

Richard & Valerie Constable
Courtfield
Norton-sub-Hamdon
Stoke-sub-Hamdon
Somerset TA14 6SG
Tel: 01935-881246

Take either of two lanes off A30. Follow sign for West Chinnock but ignore left turn to West Chinnock itself. House is on right about 100m after Middle Chinnock church on left.

Map Ref No: 3

Guy & Charmian Smith
Chinnock House
Middle Chinnock
Crewkerne
Somerset TA18 7PN
Tel: 01935-881229

It really does feel as if you matter here. Sally is as warm as can be, solicitous and friendly... and an excellent cook to boot. There's a small upstairs sitting room to withdraw into, a larger one with an open fire downstairs. This is simple, old fashioned B&B comfort... with an unheated swimming pool for the spartan. The house is a 16th-century listed former farmhouse in 2 acres of garden and a quiet corner of the village.

Rooms: 2 twin: 1 with en suite shower, 1 sharing bath, shower & wc with 1 single.

Price: £19-£21 p.p. doubles, £19 single.

Breakfast: Included – full English/continental/other.

Meals: Dinner £12 p.p., light supper also available: £7.

Closed: Christmas.

Christopher and Veronica Colley take justifiable pride in the comments made by departing guests in their visitor's book. 'Delicious', 'superb' and 'every reason to return' give an idea. A listed Georgian dower house in 3.5 acres of garden, the hotel has fine bedrooms with the usual comforts, an air-conditioned dining room and deep chairs by the winter log fire.

Rooms: 2 twins, 4 doubles, all with en suite bath &/or shower.

Price: £41 p.p. doubles, £51 p.p. singles, £62 p.p. including dinner.

Breakfast: Included – full English/continental.

Meals: Dinner £18.90-£26.90 p.p. for non-residents.

Closed: Christmas & New Year.

From Crewkerne A356 towards Dorchester. In Misterton pass Globe Inn and garage on left. Left into Silver Street, left again in 175 metres into Newbery Lane. House is on right at bottom of hill.

Map Ref No: 3

John & Sally Gregory
Dryclose
Newbery Lane
Misterton
Somerset TA18 8NE
Tel: 01460-73161

Turn left off A37, Yeovil/Dorchester road. At the first roundabout onto narrow lane through a sandstone cutting. House is on left after about 0.25 mile.

Map Ref No: 3

Christopher & Veronica Colley
Little Barwick House
Barwick Village
Nr. Yeovil
Somerset BA22 9TD
Tel: 01935-423902
Fax: 01935-420902

Excellent as a base for the delights of Somerset. The walls of this 15th-century coaching inn contain stones from the demolished 12th-century castle, the roof is thatched, the ceilings beamed, the floorboards slanting, the inglenook fireplaces huge. Bedrooms are individually and cutely decorated and some are being redecorated. Atmospheric low light in the dining room where honest, delicious English fare is served, using every sort of local produce with a sophisticated touch here and there.

Rooms: 4 twins, 7 doubles, 4 singles, all en suite with bath &/or shower.

Price: £35 p.p. doubles, £35-£40 p.p. deluxe doubles, £40-£45 single.

Breakfast: Included – full English.

Meals: Dinner from £17.50 p.p. Lunch also available.

Closed: Never!

From M3 take A303 Wincanton junction. Castle Cary is signposted off A303. The George Hotel is in centre of town, opposite market place.

Map Ref No: 3

Sue & Greg Sparkes
The George Hotel
Market Place
Castle Cary
Somerset BA7 7AH
Tel: 01963-350761
Fax: 01963-350035

As rural as you can get, with a view over fields of Wells Cathedral tucked into the hills. Rosalind Bufton was in the catering business so her breakfasts are mightily good, as are her cream teas in summer. The ground floor Garden Suite with sitting room and inglenook is beautiful, especially cosy in winter; other rooms are simple and large. Walk 20 minutes to hear evensong in the Cathedral any day except Wednesday – soul stirring. Rosalind also runs cookery or geology (!) weekend breaks by arrangement.

Rooms: 1 twin with separate private bathroom; 2 doubles: 1 en suite, 1 with shared bathroom; 1 single with shared bathroom.

Price: £17.50-£22 p.p.

Breakfast: Included – full English/continental/vegetarian.

Meals: Light refreshments available by arrangement. Dinner available locally.

Closed: Never!

Take A371 E towards Shepton Mallet. Dulcote is first village 1 mile from Wells. Right at stone fountain in village. Farmhouse clearly marked 4th on right.

Map Ref No: 3

Rosalind Bufton
Manor Farm
Dulcote
Wells
Somerset BA5 3PZ
Tel: 01749-672125

Hillview was originally a one-up-one-down quarryman's cottage. Much enlarged since then, it has wisteria growing over the door and 8 acres around it. This is superb walking country. The Hays can arrange escorted walks and provide plenty of space for muddy boots as well as a great welcome into their cosy Aga-warmed kitchen. The cottage is deliciously cottagey with patchwork and antiques, lots of animals and croquet. You will be the only, and consequently spoilt, guests.

Rooms: 1 twin with en suite bath, shower, wc & basin.

Price: £20 p.p.

Breakfast: Included – full English/continental.

Meals: Dinner available locally.

Closed: Christmas & New Year.

The endearing intimacy of this 17th-century cottage puts you instantly at ease. Naturalists and walkers especially will love it, given the hosts' passion for local natural history. Malcolm has written a guide for guests on walks from the garden gate, leading out onto the Mendip Hills and beyond to the Somerset Levels. The bedrooms are cosy and light; some look onto the busy village street. One has a fine stash of old family books.

Rooms: 1 twin with shared bathroom, 2 doubles en suite, 1 single with shared bathroom.

Price: From £17 p.p.

Breakfast: Included – full English/continental/wholefood.

Meals: Dinner from £7.50 p.p. Available by arrangement.

Closed: Christmas.

Take A371 to middle of Croscombe. Right at red phone box and then immediately right into lane. House is up hill on left after 0.25 miles. Drive straight ahead into signed field.

Map Ref No: 3

Michael & Catherine Hay
Hillview Cottage
Paradise Lane
Croscombe, Nr Wells
Somerset BA5 3RL
Tel: 01749-343526

The house is in the village, on the A371 (Wells to Cheddar road), directly opposite the Westbury Inn.

Map Ref No: 3

Malcolm & Linda Mogford
The Old Stores
Westbury-sub-Mendip
Wells
Somerset BA5 1HA
Tel: 01749-870817

A large old Mendip-style 'long cottage' with mullioned windows, beams made of ships' timbers and... a vineyard! One Roman reporter said the worst wine in the Empire was made in Britain (it has improved since then). With its gentle flower garden and old stone barns Melon Cottage is a perfect base for discovering the treasures of Bath and Wells, the gardens and concerts at Stourhead and the daily Gregorian chant in Downside Abbey. No sitting room but interesting people and excellent value.

Rooms: 1 twin/double, 1 double, 1 single – all sharing 1 bathroom.

Price: £15 p.p.

Breakfast: Included – full English.

Meals: Available locally at excellent pubs.

Closed: Never!

You may expect a formidable landlady but you get Jayne – engagingly easy-going and bustling about in the friendliest way. Her welcome, and that of her dogs, is a counterpoint to the formality of the handsome corniced sitting room where you will be offered tea when you arrive and a drink before you go out to dinner. In summer you can breakfast under glass looking over the big walled garden. The rooms are comfortable enough but it is Jayne who adds the something special.

Rooms: 2 main twin/doubles: 1 with en suite bath, 1 sharing sep. bathroom with an extra double if same party.

Price: From £26 p.p. double.

Breakfast: Included – full English.

Meals: Available locally.

Closed: Christmas & New Year.

A367 Wells Road from Bath through Radstock. After 3 miles at large roundabout B3139 towards Trowbridge. After 1.1 miles right up short tarmac drive. Pale pink Melon Cottage is at top of hill, visible from road.

Map Ref No: 3

Virginia & Hugh Pountney
Melon Cottage Vineyard
Charlton, Radstock
Nr. Bath
Somerset BA3 5TN
Tel: 01761-435090

Follow A36 from Bath to Woolverton. Turn left at Woolverton House Hotel. After 1 mile cross bridge and take third right. House is signed, 4th on right.

Map Ref No: 4

Jayne & Oliver Holder
Irondale House
67 High Street
Rode, Bath
Somerset BA3 6PD
Tel: 01373-830730
Fax: 01373-830730

THE WEST COUNTRY

'God's Pocket' is this area's name, referring to its position at the foot of Ham Hill – reputedly Europe's largest Iron Age hill fort. The cottages were made from a sensitive barn conversion next to the older Mill House – first mentioned in the Domesday Book. With part of the cottage standing on the river, the scene is almost Venetian – with ducks instead of gondolas. A special 3-acre garden, rare trees, orchards, ponds and much more. Although busy, Lynn Hart still makes time to chat.

Rooms: 4 cottages with a double room: 2 with en suite shower & bath, 2 with shared bathroom.

Price: £159-£418 per cottage per week.

Breakfast: Self-catering.

Meals: Dinner available locally.

Closed: Never!

This house grew over three centuries (14th to 17th). The dovecote is 14th century, the 20th-century Aga hides the entrance to a Reformation priesthole. The stone courtyard and the gardens are of the same period and '1630' is carved into the lintel of the porch. Carvings abound inside too. The whole house is elegant, peaceful and welcoming with old furniture and lots of books. Sarah makes her own bread and serves cream teas in the bakery in summer.

Rooms: 1 twin en suite, 1 double en suite, 1 single with shared bathroom.

Price: £20 p.p. double/twin, £18 single.

Breakfast: Included – full English.

Meals: Not available.

Closed: Christmas.

A303 to Yeovil, exit to Crewkerne A356. 2nd left to Norton-sub-Hamdon. Through village past Lord Nelson until road turns hard right – turn left. Mill is 200m on the right.

Map Ref No: 3

Lynn & Tom Hart
Little Norton Mill
Little Norton
Norton-sub-Hamdon
Somerset TA14 6TE
Tel: 01935-881439
Fax: 01935-881337

From Bath A367 Exeter road. After 3 miles. Left opposite Burnt House Inn at sign for Wellow. Once in Wellow turn left. House is 85 metres down on left-hand corner of crossroads diagonally opposite village school.

Map Ref No: 4

Sarah Danny
The Manor House
Wellow
Bath
BA2 8QQ
Tel: 01225-832027

A spring blaze of sulphur-yellow rapeseed or a summer haze of linseed blue blankets the Addicotts' acres. Theirs is a sturdy 17th-century Grade 11 listed farmhouse with stone mullion windows, open fires and big wholesome bedrooms. There are dressers full of old china, Chinese rugs on wooden floors and swathes of exposed Bath stone. The owners are involved in Ugandan women's issues and agriculture so there is a smattering of Africana around the house and interesting conversation to be had. They are also passionate supporters of Bath Rugby Club.

Rooms: 1 twin with shared bathroom, 1 double with shared bathroom, 1 double en suite, 1 triple with shared bathroom.

Price: From £20 p.p. doubles, £28 single.

Breakfast: Included – full English/continental.

Meals: Dinner available locally.

Closed: Christmas & New Year.

From A4 W of Bath take A39 through Corston. 1 mile on just before Wheatsheaf Pub (on right) turn right. Signposted 200m along lane on right.

Map Ref No: 3

Gerald & Rosaline Addicott
Corston Fields Farm
Corston
Bath
Somerset BA2 9EZ
Tel: 01225-873305
Fax: 01225-873305

John Wood built this as a private house for the Marquess of Queensberry within a stone's throw of the Assembly Rooms in 1772 and it still has that Regency combination of elegance and intimacy. Lovely ceiling mouldings, cornices and fireplaces marry perfectly with quiet, pale colour schemes, generous spaces and neo-classical draperies. The bathrooms are wholly modern; the restaurant well-reputed; the service professional with the personal touch of the real small hotel.

Rooms: 21 double & twins with en suite bath; 1 double with en suite shower.

Price: £65-£85 p.p.

Breakfast: Included – full English/continental.

Meals: Dinner from £25 p.p. Lunch £10.50-£12.50 p.p.

Closed: 23-30 December.

From London, follow London Road (A4) until it becomes Paragon. First right into Landsdown, second left into Bennett Street, then first right into Russel Street. The Queensberry is on your left.

Map Ref No: 4

Stephen & Penny Ross
The Queensberry Hotel
Russel Street
Bath
Somerset BA1 2QF
Tel: 01225-447928
Fax: 01225-446065

The urban exterior of this early Georgian house conceals half an acre of superb garden and magic 180° views of the city. The welcoming and enthusiastic Cuttings love their house, do the garden, make their own curtains and show designer talent in their mix of contemporary and trad. The pretty sitting room has Liberty prints and maple-framed pictures, the breakfast room feels French with parquet floor, heavy lace at the windows and geraniums outside. In a quiet cul-de-sac only 7 minutes walk from the town centre.

Rooms: 8 twin/doubles, all en suite.

Price: £36-£39 p.p. doubles, £57-£63 single.

Breakfast: Included – full English/continental.

Meals: An easy walk to all Bath's restaurants.

Closed: Christmas week.

Victorian red bricks are rare in Bath, so is an old-fashioned decor such as this. It is fun and atmospheric. The Keelings are very keen new owners and spare no effort to make your stay memorable. Gradually they are refurbishing their rooms. The reception rooms have elaborate period fireplaces and velvet, the small attic rooms are romantic with views, the bathrooms (mostly showers) are small. Susan is a Cordon Bleu cook and plans to do 'Japanese' picnics (beautiful food in a knotted cloth) and full afternoon teas.

Rooms: 12 twins/doubles/family/triples/4-posters, all en suite.

Price: £32.50-£36.50 p.p. doubles, £50-£60 single.

Breakfast: Included – full English/continental/wholefood.

Meals: Dinner £15 p.p. Picnic lunch & afternoon teas available.

Closed: Never!

From Bath train station follow 1-way system to Churchill Bridge. Take A367 exit from r-bout up hill. After 0.75 mile turn left at Day and Pierce (a shop). Left down hill into cul-de-sac. On left.

Map Ref No: 4

David & Janet Cutting
Paradise House
Holloway
Bath
Somerset BA2 4PX
Tel: 01225-317723
Fax: 01225-482005

From Bath take A36 Warminster road. Climb slight hill for 0.5 miles. Over brow of hill, hotel on left and well signposted.

Map Ref No: 4

Susan & David Keeling
The Bath Tasburgh Hotel
Warminster Road
Bath
Somerset BA2 6SH
Tel: 01225-425096
Fax: 01225-463842

A neat, professional organisation here in a 13th-century Clergy house in this charming, busy old market town. This hotel goes from strength to strength. The whole was updated a year ago but the ingredients are 'non-hotelly'. Lovely designer materials and fresh flowers in all the public rooms. Log fires, pink dining room with conservatory extension, a really lovely walled garden and terrace. More sophisticated than your average country-town hotel with personal attention from loyal staff. The restaurant has a growing reputation with discerning diners.

Rooms: 13 twin/doubles, all with en suite bath/shower.

Price: £28.50-£49.50 p.p. doubles, £53-£70 single.

Breakfast: Included – full English/continental.

Meals: Dinner £18.95 p.p. Lunch available.

Closed: Never!

A fabulous getaway surrounded by 10 acres of orchard, enveloping valleys and wooded hills. Guests have absolute privacy in their own converted 17th-century wing. The rooms are thoroughly French in flavour with antique French beds, French furniture, French colours. This and the Englishness of exposed beams and a snug open log fire, stone walls and soft, deep chairs. Irresistible. The breakfast is excellent – cured ham, 100% meat sausages, local kippers give an idea. To-die-for sunsets... do you need more?

Rooms: 1 twin, 3 doubles, all en suite.

Price: £29-32.50 p.p. doubles, £16 p.p. single supp.

Breakfast: Included – full English/continental.

Meals: Dinner available locally.

Closed: Christmas.

Beaminster is just off the A3066 Bridport to Crewkerne road. The hotel is 100 metres down the hill from the town centre. There is a red phone box outside.

Map Ref No: 3

Peter Pinkster & Sharon Baxter
The Bridge House Hotel
Beaminster
Dorset
DT8 3AY
Tel: 01308-862200
Fax: 01308-863700

From Dorchester on A35, after 13 miles take second road signposted left to Shipton Gorge and Burton Bradstock. First left to farmhouse.

Map Ref No: 3

Sydney Davies & Jayne Turner
Innsacre Farmhouse
Shipton Gorge
Bridport
Dorset DT6 4LJ
Tel: 01308-456137
Fax: 01308-456137

You could scarcely find a more typical English cottage – it's got the lot. A lovely village, fields and hills all around, a thatched roof, a stream to cross, a pretty garden, a stone-flagged hall... and small to very small attic bedrooms with dormer windows and simple pine furniture. A huge (but redundant) stone fireplace dominates the dining room. Nicky is enthusiastic and knowledgeable about walks and visits in the area but will leave you to your own devices.

Rooms: 2 doubles (1 with room for extra bed), 1 twin. All with basins. 1 bathroom with bath, 1 bathroom with shower to be shared by all.

Price: £19 p.p. doubles/twin, £22 single.

Breakfast: Included – full English/continental/health food.

Meals: No, but good food locally available.

Closed: Christmas.

From Dorchester A37 north. After 5 miles in Grimstone, right under railway bridge to Sydling St. Nicholas. Lamperts is first thatched cottage on right in village.

Map Ref No: 3

Nicky Willis
Lamperts Cottage
Sydling St. Nicholas
Dorchester
Dorset DT2 9NU
Tel: 01300-341659
Fax: 01300-341699

A big black labrador and 6-year-old Clemmie will greet you; Sir Percival, the cockerel, may wake you. A very cosy and typical country house with owners to match; they are keen sportspeople and Julian (an estate agent) plays cricket for a nearby village. There is a walled ½ acre garden and herbaceous border (Tia's passion). Feel at home and hunker down with a pile of their books in front of a blazing log fire. A lovely old house, comfortable and easy.

Rooms: 1 twin/double, 1 double, 1 single, 2 bathrooms.

Price: £19 p.p.

Breakfast: Included: full English/continental.

Meals: By prior arrangement £10 p.p.

Closed: Christmas.

From Dorchester, B3143 into Buckland Newton over crossroads, Holyleas on the right opp. village cricket pitch.

Map Ref No: 3

Mrs Tia Bunkall
Holyleas House
Buckland Newton
Dorchester
Dorset DT2 7DP
Tel: 01300-345214
Fax: 01305-264488

Oh rural England! In a picture of a quaint little Dorset village, a 16th-century cottage that's got it all – thatch, roses climbing, sunflowers turning, open fireplaces, flagstone floors, oak beams, twisty corridors, good country furniture in the big dining room, simple welcoming guestrooms and a gentle light-hearted atmosphere. Your hostess talks and laughs her way enthusiastically through life and also provides amazing breakfasts with fruit salad and kippers (for example).

Rooms: 1 twin shared bathroom & wc; 2 doubles sharing bath, shower & wc.

Price: £15-£18 p.p.

Breakfast: Included – full English/continental/health food.

Meals: Dinner £8-£10 p.p, prior notice required.

Closed: Never!

Sir James Thornhill painted the fabulous ceiling at Greenwich before building this remarkable house, still surrounded by park, pasture and woodland. Cary is a garden designer and is working miracles on her own acres. Hurdles, furniture and charcoal are also made from their own hazel. You may use the beautiful reception rooms, including the fine vaulted library. It is all very elegant and comfortable – but the Goodes are delightfully unstuffy. Dine at one huge table. Flagstone floor, huge staircase, galleried landing.

Rooms: 1 twin, 2 doubles, all en suite.

Price: £30 p.p.

Breakfast: Included – full English.

Meals: Not available.

Closed: Never!

4 miles west of Dorchester on A35, take sharp left at bottom of steep hill signed Winterborne Steepleton. Follow road for 0.75 miles, stream on right, until S-bend. House on right.

Map Ref No: 3

Charmian Goodenough-Bayly
Old Manor Cottage
Winterborne Steepleton
Dorchester
Dorset DT2 9LZ
Tel: 01305-889512

From A303 take A357 towards Blandford. Through Stalbridge and in about 1 mile you see T-junction with lodge gates of house opposite. Go down drive for about ¾ mile.

Map Ref No: 4

Mrs Cary Goode
Thornhill Park
Stalbridge
Dorset
DT10 2SH
Tel: 01963-362746
Fax: 01963-363751

General Pitt-Rivers, of famously eclectic tastes, lived here. Across the road the water meadows descend to the river that winds round Sturminster Newton. Australian Margie is fun and easy-going; the house is the same, with a huge fireplace in the hall and a smaller one in the snug sitting room. Bedrooms are big and unpretentiously attractive with plain Wilton carpets. Breakfasts, served from the vast and friendly kitchens, are feasts of local sausage, homemade yoghurts and fruit salad, etc. A wonderful house.

Rooms: 2 doubles with bath & wc., 1 twin & 2 singles sharing bath & wc.

Price: £20 p.p.

Breakfast: Included.

Meals: Supper £12 'en famille' by arrangement. BYO wine. Meals also available locally.

Closed: Christmas.

A magical place. Complete peace; the garden runs down to the river Stour and has uninterrupted views over the water meadows. The millhouse, 16th-cent.ury and Grade 1 listed, is as warm and vibrant as the owners. The inside is no surprise: an original moulded plaster ceiling and open fireplace in one room, a real four-poster in another, rich decoration and large table in the dining room. There is no sitting room for guests but the rooms are big and who cares when the house is so magnificent?

Rooms: 1 double en suite; 1 double sharing bathroom with a 4-poster double.

Price: £15-£17.50 p.p. doubles, from £25 single. £5 p.p. extra Saturday nights.

Breakfast: Included – full English.

Meals: Not available.

Closed: Never!

On A357 Sherborne to Blandford road. House is 0.25 miles west of Sturminster Newton Bridge, on south side of road.

Map Ref No: 4

Charles & Margie Fraser
Newton House
Sturminster Newton
Dorset
DT10 2DQ
Tel: 01258-472783

House is on A357 between Sturminster Newton and Blandford. Look for well-marked turning on north side between Lydlinch and Fiddleford.

Map Ref No: 4

Mr & Mrs A Ingleton
Fiddleford Mill
Fiddleford
Sturminster Newton
Dorset DT10 2BX
Tel: 01258-472786

Our front cover hints at what Plumber Manor is about; no ducks but deck chairs, a white bridge over the river, a well-manicured garden. A family triumvirate own and run this special place – Brian being brilliant in the kitchen, Richard behind the bar (guaranteed to provide laughter, we hear) and Alison everywhere. Their family demesne since the 17th-century keeps the ancestral atmosphere by avoiding 'hotelisms' - no room numbers for example. Homely, big, elegant rooms, delectable food and lots of family portraits complete the picture.

Rooms: 14 twins/doubles: 1 with separate private bathroom, 13 en suite; 2 doubles, both en suite.

Price: £90-£120 p.p. doubles, £130-£160 single, all prices quoted for minimum of 2 nights.

Breakfast: Included – full English/continental.

Meals: Dinner £15-£27.50 p.p. Sunday lunch available.

Closed: February.

Piddle is a fine name for a valley. Here is this charming traditional Dorset country house built in 1792, solid and comfortable with touches of elegance even in the corridors. The bedrooms are marvellous, with old furniture, easy chairs, books, radio etc and lovely views. No sitting room but a fine drawing room and an equally beautiful furnished hall. The dining room has been described as one of the prettiest in any B&B, with fine white oak furniture.

Rooms: 2 double/twin with private bathroom, 1 double en suite.

Price: £20-£25 p.p.

Breakfast: Included – full English.

Meals: Supper £8-£9 in winter on request.

Closed: Christmas – New Year.

Plumber Manor is 1.5 miles SW of Sturminster Newton on the Hazlebury Bryan road. Turn off A357 to Hazlebury Bryan; hotel is 2 miles along.

Map Ref No: 4

Richard, Alison & Brian Prideaux
Brune
Plumber Manor
Sturminster Newton
Dorset DT10 2AF
Tel: 01258-472507
Fax: 01258-473370

From A35 towards Dorchester, left onto B3390. On for 1 mile, then right. 50m along on right next to church.

Map Ref No: 4

Anthea & Michael Hipwell
The Old Vicarage
Affpuddle
Dorchester
Dorset DT7 7HH
Tel: 01305-848315
Fax: 01305-848315

A busy, thriving organic farm offering totally organic farmhouse food with all the trimmings. There are cart horses, sheep, cows, dogs; you can even stable your own horses here. There is also a farm shop, so the place is a constant bustle. Nevertheless, guests are greeted by the Crosses with utmost warmth, enthusiasm and cups of tea. Children are welcome and would love it. A very comfortable, companionable place to stay without frills. Thomas Hardy country around and it is only 1 hour to the sea.

Rooms: 2 twins with shared bathroom, 1 double en suite, 1 annexe for two persons.

Price: £18-£22 p.p.

Breakfast: Included – full English/continental.

Meals: Dinner available locally.

Closed: Never!

A large, heavy-roofed, rather gloomy-looking late Victorian manor, this house is surprisingly light and pretty inside. It has panelling (not original and older than the house), old pine furniture, traditional decor and a gallery/landing with chairs, an oak chest and big windows instead of a sitting room. The bedrooms have a homely feel, the breakfast room is lovely with its stripey walls and big fireplace and your hostess is a gentle and charming person. Children over 12 welcome.

Rooms: 1 twin en suite shower, 2 doubles, 1 en suite bathroom, 1 adj. private bathroom.

Price: £22 p.p. double, £25 single.

Breakfast: Included – full English/continental.

Meals: Available within walking distance.

Closed: Christmas.

From Sturminster Newton A357 to Blandford Forum. At T-junction pass village cross on the left. Farm is signed 0.25 miles on the left.

Map Ref No: 4

Ann & David Cross
Gold Hill Organic Farm
Child Okeford
Blandford Forum
Dorset DT11 8HB
Tel: 01258-860293

From Shaftesbury A30 signed Sherborne. Left onto B3092. 4 miles to Marnhull church, right down Church Hill. After ¼ mile Lovells Court is on left just beyond village shops but before Blackmore Vale Inn.

Map Ref No: 4

Mary-Ann & Peter Newson-Smith
Lovells Court
Marnhull
Dorset
DT10 1JJ
Tel: 01258-820652
Fax: 01258-820487

Built in 1700, the forge, once used by the local estate wheelwright, now houses a museum of Dorset blacksmithing. There is still an eclectic array of old ironmongery here. In the sitting room the wheelwright's tools lie alongside an ancient vacuum cleaner. In the workshop Tim restores post-war classic cars. An intriguing corner of mechanical history hidden in the hills of Hardy country. Wonderful place for children. Bedrooms are pretty, mostly pine-furnished. Lucy serves a feast of local, organic produce for breakfast.

Rooms: 1 double/family room en suite; 1 double and 1 single sharing adjacent bathroom but only if same party.

Price: £20-£22.50 p.p. doubles, £25 single. Extra £2.50 p.p. for bookings of one night only.

Breakfast: Included – full English.

Meals: None, but good food locally.

Closed: Never!

From Shaftesbury take A350 to Compton Abbas. The Old Forge is the first property on left before C. Abbas sign. Turn immediately left there off main road. Entrance on left through five-bar gate.

Map Ref No: 4

Tim & Lucy Kerridge
The Old Forge, Fanners Yard
Compton Abbas
Shaftesbury
Dorset SP7 0NG
Tel: 01747-811881
Fax: 01747-811881

The Turnbulls are as thoroughly English as their 1930s thatched house and huge totally unmechanised garden (John mows by hand because a machine cannot give the effect he craves). Sara keeps a large welcoming home with impeccable taste, mixing antique and modern, whites and pastels and paying attention to detail such as a new toothbrush for the forgetful, linen table napkins and two sorts of tea.... Every view is into lush green countryside.

Rooms: 1 double, 1 twin, 1 single. All share 2 sep. adj. bathrooms with wcs. Can arrange for 1 couple to have private bathroom.

Price: £20 p.p.

Breakfast: Included – full English.

Meals: Dinner available on request.

Closed: Never!

B3078 from Wimborne to Cranborne. Turn right to Holt. After 2 miles Thornhill is on right, 200 metres beyond Old Inn.

Map Ref No: 4

John & Sara Turnbull
Thornhill
Holt
Wimborne
Dorset BH21 7DJ
Tel: 01202-889434

Tony is an early-retired naval officer and the house is as solid and well-run as a ship. Nothing is out of place and the hospitality is meticulous and old-fashioned. The house was built in the '20's and is special for its commanding views over Lyme Bay and 30 miles of Dorset coast, and it is only a 15-minute walk down to the town centre and sea. The Normans have travelled far and wide with the Navy. Vicky runs doll-making courses from her studio in the well-kept garden.

Rooms: 1 double/twin/family; 2 twins. All en suite bathrooms.

Price: £40-£48 p.p. double, £30-£36 single.

Breakfast: Included – full English.

Meals: Supper tray £7.50 p.p., order in advance.

Closed: Mid-November – early March.

The style is Grand Victorian Jacobean, the view is panoramic. An opulent place with 10 acres of garden that are glorious with bulbs in the spring (and the source of the River Parrot), and a solid reputation for excellent food. Inside it is equally large and luxurious with Persian rugs, carved fireplaces, antiques, books and paintings galore, but light and airy throughout. A country house hotel for an interlude of complete self-indulgence.

Rooms: 1 twin, 5 twin/doubles, 4 doubles, all en suite.

Price: £82-£95 p.p. doubles, £92-£105 single, prices inclusive of dinner.

Breakfast: Included – full English/continental.

Meals: Dinner.

Closed: 2 – 31 January.

Entering Lyme from A3052, The Red House is first left past Blue Water Drive on left and 'Welcome to Lyme' sign on right. From Lyme go up Sidmouth Rd, past Morgan's Grave & Somers Rd., then enter first driveway on right.

Map Ref No: 3

From Crewkerne take A356. Turn off A356 at Winyards Gap. House is 0.25 miles further along the lane.

Map Ref No: 3

Tony & Vicky Norman
The Red House
Sidmouth Rd
Lyme Regis
Dorset DT7 3ES
Tel: 01297-442055
Fax: 01297-442055

Philip & Hilary Chapman
Chedington Court
Chedington
Beaminster
Dorset DT8 3HY
Tel: 01935-891265
Fax: 01935-891442

A great escape from usual Dorset tourist routes into this magical wooded valley. The Scotts have laboured devotedly to transform the 17th-century buildings – their own cottage and a separate barn. Cottage rooms have what you would expect: low ceilings, beams, pretty floral cottage style. The barn has its own sitting room and balcony onto the garden. An enthusiastic welcome and if you're superstitious you can throw a coin into the village wishing well.

Rooms: 1 twin with shared bathroom; 3 doubles, 2 en suite, 1 with shared bathroom.

Price: £19-£22 p.p. doubles, £25 single.

Breakfast: Included – full English/continental.

Meals: Dinner available locally. Packed lunch available on request.

Closed: Christmas.

A beautiful Queen Anne farmhouse, its architectural integrity intact: flagstones, original windows, exposed beams. Unpretentious bedrooms are large with country-style fabrics. Janice Hyde, who has a ceramic gallery in the stable across the gravelled yard, has given her easy, warm personality to the house. Fresh milk and cream come straight from the farm and in winter there may be a roaring fire lit during breakfast. The farm's fourth generation continue the family's vocations as cook, thatcher and farmer.

Rooms: 1 twin en suite, 1 double with separate, private bathroom.

Price: £25 p.p. doubles, £30 single.

Breakfast: Included – full English/continental.

Meals: Dinner available locally.

Closed: 1 December – 28 February.

On B3159 between Martinstown and Weymouth and signed opposite St. Laurence parish church car park.

Map Ref No: 3

Christina & Les Scott
Friars Way
Church Street
Upwey
Dorset DT3 5QE
Tel: 01305-813243

Milton Farm is 0.25 miles off the A350 at the NW end of East Knoyle (signed for Milton). Follow the signs for Janice Hyde Ceramics.

Map Ref No: 4

Janice & Richard Hyde
Milton Farm
Milton
East Knoyle, Salisbury
Wiltshire SP3 6BG
Tel: 01747-830247

The name Little Langford belies the true size of this rather grand Victorian gothic farmhouse. It is a working, tenanted farm owned by the Earl of Pembroke, with arable and dairy, plus chickens scratching about. There are very large bedrooms with grand garden views, a cosy sitting room and a billiard room. Open fires in winter and fresh milk straight from the dairy. The whole estate is 1400 acres and a Site of Special Scientific Interest, treasured for its wild flowers and butterflies.

Rooms: 2 twins: 1 en suite, 1 with private shower room; 1 double/family room with private bathroom.

Price: £20-£25 p.p.

Breakfast: Included – full English/continental.

Meals: Dinner available locally.

Closed: Christmas & 31 December.

How about a picnic with a difference? Transportation: donkey trap. Destination: Salisbury Plain. Chris and Emma have all that it takes to give their guests a good time. Emma has 9 years of cooking experience and uses 90% organic ingredients in her Thai, French and English dishes and finds time to make bread, jams, chutneys. Chris knows all about wine – even of organic type. The house, described as 'a Victorian Villa type affair', is an understated glory; newly decorated with tartans, creams, seagrass flooring.

Rooms: 1 twin with shared bathroom, 1 double with shared bathroom, 1 double with private bathroom.

Price: £18-£20 p.p.

Breakfast: Included – full English/continental.

Meals: Dinner £15 p.p. Lunch & picnics also available on request.

Closed: Never!

From Salisbury A36 towards Warminster/Bath. Left at Stoford into Great Wishford. Pass church and turn right at Royal Oak pub. House signed on right after 2 miles.

Map Ref No: 4

From Salisbury A345 towards Marlborough. Right into Enford village, cross Avon. At T-junction right and then immediately left. House is signed.

Map Ref No: 4

Patricia Helyer
Little Langford Farmhouse
Little Langford
Salisbury
Wiltshire SP3 4NR
Tel: 01722-790205
Fax: 01722-790086

Christopher & Emma Younghusband
Hill House
Long Street
Enford Pewsey
Wiltshire SN9 6DD
Tel: 01980-671202
Fax: 01980-671212

A little old (1700?) wisteria-clad manor house in a peaceful hamlet, as attractive as they come. The house feels old, not least because so many bits have been added over the years. It is full of skewy angles and hotch-potch alterations... all delightful. There is an Aga, flagstones throughout the ground floor, a wood-burning stove... and central heating. During term-time guests can use the children's bedrooms. Three horses, a dog and two cats, plus ten Black Welsh mountain sheep.

Rooms: 1 twin with adjoining private bath, 1 twin with private shower.

Price: £18 – £20 p.p., £20 p.p. single.

Breakfast: Included: full English/continental.

Meals: Available locally.

Closed: Christmas and New Year.

Hooray! A child-friendly hotel with nursery, full-time nanny, nipper-friendly food.... But Woolley Grange offers much more and you don't have to bring the children. With a triumphant reputation already marching before them, Nigel and Heather Chapman (4 kids, 1 springer spaniel) have created an unstuffy, blissfully comfortable country house hotel at the doorway to utterly delightful Bradford-on-Avon. Esoteric decoration, a Victorian gothic conservatory, oak-panelled drawing room and mouth-watering food at every meal.

Rooms: 3 twins, 18 doubles, 1 single, all with en suite bath &/or shower.

Price: £42.50-£110 p.p.

Breakfast: Included – full English/continental.

Meals: Dinner £29 p.p. Lunch £15 p.p.

Closed: Never!

From Pewsey west on A345 towards Devizes. Right to Manningford Abbots. 0.5 mile, chicken farm on left, over cattle grid.

Map Ref No: 4

Priscilla Gamble
The Manor
Manningford Abbots
Pewsey
Wiltshire SN9 6HZ
Tel: 01672-564292

From M4 junction 17. Follow A350 to Melksham; B3107 to Bradford-on-Avon; right to Woolley Green. Hotel signed after 0.5 mile on left.

Map Ref No: 4

Nigel & Heather Chapman
Woolley Grange Hotel & Restaurant
Woolley Green
Bradford-on-Avon
Wiltshire BA15 1TX
Tel: 01225-864705
Fax: 01225-864059

On a steep hillside is this old windmill, now something of a folly... with a Victorian spiral staircase and pointed Gothic windows. But the restored oak sail gallery speaks of an honest mill. Sleep comes easily in the round womb-like rooms with spectacular views over the lovely old Cotswold-stone town. The rooms are self-conscious but fun: waterbed and whirlpool bath here, vast round bed there, minstrels' gallery and box bed elsewhere. Dinners at the refectory table are eclectic, exotic and delicious. Books and log fires... come and wallow.

Rooms: 1 twin, 3 doubles: 3 en suite bathrooms, 1 with private bathroom.

Price: £25-£37.50 p.p. £15-£27.50 single.

Breakfast: Included – full English/continental/vegetarian/health foods.

Meals: Dinner £18 p.p. Mon, Thurs, Sat only. 'Ethnic' by prior arrangement.

Closed: December, January, February.

Travelling from N on A363, mini-roundabout at Castle Pub, take road downhill to town centre. After 50m turn left into private drive, immediately before first house on pavement.

Map Ref No: 4

Peter & Priscilla Roberts
Bradford Old Windmill
Masons Lane
Bradford-on-Avon
Wiltshire BA15 1QN
Tel: 01225-866842
Fax: 01225-866648

Walk out of the house up hill for horizon-sweeping views. Or bring your own horse and ride it up. You are wrapped in farmland, cossetted by two charming hosts (Richard a wine buff and Pippa a skilled organiser of social events), fed food cooked with passion and given the run of an elegant but easy house and its gardens. The grass tennis court is one of the best, the chickens range free, the bedrooms are vast and luxurious and the three dogs (Pippa trains them) and log fires make the house cosy. Beautifully furnished and decorated. Children over 13 welcome.

Rooms: 2 double/twin with bathroom en suite. 1 small double with private bathroom.

Price: £26-£28. Single £28 in small double.

Breakfast: Included – full (seasonal) English.

Meals: Dinners on request in advance £18.

Closed: Christmas and Easter

West along A4. Left just before Calne signed Heddington. 2 miles to Ivy Inn and T junct. Left. House on left opposite church 50 yards on.

Map Ref No: 4

Richard & Pippa Novis
Heddington Manor
Heddington
Nr. Calne
Wiltshire SN11 0PN
Tel: 01380-850240

Where there isn't a picture there are books: the friendly, gentle Harveys are painters and book buffs. Theirs is a dream house, a finely-furnished 17th-century mill cottage with something French about it. Each room is utterly individual; one has a half tester bed and steps down to the source of the Bybrook, right here! In the organic garden, floods of colour and secret paths lead past laden fruit trees to the stream-side water garden or through the vegetable garden to the summer house. A dream, we said.

Rooms: 1 twin with private bathroom, 2 doubles with en suite bathrooms.

Price: £21.50-£25 p.p. doubles, £20-£25 single.

Breakfast: Included – full English/continental.

Meals: Dinner £20 p.p. on request. Very good local pubs.

Closed: Never!

A traditional Cotswold-stone cottage (with recent additions), Bullocks Horn is in a peaceful hamlet well away from the main road: on one side the garden, on the other the open fields. Warmth comes from log fires and a sunny human welcome; colour schemes are sunny too. Liz Legge is very flexible and clearly enjoys meeting people. There is an arbour for summer dining in the delightful garden, the conservatory for cooler days. Over 16s welcome.

Rooms: 1 twin en suite, 1 twin with private bathroom.

Price: £20-£25 p.p.

Breakfast: Included – full English/continental/health food.

Meals: Dinner £14 p.p. by arrangement.

Closed: Christmas & Easter.

From Chippenham A420. After 0.5 mile right onto B4039. After 3 miles through hamlet of Gib. Drive is opposite turn signposted Littleton Drew on right.

Map Ref No: 4

Mike & Alison Harvey
Goulters Mill
Nettleton
Nr. Chippenham
Wiltshire SM14 7LL
Tel: 01249-782555

From A429 take B4040 E through Charlton, past Horse & Groom pub, turn left signposted 'Bullocks Horn – No Through Road'. Continue to end of lane. Turn right. House is first on left.

Map Ref No: 4

Colin & Liz Legge
Bullocks Horn Cottage
Charlton
Malmesbury
Wiltshire SN16 9DZ
Tel: 01666-577600
Fax: 01666-577905

THE WEST COUNTRY

In one room you have a view of the village duck pond. The ducks happily and often cross the road so it can't be very trafficked. The Corner House was built in about 1700 and built to last – well-grounded square-set Cotswold dwelling. Margaret, a Scottish exile, is a sweetheart, her little old cottage has all the right things: beams, ship's timbers, old stones, flagged floors, log fire, a walled garden and a lovely kitchen that guests can use.

Rooms: 1 double en suite, 1 twin, 1 single, sharing bathroom.

Price: From £17.50 p.p.

Breakfast: Included – full English/continental.

Meals: No, but available locally.

Closed: 31 October – 1 March.

What could be more seductive than the smell of home-baked bread wafting out of the kitchen? It sets the scene for this fine George1 farmhouse in a quiet spot off the main road, on the edge of the New Forest. The rooms are full of character; ample and charming, with patchwork quilts, brass beds, stencils. Sue Berry is equally characterful and as a Blue Badge Guide is well qualified to tell you about the area. Homemade jams, honey and elderflower cordial. Several black labradors snuffling about.

Rooms: 1 twin/family en suite, 2 doubles en suite, 1 single with private bathroom.

Price: £20-£22 p.p. doubles, £25 single.

Breakfast: Included – full English/continental.

Meals: Dinner available locally.

Closed: Christmas & New Year.

From M4 take junction 17 to Chippenham. Join the A420. Biddestone is signed. House is in the village on the corner by the duck pond.

Map Ref No: 4

Margaret Kerr
Corner House
Biddestone
Nr. Chippenham
Wiltshire SN14 7DF
Tel: 01249-714141

From Salisbury A36 towards Southampton. After about 5 miles look for sign on left before lights. Follow the signs.

Map Ref No: 4

Sue Barry
Brickworth Farmhouse
Brickworth Lane
Whiteparish
Wiltshire SP5 2QE
Tel: 01794-884663
Fax: 01794-884581

So long as you are not a 6'6"
claustrophobic you will love this ancient
hostelry in the jewel of National Trust
villages, only yards from the church.
There are lots of low beams and doors
to navigate, plus flagstone floors,
panelling, warm old antiques and so on.
Very comfortable, cottagey bedrooms
with 20th-century, not 15th-century,
plumbing. There is a charming garden
behind the inn, complete with stream,
bridge and chickens. Their eggs are
presented for breakfast along with
homemade bread and marmalade.

Rooms: 1 twin, 3 doubles, (2 with 4-
posters), all en suite. In the cottage: 1
twin, 3 doubles, all en suite.

Price:£37.50-£46.50 p.p. doubles, £55
p.p. single.

Breakfast: Included – full English.

Meals: Lunch from £5 p.p., dinner from
£10 p.p..

Closed: 22-30 December.

*From M4 junction 17, follow A350
south past Chippenham. Follow signs left
into Lacock. Hotel is at bottom left of
village by church.*

Map Ref No: 4

George Hardy
At the Sign of the Angel
Church Street
Lacock
Wiltshire BN15 2LB
Tel: 01249-730230
Fax: 01249-730527

Superlatives are permitted – vast, lavish,
luxurious. The quality of the light in the
bedrooms is very special as is the restful
mood emanating from the soft decor
and the space. There are long views
across Salisbury Plain. The great
drawing room, once a ballroom, is
softened with pale colours and period
pieces. Dinner in the red-lacquered
dining room with candles and Georgian
glasses at one long table is a rare
experience. It may be too coolly grand
and formal for some, but there is no
doubting the splendour of it all.

Rooms: 1 twin, 2 doubles, all with en
suite bathrooms.

Price: £40 p.p. doubles.

Breakfast: Included – full
English/continental.

Meals: Dinner from £20 p.p. Available
on request.

Closed: Christmas.

*Take A3102 from Melksham. After 2
miles and half-way up hill, entrance is
on left between 2 short stretches of stone
walls.*

Map Ref No: 4

Annette & Andrew Hoogeweegen
Sandridge Park
Melksham
Wiltshire
SN12 7QU
Tel: 01225-706879
Fax: 01225-702838

In one of the first villages on the infant River Thames, this is one half of an early 18th-century manor and many of the rooms have the gracious proportions of Georgian architecture. There is a big ballroom that you cross to reach the garden room, the dining room's natural elegance is enhanced by Valerie's flair for interior design and everywhere you will be reminded that she is a collector of and authority on historical costume. You can also tell that she loves gardening... and people.

Rooms: 1 double en suite bath; 1 twin en suite shower; 1 double with 4-poster, shower & wc.

Price: £22-£27 p.p.

Breakfast: Included – full English.

Meals: Available locally.

Closed: Christmas & New Year.

In the midst of poppy-strewn fields, Cotswold stone is star here: house, yard, flower beds, delicious walled garden are all softly golden. Tony's mother made the lovely vine-hung thyme-carpeted arbour. Easy-going Doi does B&B because she simply loves it; breakfast is when you want, dinner is if you want. Gently-decorated bedrooms have space, views, flowers and old photographs. The sitting and dining rooms are beamed and quiet. You may not want to leave.

Rooms: 2 doubles: 1 en suite, and 1 with private bath & shower.

Price: £18-£20 p.p.

Breakfast: Included – any type as requested.

Meals: Dinner £12.50 p.p. By arrangement. Also local pub food.

Closed: Christmas.

In the centre of the village is the White Hart pub. 100 metres due east is a tall Cotswold stone wall with stone pillars. Turn in and the house is on the right.

Map Ref No: 4

Valerie & Roger Threlfall
1 Cove House
Ashton Keynes
Wiltshire
SN6 6NS
Tel: 01285-861226
Fax: 01793-814990

Take B4042 from Malmesbury towards Wootton Bassett. Left turn to Lea & Charlton. In Lea village, take right opposite primary school. House is along drive through fields.

Map Ref No: 4

Tony & Doi Newman
Winkworth Farm
Lea
Nr. Malmesbury
Wiltshire SN16 9NH
Tel: 01666-823267

The oldest hotel in Britain? Founded as the abbey guest-house in 1220 it may very well be. It is a superb old building. The 'traditional' wing has oak beams and floors, large mirrors, tartan sofas: quintessential England. The recent cleverly-designed 'oriental' wing fits perfectly and recalls the Bell's monastic past in its elegant simplicity. Wonderful for families, with children's meals and mealtimes, a crèche, baby-sitting and superb food for adults. And the ever-dazzling Abbey, of course.

Rooms: 31 rooms (all en suite) of which 16 are in main building.

Price: £35-£62.50 p.p. doubles. Singles from £60.

Breakfast: Included – full English/continental.

Meals: Dinner £18.50-£24 p.p.

Closed: Never!

A treat – big beds! Not American big, but generous. The Coach House hides inside 8 acres of parkland and gardens within an ancient hamlet, hunkering down against winter gales. A clever conversion makes use of all space – immaculate rooms with sloping ceilings and skylights. Chintzy, very English, very elegant and very right for this situation. Plusses: huge sitting room, dining room, patio and adorable chocolate labrador. Immaculate garden, with croquet and tennis at whatever time of day.

Rooms: 1 twin, 1 double, 1 single. Private or shared bathroom available.

Price: £20-£25 p.p.

Breakfast: Included – full English/continental.

Meals: Dinner £12.50-£15 p.p. Available on request.

Closed: Never!

At top of High Street turn left in front of Market Cross and drive round corner. The Old Bell is directly in front of you next to Abbey.

Map Ref No: 4

Nicholas Dickinson & Nigel Chapman
The Old Bell
Abbey Row
Malmesbury
Wiltshire SN16 0AG
Tel: 01666-822344
Fax: 01666-825145

West along A420. Take exit to Upper Wraxall. Take first left in village opposite pond. Coach House at end of this private drive.

Map Ref No: 4

Helga & David Venables
The Coach House
Upper Wraxall
Nr. Bath
Wiltshire SN14 7AG
Tel: 01225-891026

From the front it is a characteristic townhouse in sight of the Benedictine Abbey; from the back it is a country house with views over the Avon River and Wiltshire. Inside there is a sense of sunlit space, the foyer/dining room has a gallery, there are old, rare, well-loved possessions, books (Dick used to run a book shop here) and a fine conservatory. There is also a meditation room. Your hostess is fun and chatty; both she and Dick enjoy having guests in this, the oldest borough in England.

Rooms: 1 twin en suite, 1 single with private bathroom. 1 separate shower also available.

Price: £20 p.p.

Breakfast: Included – full English/continental.

Meals: Dinner available locally.

Closed: Never!

Picture perfect, outside and in: it's everything that you'd expect to see in the best glossy interior magazines, but with human beings in it. A doll's house façade looks onto a gently sloping garden with river and swans. Inside, not a tacky thing in sight, just huge pillows, lovely linen, perfect furniture, style everywhere. Breakfast in the conservatory which leads off the kitchen, so you are in touch with the heart of the house. Heather is a professional flower arranger and it shows.

Rooms: 1 double en suite, 3 singles with shared bathroom.

Price: £22.50 p.p. double, £20 single.

Breakfast: Included – full English/continental.

Meals: Dinner available locally. Lunch & packed lunch available on request.

Closed: Christmas.

From top of High Street turn left at Market Cross. House is 100m on left-hand side next to the large traffic mirror.

Map Ref No: 4

Dick & M.E. Batstone
St. Aldhelms
14 Gloucester Street
Malmesbury
Wiltshire SN16 0AA
Tel: 01666-822145

From Hungerford A4 towards Marlborough. After 7 miles right towards Stitchcombe, down hill (bear left at barn) and left at T-junct. On entering village house is on left.

Map Ref No: 4

Jeremy & Heather Coulter
Fisherman's House
Mildenhall
Nr. Marlborough
Wiltshire SN8 2LZ
Tel: 01672-515390

A comfortable, traditional Cotswold farmhouse, set in open countryside on the Fosseway (on the road, but not a busy one). Mr Owen is a cabinet-maker and specialises in gilding restoration, working from home. The house immediately reveals the artistic interests of its owners and is happily full of books. They have created a shady courtyard, now dominated by a splendid acacia, and a lovely walled garden.

Rooms: 1 twin with separate private bathroom, 1 double with en suite bath.

Price: £20 p.p.

Breakfast: Included – full English/continental.

Meals: Dinner available locally. Packed lunch available on request.

Closed: Occasionally – please check.

From Chippenham A420 west to Shoe. Just past garage on left, turn sharp right before pub, signed to Grittleton. Over crossroads. House first on left with gates.

Map Ref No: 4

John & Heather Owen
Halls Barn Farm
North Wraxall
Chippenham
Wiltshire SN14 7AQ
Tel: 01225-891542
Fax: 01225-891904

An endlessly rambling house in an unusually secluded spot just one mile from the south coast where salt smuggling barons used to meet, Chequers Green has a warm and happy feel about it now – it is quite naturally, almost guilelessly itself. Guests have very fine bedrooms and their own sitting and breakfast rooms. Plants and sailing are the family's passions – you can walk in the lovely garden or rush to the sea and be active. Anyone would feel welcome here; sailors would find soul mates.

Rooms: 2 twins with en suite bath & hand showers.

Price: £29 p.p. twins, £39 single.

Breakfast: Included – full English/continental.

Meals: Dinner available locally.

Closed: Christmas & New Year.

The South Coast

From Lymington A337 towards New Milton. After 0.5 mile left at roundabout by White Hart and immediately left again. Continue 0.75 miles to Chequers Inn. Right by post box and immediately right again.

Map Ref No: 4

Caroline & Jamie Heron
Chequers Green
Lymington
Hampshire
SO41 8AH
Tel: 01590-674660
Fax: 01590-679044

Beware the bear in the corner if you pass in the dark. He is just one of the antiques and heirlooms that fill this elegantly-proportioned Georgian townhouse. There are ancestors and a rocking horse too. The Jeffcocks are cultured, travelled and welcoming. He chairs the Hants European Movement and 'is a fount of useless information'. They have a top-floor conservatory drawing room overlooking the harbour and a perfect central position for visiting pretty Beaulieu.

Rooms: 1 twin with separate bathroom; 1 double, with en suite shower.

Price: £24 p.p.

Breakfast: Included – full English/continental.

Meals: Dinner available by arrangement (£10), communal dining. Restaurants available locally.

Closed: December 23 to January 2.

Go down High Street (steep hill leading to sea). Captains Row is at bottom on right. House is about 70 metres on left.

Map Ref No: 4

Josephine and David Jeffcock
Wellington House
Captains Row
Lymington
Hampshire SO41 9RR
Tel: 01590-672237
Fax: 01590-673592

One of the best. A beautiful old house, full of history, with panelling, antiques, decorated ceilings, nooks and crannies, odd steps and low corners living in symbiotic partnership with gardens that lead into each other from terrace to lawn to apple orchard to lily pond. A Victorian dining room balances a silvery damask and turquoise sitting room. Great bedrooms too. Anthea is a dynamo doing B&B for the fun of it... and to pay for ever better furnishings.

Rooms: 3 twin/doubles, 1 en suite, 2 with separate, private bathrooms.

Price: £22-£24 p.p. doubles, £25-£35 single.

Breakfast: Included – full English/continental.

Meals: Dinner £15 p.p. (24 hours notice).

Closed: Christmas Day.

Between Romsey and White Parish on the A27, 0.75 miles from the Romsey turning towards Salisbury. The driveway to the house is directly off the A27.

Map Ref No: 4

Anthea & Bill Hughes
Spursholt House
Salisbury Road
Romsey
Hampshire SO51 6DJ
Tel: 01794-522670
Fax: 01794-523142

Jeremy Whitaker, a Guards officer turned architectural photographer, will tell you the story of the name. His is an 'Edwardian' house (built in 1939) in 7 acres of fabulous mature English garden with formality here, wildness there, a Japanese garden, a Wendy house, a tennis court and more. The Whitakers are natural hosts, the bedrooms the epitome of country house comfort. The Major will knowledgeably and entertainingly conduct you round the local stately homes (if you wish). Children over 12 welcome.

Rooms: 2 twins: 1 en suite and 1 with private bathroom.

Price: £25 p.p. twins, £35 p.p. single occupancy.

Breakfast: Included – full English/continental.

Meals: Dinner £20 p.p. Available on request.

Closed: Christmas day.

The long brick barn with its vast expanse of low-sloping russet-tiled roof has been carefully converted and extended. There is a secluded terrace by the lily pond for sitting out on fine days, a sunny, armchaired old-timbered sitting room for cooler moments and twenty acres of paddocks and flower-filled gardens to protect you from the outside world and all the din that therein is. Your hosts are relaxed, agreeable folk and your bedroom is furnished for true English comfort.

Rooms: 1 twin en suite, 1 twin/double en suite.

Price: £22.50-£24 p.p. twins, £30 single.

Breakfast: Included – full English/continental.

Meals: Dinner available locally.

Closed: Never!

South on A3 to traffic lights at Hindhead. Go straight across & turn right onto B3002 for Bordon. Through Grayshott. Church on right, house is signed on right, in wood two miles beyond church.

Map Ref No: 5

Jeremy & Philippa Whitaker
Land of Nod
Headley
Bordon
Hampshire GU35 8SJ
Tel: 01428-713609

From A272 turn at Seven Stars pub in Stroud towards Ramsdean. At T-junction by small village green and phone box, turn left. Twentyways Farm is 300 yards on left.

Map Ref No: 5

David & Maureen Farmer
Twentyways Farm
Ramsdean
Petersfield
Hampshire GU32 1RX
Tel: 01730-823606

'Just like home'... but this home is your own terrace house (your hosts are next door) in the village of St Cross, just 12 minutes walk from the centre of Winchester's cathedral, college and water meadows. The whole house is very newly fitted, the rooms are small and cosy and there is a log fire in the sitting room. Fizzy is Constance Spry trained, serves sumptuous breakfasts and keeps the flowers fresh. You are also left with an 'honesty box' so you may help yourselves to drinks.

Rooms: 1 twin, 1 double, both with en suite shower & bath.

Price: £22.50 p.p. doubles, £35 single.

Breakfast: Included – full English.

Meals: Available nearby.

Closed: Please check.

The breakfasts at Mizzards certainly live up to the superb vaulted dining room where they are served – traditional English with porridge, Isle of Man kippers, kedgeree... and one of the beds is a four-poster with an electrically-operated curtain! Despite the general grandness and elegant taste, the atmosphere is relaxed, the big house and gardens (lake and river thrown in) are welcoming and your excellent, caring hosts will make you feel instantly at home.

Rooms: 1 twin en suite, 1 double en suite, one 4-poster en suite.

Price: £24-£28 p.p.

Breakfast: Included – full English.

Meals: Dinner available locally.

Closed: Christmas.

Leave M3 at junction 9 and follow signs for Winchester Park & Ride. Under motorway, straight on at roundabout signed to St Cross. Left at T-junction. St Faith's Road about 200 metres ahead.

Map Ref No: 4

Guy & Fizzy Warren
Brymer House
29/30 St Faith's Road
St Cross, Winchester
Hampshire SO23 9QD
Tel: 01962-867428
Fax: 01962-868624

From A272 at Rogate, turn towards Harting/Nyewood. Cross hump back bridge, the drive is the first turning on the right. Signed.

Map Ref No: 5

Harriet & Julian Francis
Mizzards Farm
Rogate,
Petersfield
Hampshire GU31 5HS
Tel: 01730-821656
Fax: 01730-821655

Once an inn, always an inn. The George has been tending tired travellers since 1540 and bears many marks of history. The oak-panelled restaurant was once the Assize Court, the Whipping Post was in the room above – a quick trip. The rooms in the main building have old timbers and furniture (four-posters in some), those in the converted coach house are modern and functional. The George is still a meeting place for local country folk and the ancient fabric imparts an authentically rustic atmosphere.

Rooms: 6 singles, 8 doubles, 2 twins, two 4-posters, all en suite.

Price: £32.50-£37.50 p.p. twin/doubles, £45 p.p. 4-posters, £45-£65 single.

Breakfast: Included – full English/continental.

Meals: Lunch & dinner available. Packed lunch on request.

Closed: Christmas Day.

It's not surprising that people love to hold their wedding and anniversary parties here because it is very good looking, has friendly and professional management and the food is ambrosial. Rooms are distributed between the c1520 house and a c1990 addition but all have a smart country-house look helped along by lots of antiques and, predominantly, Colefax & Fowler and Zoffany materials and papers. Business people and those wanting a quick dose of spoiling come here in winter and many Americans and Europeans in summer.

Rooms: 4 twins, five 4-posters, 12 doubles, 1 single, all with en suite facilities.

Price: From £49-£104 p.p.

Breakfast: Included – continental. Full English £5 p.p.

Meals: Lunch & dinner available.

Closed: Never!

M3 exit at junct. 5. A287 towards Odiham/Farnham. The George Hotel is half-way up High Street with car park at the back.

Map Ref No: 5

Peter & Moira Kelsey
The George Hotel
High Street
Odiham, Hook
Hampshire RG29 1LP
Tel: 01256-702081
Fax: 01256-704213

4.5 miles after end of M23 (south), left onto B2115 towards Haywards Heath. Cuckfield 3 miles on & hotel at end of Ockenden Lane, just off High Street opposite Talbot Inn.

Map Ref No: 5

Sandy & Anne Goodman
Manager: Mr Kerry Turner
Ockenden Manor
Ockenden Lane, Cuckfield
West Sussex RH17 5LD
Tel: 01444-416111
Fax: 01444-415549

Olde Worlde charm at its most authentic. The Lodge was built in pure Neo-Gothic style as the gatehouse to the local manor and has kept its other-world, other-age atmosphere (delicious church windows). It sits in a large rambling garden, is totally secluded and instantly wraps you in peace. There is a wood-burning stove in the garden room for chilly days, a plant-filled conservatory to introduce the garden, two warm, elegant bedrooms and a delightful hostess who bakes a delicious cake.

Rooms: 3 doubles, all with en suite bathrooms.

Price: £22.50 p.p. doubles, £35 p.p. single.

Breakfast: Included – full English/continental.

Meals: Dinner available locally.

Closed: Never!

The Bonds enjoy the superbly isolated position of the old tidal mill (now demolished) on Manhood Peninsula. It is on the quay beside the peaceful waters of Pagham Harbour. There is a tennis court in the walled garden and you can also play croquet. Your hosts live in the 16th-century former miller's house, you stay in the delightful recently-converted little self-catering cottage. Chris takes his hosting very seriously and has been doing it for years.

Rooms: Twin bedroom, bathroom, separate shower, kitchenette.

Price: £27.50 p.p.

Breakfast: Not included.

Meals: Self-catering or available locally.

Closed: Christmas, New Year & Easter.

Village is 3 miles W of Chichester on the B2178. The lodge is 170 metres on the left after Salthill Road. Look for the sign for Oakwood School.

Map Ref No: 5

Jeanette Dridge
Chichester Lodge
Oakwood School Drive
East Ashling, Chichester
Sussex PO18 9AL
Tel: 01243-786560

From Chichester B2145 towards Selsey. Just before leaving Sidlesham, left into Mill Lane. Old Mill House is on the quayside 350 m down Mill Lane.

Map Ref No: 5

Chris & Gill Bond
The Cottage, Old Mill House
Sidlesham
Chichester
West Sussex PO20 7LX
Tel: 01243-641595
Fax: 01243-641140

The Spread Eagle has always housed travellers. It opened in 1430 and was extended in 1650 to meet increasing demand. If this all sounds rather contemporary, the facilities are, the fabric is not. Exposed beams and rafters, bricks and stones, level changes, arrow-slit and Flemish stained-glass windows are visible parts of the hotel's long story. Bedrooms are big, light and soft-furnished (some have four-posters). The public rooms look authentically ancient and can be hired for private occasions.

Rooms: 37 twin/doubles/suites, 4 singles, all en suite.

Price: £47.50-£67.50 p.p. doubles, £135-£175 suites, £75 single.

Breakfast: Included – full English/continental.

Meals: Dinner £27 p.p. Lunch £12.95-£16.50 p.p.

Closed: Never!

A 'genuine fake', this very beautiful 15th-century mansion was built at vast expense in the 1930s out of innumerable mediæval bits – stone mullions, moulded doorways, oak beams, carved doors – recovered from the original courthouse and other ancient ruins. It rambles, has nooks and crannies, tapestries and all things Gothic and big, high-ceilinged, old-furnished, new-bathroomed bedrooms. Only the (much-renovated) chapel is authentic. Superb public rooms and a magnificent garden complete the picture.

Rooms: 26 doubles, 1 single, all with en suite bath & shower.

Price: £57.50-£125 p.p. doubles; from £80 single.

Breakfast: Included – full English.

Meals: Lunch £17.50, Dinner £29.50.

Closed: Never!

In Midhurst off A272, 20 miles north of Chichester on A286.

Map Ref No: 5

Sandy & Anne Goodman
Manager: Martin Harris
The Spread Eagle Hotel
South Street, Midhurst
West Sussex GU29 9NH
Tel: 01730-816911
Fax: 01730-815668

From Littlehampton A259 W to Climping. At blue sign for Bailiffscourt turn into Climping Street and continue up lane to reach hotel.

Map Ref No: 5

Sandy & Anne Goodman
Manager: Pontus Carminger
Bailiffscourt Hotel
Climping
West Sussex BN17 5RW
Tel: 01903-723511
Fax: 01903-723107

A Lutyens manor – 'The best of the bunch', he called it himself – of mighty Elizabethan proportions, proudly displaying dressed stone inside and out, a great sitting hall with minstrels' gallery, vaulting stone doorways, high mullioned, leaded windows and a glorious Lutyens garden as well. The wood and leather in library/bar and hall are properly in keeping, the dining tables less so. Guest suites are exquisite, each seductive and different, all very smart, perhaps even grand, as is the gourmet food.

Rooms: 7 twin/doubles en suite facilities, 2 doubles with private facilities.

Price: £76-£100 p.p. doubles, £105.75 single.

Breakfast: Included – full English.

Meals: Lunch and dinner available on request.

Closed: Christmas & New Year.

We had forgotten that Sussex had so many beautiful old houses. Lywood House is a large 17th-century yeoman's home set in perfect Sussex Weald countryside, up a long lane in its own world. (However, London is only 40 miles away and Brighton 25.) Very pretty rooms, a drawing room with open fire, a fun swimming pool and a warm, not grand, mellow atmosphere. Superb food from Cleone Pengelley. Both Cleone and Max are affable hosts, described by visitors as 'real stars'.

Rooms: 2 twins: 1 en suite and 1 with private bathroom; 1 double with private bathroom.

Price: £35 p.p. doubles, £10 singles.

Breakfast: Included – full English/continental.

Meals: Dinner £15-£22 p.p.

Closed: Christmas & New Year.

Little Thakeham lies off the A24 1.5 miles north of Storrington. The hotel is on Merrywood Lane.

Map Ref No: 5

Tim & Pauline Ractliff
Little Thakeham
Merrywood Lane
Storrington
West Sussex RH20 3HE
Tel: 01903-744416
Fax: 01903-745022

Go south through Ardingly on B2028 and 1 mile after road turns to left take first lane to right. House is first on left.

Map Ref No: 5

Max & Cleone Pengelley
Lywood House
Ardingly
West Sussex
RH17 6SW
Tel: 01444-892369
Fax: 01444-892291

Jenny Maddock's house is a charming rambling 200-year-old flint cottage with creepers up the walls, little-paned windows and a warm family kitchen where breakfasts are cooked on the Aga and served piping hot on the spot (you may use the dining room if you prefer a bit of formality). Jam is made on the Aga too. As well as fresh apple juice from garden apples there are books and other touches that give that 'homely' feel. Jenny is energetic, chatty, full of local lore and loves entertaining.

Rooms: 2 twins, 1 en suite, 1 with shared bathroom, 2 singles, both with shared bathrooms.

Price: £18-£21 p.p. twins, £16-£18 p.p. singles.

Breakfast: Included – full English/continental.

Meals: Dinner available locally.

Closed: Christmas.

The Stone House has belonged to the Dunn family for 500 years and Peter and Jane Dunn have managed to keep the feel of 'home'. The decorations are fabulous – nothing 'hotelly' here, except luxury and service you won't find in many grander establishments, plus croquet and billiards. Jane cooks (Master Chef Award!): fresh fish every day, game from the estate, specially selected wines at reasonable prices. Sumptuous picnic hampers for Glyndebourne (chairs and tables provided) are an added treat.

Rooms: 1 double/single, 3 twin/doubles, 2 four-posters – all en suite. 1 suite with 2 rooms & bathroom.

Price: £42.50-£83.75 p.p. doubles, £55-£71.25 single.

Breakfast: Included – full English/continental.

Meals: Lunch available on request. Dinner £24.95 p.p.

Closed: Christmas and New Year.

South from B2096 to Rushlake Green. With village green on right, go to end of green and turn left. Stone House is to left of crossroads, signed.

Into the centre of the village – the cottage is signed on left before church.

Map Ref No: 5

Map Ref No: 6

Jenny Maddock
Hyde Cottage
The Street
Kingston
East Sussex BN7 3TB
Tel: 01273-472709

Peter & Jane Dunn
Stone House
Rushlake Green
Heathfield
East Sussex TN21 9QJ
Tel: 01435-830553
Fax: 01435-830726

Simply arriving here is special – the view takes the breath, the blue lake shimmers, the weathered bricks and tiles of the 18th-century farmhouse promise warmth and welcome, a promise kept by charming Pauline. They run a Shetland pony stud in this waterside retreat, their garden runs down to the lake (trout fishing is possible), Pauline will serve tea on the terrace but guests may also use her Aga. The bedrooms have glorious views and fluffy towels. Children over 12 welcome.

Rooms: 1 twin, 1 double, 1 single, all sharing bathroom with bath, shower & w.c. One w.c downstairs.

Price: £25 p.p.

Breakfast: Included – full English/continental/health food.

Meals: Not available.

Closed: Christmas.

If the words 'self-catering' chill your soul with thoughts of chipped cups and cheap furniture, take heart! This 17th-century oasthouse has enough character to change your mind. Two of the rooms are actually in the Roundel, which makes furniture arrangement a challenge. Large and lovely traditional kitchen, flagstone and polished brick floors. Beautiful surroundings and chickens clucking about outside your door. Fresh milk, home-laid eggs and bread will be produced on your arrival.

Rooms: 2 twins with shared shower-room, 2 doubles both en suite.

Price: £700 per week (sleeps 8-10).

Breakfast: Self-catering. Fresh milk, bread eggs, tea/coffee available on arrival.

Meals: Cook your own!

Closed: 1 November – mid-March.

From Wadhurst take B2099 for approx 1.5 miles, left into Wards Lane, follow road for 1.5 miles to Newbarn. Last part of road is unpaved.

Map Ref No: 6

Chris & Pauline Willis
Newbarn
Wards Lane
Wadhurst
East Sussex TN5 6HP
Tel: 01892-782042

From A21 south towards Hastings turn left to Sedlescombe opposite Blackbrooks Garden Centre. After 300m take sharp right to Westfield. Farm is on left-hand side after 1.25 miles.

Map Ref No: 6

Mrs Benedetta Howard
The Old Oasthouse
Platnix Farm, Harts Green
Sedlescombe, Nr. Battle
East Sussex TN33 0RT
Tel: 01424-870214

Jeake's House positively creaks with history. It and the next-door Quaker's House have been wool store, Baptist chapel (breakfast is here with piped chamber music), school, Quaker meeting house, Men's Club, even Conrad Aiken's home, now hotel. The old cobbled street in central Rye is a fitting approach indeed. Bedrooms have brass beds or four-posters, cushions and pelmets; in the public rooms there are pictures and books to browse through. There is a Honeymoon Suite too.

Rooms: 10 double en suite bathroom, 1 double shared bathroom, 1single shared bathroom.

Price: £22-£54 p.p.

Breakfast: Included – full English/continental/health food.

Meals: No.

Closed: Never!

'Teddy bears inside, hedgehogs outside and a really excellent cat'. This most welcoming, rule-free townhouse in lovely history-laden Rye also boasts fine antiques, masses of books and paintings, occasional groups of amateur dramatists in the big and otherwise quiet garden, a Smugglers' Watchtower and a small library for rainy days. Sara is lively, attentive and fun and will give you big organic/free-range breakfasts as well as all info about what to do and see. Children over 12 welcome.

Rooms: 2 doubles, 1 twin: all en suite.

Price: £30-£42 p.p. doubles, £45-£65 single.

Breakfast: Included – full English/continental, in bedroom if requested.

Meals: Dinner available nearby.

Closed: Never!

From London A268 drive straight into centre of Rye onto the High Street. Turn left off the High Street onto West Street then take the first right into Mermaid Street. Jeake's House is on the left. Pay & display parking nearby.

Map Ref No: 6

Francis & Jenny Hadfield
Jeake's House
Mermaid Street
Rye
East Sussex TN31 7ET
Tel: 01797-222828
Fax: 01797-222623

In Rye follow signs to town centre and enter Old Town through Landgate Arch into High Street. West Street is third turning on left. House is half way up on left.

Map Ref No: 6

Sara Brinkhurst
Little Orchard House
West Street
Rye
East Sussex TN31 7ES
Tel: 01797-223831

The oast house is the main horizontal building; the familiar round tower with the skewy thing on top is the kiln. Egypt Farm has two of these and oval is the home shape. Two oval bedrooms – antiques, evening sun, pretty papers – and an oval dining room with an oval table with beams, more antiques. House and owners have character and elegance. There is the drawing room, the sun room or the conservatory for the contemplative; the pool or the tennis court for the active. The 4-acre sloping garden is a delight for the potterer.

Rooms: 2 twin/doubles: 1 with private sep. bathroom and 1 with shower room almost en suite.

Price: £35-£40 p.p.

Breakfast: Included – full English.

Meals: Dinner £22 p.p. on request.

Closed: Christmas.

A working farm and fine Georgian manor house in quintessential Garden of England countryside, in the family since 1760. Not a road, railway line or telegraph pole in sight. Fine mahogany furniture, enormous dining table, old racing prints... and sherry. Rosemary Piper pampers her guests, even providing hot drinks in the sitting room after an evening out and, on request, dinner of seasonal, locally-produced foods. The rooms are traditionally decorated with superb bathrooms, flowers everywhere and great views of the Weald of Kent.

Rooms: 2 twins, 1 en suite, 1 with separate private bathroom; 1 double with separate private bathroom.

Price: £22.50-£25 p.p.

Breakfast: Included – full English/continental.

Meals: Dinner £10 p.p. Mon-Thurs & £13.50 p.p. Fri-Sun. Available on request.

Closed: 1 December – 31 January.

From Borough Green turn right off Maidstone road into Crouch Lane just before Esso station. Follow signs to West Peckham & Mereworth for about 3 miles. Down hill & right at crossroads to Tonbridge. Farm on right after fork.

Map Ref No: 5/6

Francis & Helen Bullock
Egypt Farm
Hamptons
Nr. Tonbridge
Kent TN11 9SR
Tel: 01732-810584
Fax: 01732-810584

At traffic lights in centre of Hawkhurst, A268 towards Rye. At Shell garage 1.5 miles after lights, immediately right into Conghurst Lane. After 1.25 miles on left is signed driveway.

Map Ref No: 6

Mrs Rosemary Piper
Conghurst Farm
Hawkhurst
Kent
TN18 4RW
Tel: 01580-753331
Fax: 01580-754579

We fell in love with this delicious watery place and its fabulous wildlife, natural architecture, real attention to detail and intensely warm welcome. The tea tray is laid with fine china, towels are fluffy and match the decor, baths are old-fashioned and match the house. Guests sleep and sit (the large light drawing room straddles the very mill race) in the converted mill and eat with their hosts in the mill house's beamed, inglenooked, antique-furnished dining room. Too much water for children under 12.

Rooms: 1 twin/double en suite, 1 double en suite, 1 twin with private adjacent bathroom.

Price: £29.35 p.p. doubles, £39.45 single.

Breakfast: Included – full English.

Meals: Dinner £19 p.p.

Closed: Christmas – New Year.

A lovely Georgian house where attention to detail is paramount . The comfortable bedrooms are made even more inviting with the addition of pretty china, writing paper, biscuits and sweets and bathrobes. Your hostess lays breakfast in the large conservatory (glorious all-round views over the 10-acre garden and countryside). Later she will cook you a 4-course dinner, taken 'en famille' in the comfortable dining room lit by masses of floating candles. The cosy, beamed drawing room leads onto a terrace with tables and chairs and an optimistic sun umbrella.

Rooms: 1 twin with en suite shower; 2 doubles, both with en suite shower; 1 single with separate private bathroom.

Price: From £27.50-£30 p.p. doubles, from £38-£42 sing. supp; from £29-£35 single.

Breakfast: Included – full English/continental/health foods.

Meals: Dinner £17.50 p.p. BYO wine.

Closed: Christmas & New Year.

Take A229 south from Maidstone. After Staplehurst take left to Frittenden. In about 1 mile take narrow lane to right opposite white house. Right again at end of lane – house is first on right, through the wood.

Map Ref No: 6

Kenneth & Heather Parker
Maplehurst Mill
Frittenden
Kent
TN17 2DT
Tel: 01580-852203
Fax: 01580-852203

On A28 from Tenterden towards Hastings, take right into Cranbrook Road. Go over the level crossing. Brattle House is on the left.

Map Ref No: 6

Mo & Alan Rawlinson
Brattle House
Watermill Bridges
Tenterden
Kent TN30 6UL
Tel: 01580-763565

The charming, friendly, informative Watsons know how to coddle their guests – there are big thick towels on heated towel rails and super goodies in the bathrooms, electric blankets if needed, maps in the bedrooms... and a sense of English comfort throughout this antique-filled, beam-ceilinged 18th-century manor house with its lovely garden. It is near places of interest such as Leeds Castle, Bodiam, Sissinghurst and Romney Marsh. Over 14's welcome. Definitely no pets.

Rooms: 1 twin and 1 double with private bathrooms; 1 double with en suite shower & w.c.

Price: £30 p.p. doubles, £12 single supplement.

Breakfast: Included – full English/continental/health food.

Meals: Dinner £20 p.p.

Closed: Christmas & New Year.

An ancient building, built in the 14th century by the powerful Hales family and then after being burnt down by Watt Tyler, it now has wildlife ponds, farmyard animals and barns converted into studios and an art gallery. Your artist host also has a huge collection of old films. A gentle place where flowers reign supreme, three-course candlelit dinners containing lots of homegrown organic vegetables are served in the beamed dining room and guests have their own sitting room.

Rooms: 3 twins: 1 with en suite shower, 1 with en suite bath, 1 with private adjacent bathroom.

Price: £23.50-£24.50 p.p.

Breakfast: Included – full English/continental/vegetarian.

Meals: Dinner £19 p.p.

Closed: Christmas & New Year.

Take B2082 from Tenterden, signed Wittersham & Rye. Turn right at War Memorial, go for 275 metres, entrance on left just past school sign and before church.

Map Ref No: 6

Ian & Mim Watson
Wittersham Court
Wittersham
Tenterden
Kent TN30 7EA
Tel: 01797-270425
Fax: 01797-270425

In High Halden, off A28, follow Tourist Board sign to 'Art Studio' – part of Hales Place.

Map Ref No: 6

Roger & Ellen Green
Hales Place
High Halden
Nr. Ashford
Kent TN26 3JG
Tel: 01233-850219
Fax: 01233-850716

THE SOUTH COAST

The Latham area is rich in historical incident (including Caesar's invasion). The house is a mélange of styles and ages from redbrick beamed Tudor, via a fine Georgian 'extension' with pillars and high ceilings, to a modern conservatory. The Lathams are a well-travelled, friendly and active couple. Bedrooms are pleasant (some beds firmer than others), two have glorious views; bathrooms are traditional (no showers). Guests have a log-fired drawing room. It is all full of sober taste and very easy to live in. Children over 10 welcome.

Rooms: 3 twins: 2 with private bathroom; 1 let only to members of same party willing to share bathroom.

Price: £18 p.p.

Breakfast: Included – full English/continental.

Meals: Dinner £12 p.p. and packed lunches available on request.

Closed: Christmas & New Year.

When house and garden are gorgeous, hosts enchanting and all places around hum with history, what more can one ask? Katie is a flower arranger, the elegant Georgian house shimmers with her art; Neil runs an Audio Book Library in the stables so they are both very present to enjoy guests' company. The guestrooms have big windows, fine English furniture and plenty of reading matter. Only one room is let at a time unless to a family, so no sharing a bathroom with strangers.

Rooms: 2 doubles, 1 single, all with handbasins, sharing 1 bathroom.

Price: £22.50-£25 p.p.

Breakfast: Included – full English.

Meals: Dinner £17.50 p.p. on request.

Closed: Christmas & New Year.

From M20 junction 11 take B2068 north. After 4.6 miles left opposite BP garage. House is at bottom of hill on left after 1.7 miles. Turn left into drive.

Map Ref No: 6

Take A257 from Canterbury. Pass Wingham, take fourth left. House on left.

Map Ref No: 6

Richard & Virginia Latham
Stowting Hill House
Stowting
Nr. Ashford
Kent TN25 6BE
Tel: 01303-862881
Fax: 01303-863433

Neil & Katie Gunn
Great Weddington
Ash
Nr. Canterbury
Kent CT3 2AR
Tel: 01304-813407
Fax: 01304-812531

This beautiful porticoed brick house has a gorgeous sitting room, some fabulous antiques, gardens to dream of with romantic arbours, a pond, a secret garden and an utterly English atmosphere. The gregarious Yerburghs genuinely enjoy entertaining and hope you will feel you are their friends. Her sociable and somewhat eccentric art historian father lives in the extension. They are animal-lovers too, especially of their pot-bellied pig. Children over 12 welcome and pets by arrangement.

Rooms: 3 doubles, 1 en suite, 2 with private bathrooms.

Price: £35 p.p.

Breakfast: Included – full English/continental.

Meals: Dinner £20 p.p.

Closed: Christmas & New Year.

From Dover M2 to Pavillion Services. Drive into station, continue on road past pumps. Ignore exit signs. Left at T-junction, first left & continue for 200m. Left at next T-junction, left again. House is third on left.

Map Ref No: 6

Lt. Col. & Mrs John Yerburgh
Hartlip Place
Place Lane
Nr. Sittingbourne
Kent ME9 7TR
Tel: 01795-842583

A spotless, close-carpeted, upside-down 1930s weatherboarded house on a hillside where you go down to bed and up to sit and admire the views to the North Downs and the sea beyond. The Bigwoods are cheerful, unpretentious hosts who have been cherishing guests for years and have comforted many a weary pilgrim (the pilgrims' path is just here). The rooms are not large but well-designed and practical. The main road is close but the house is set well down on the hillside and windows double-glazed.

Rooms: 1 triple en suite, 1 double en suite, 1 single with private bathroom, 1 single with shared bathroom if same party only.

Price: £18-£27.50 p.p.

Breakfast: Included – full English/continental.

Meals: £6-£10 p.p. on request only, with 24 hours notice.

Closed: Christmas.

From Charing take A252 up hill towards Canterbury. Half way up on right house is clearly signed.

Map Ref No: 6

Rosemary & Eddie Bigwood
Timber Lodge
Charing Hill
Charing
Kent TN27 0NG
Tel: 01233-712822

The Channel Island of Sark has no cars to spoil the tranquil pace which is what people come here for. Built as a farm, Stocks has been a hotel since 1895 and now belongs to the Armorgie family. It has a terrific reputation for exquisite food – Paul Armorgie is also head chef. Apart from the main Cider Press Restaurant, there is also a more informal Bistro for family lunches and suppers. A simple, affordable and accessible 'escape'. Wild flowers, clean air and dawn chorus will linger in the memory.

Rooms: 18 twin/doubles, 2 family rooms, 4 singles, most en suite.

Price: £18-£48 p.p. for B&B or £30-£60 p.p. dinner, B&B. Babies free, scale of discounts for children.

Breakfast: Included – full English/continental/health food.

Meals: Dinner £12-£20 p.p. Lunch also available from £2.50.

Closed: October – Easter.

Boat from Jersey or Guernsey. Guests met at the harbour. Or a 20-minute walk from harbour! A horse & carriage can be arranged.

Map Ref No: 1

The Armorgie Family
Stocks Island Hotel
Sark
via Guernsey
Channel Islands GY9 0SD
Tel: 01481-832001
Fax: 01481-832130

This is not a hotel where battalions of staff follow your every step but a small cosy place whose charming owner is there to welcome you. He has lovingly restored this pretty building on its elegant side street. The buffet breakfast is in the shrubby flowery Victorian conservatory which in turn gives onto the patio garden. The bedrooms are all different and quiet good taste is everywhere. Happy customers keep coming back. Children over 6 years only.

Rooms: 3 singles with private bathroom, 10 doubles with private bathroom.

Price: £125 per double room, £81 single.

Breakfast: Included – full English/continental.

Meals: Not available.

Closed: Never!

From South Kensington tube, head down Old Brompton Road and take first left (Sumner Place). The hotel is on your right.

Map Ref No: 5

London Area

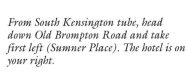

John Palgan
Five Sumner Place
South Kensington
London
SW7 3EE
Tel: 0171-5847586
Fax: 0171-8239962

This was the first private house hotel to open and privacy, attention to detail and individual treatment are the keynotes still. A lovely terrace house in a quiet cul-de-sac off Knightsbridge, it houses the world's largest collection of original English floral watercolours (Sir Michael used to work for James Goldsmith and is used to aiming high) and offers champagne on the house. Supremely elegant rooms, tip-top service and a gentle atmosphere make it exceptional in central London. Pets welcome by arrangement.

Rooms: 7 suites, 5 singles, 14 doubles, all with en suite bathrooms.

Price: £91-£145.50 p.p.

Breakfast: Not included – continental £7.50 p.p.

Meals: Room Service menu available.

Closed: Never!

At Knightsbridge tube take the Brompton Road exit. Walking away from Harrods down the Brompton Road, Beaufort Gardens is the first turning on the left (after Hans Road).

Map Ref No: 5

Sir Michael & Lady Wilmot
The Beaufort
33 Beaufort Gardens
London
SW3 1PP
Tel: 0171-5845252
Fax: 0171-5892834

Perhaps people don't often think of staying in B&Bs in central London. They miss out. Peter and Suzy Bell (respectively architect and psychotherapist working on the premises) have remodelled their home along modernist lines with distinctive understated style. Open and light, pleasing to the eye with cool colours and luxurious carpets. It is in the heart of trendy Camden Town but well set back in a quiet, wide tree-lined street round the corner from Regent's Park. This must be a more intimate and economic choice than impersonal chain hotels.

Rooms: 1 twin with bunk-beds and private bathroom, 1 twin/double with private bathroom, 1 double with en suite shower and private WC.

Price: £35 p.p. twin/doubles, £40 single occupancy.

Breakfast: Included – full English/continental.

Meals: Dinner available locally.

Closed: Open all year.

From Camden Town tube station go up Parkway. Albert Street is the second on the left. Number 78 is on the left-hand side.

Map Ref No: 5

Peter & Suzy Bell
78 Albert Street
London
NW1 7NR

Tel: 0171-3876813
Fax: 0171-3871704

A large, comfortable, Victorian family house where Carole Ingram has instilled the flavour of country living in Primrose Hill. The large, colourful kitchen, complete with Aga and wooden table, is where you take a delicious breakfast and Carole's advice on What's On For You in London. The gorgeous guestrooms are on the top floor, a mix of wood, brass and contemporary decor. In between is the temptingly-cluttered, soft-furnished drawing room. Carole is jolly and keen on the arts.

Rooms: 1 twin en suite bathroom, 2 doubles each with private bathrooms. Third bed available for twin & 1 double.

Price: £35-£40 p.p. doubles, £15 single supplement, £25 additional bed.

Breakfast: Included – full English/health food.

Meals: Not available.

Closed: Never!

Leave Chalk Farm tube station, cross Adelaide Rd., turn right for 20 steps, then left into Bridge Approach. Cross bridge, turn right and walk till you reach No. 30 on right-hand side.

Map Ref No: 5

Andrew & Carole Ingram
30 King Henry's Road
Primrose Hill
London
NW3 3RP
Tel: 0171-483 2871
Fax: 0171-483 4587

Right beside Hampstead Heath, in London's trendiest village, this hotel feels more like a private home. The coolly elegant drawing and dining rooms are classically furnished and there is a walled garden for a quiet drink. The bedrooms, all differently designer-treated, are on rambling levels in the Victorian twists of the old house, the bathrooms are amazing, the service exquisite (turned-down beds, complimentary sherry). Diana Sparks may even find time to tell her wild traveller's tales. Children over 8 welcome.

Rooms: 5 single, 8 double/twin, 2 junior suites.

Price: From £70 p.p.

Breakfast: Included – continental. Full English also available.

Meals: Room service provides excellent Italian food from local kitchen.

Closed: Never!

From Hampstead tube turn uphill into Heath St. 4th turning on right leads to Holford Road.

Map Ref No: 5

Peter Long
Sandringham Hotel
3 Holford Road
Hampstead
London NW3 1AD
Tel: 0171-4351569
Fax: 0171-4315932

Don't be deterred by 'Chingford'! The Clapps' double-fronted Edwardian house is a mere 400 yards from the splendid bosky retreat of Epping Forest. The bedrooms are large, there is a small pool in the neat garden and a terrace for breakfast (smoked salmon, Irish soda bread, kippers, homemade muesli to name a few choices). A 3-course dinner can be served on request and there are 10 places to eat within five minutes walk. The Clapps will meet guests at Chingford Station if required. Wonderful value for London.

Rooms: 1 twin, 1 double, both with shared guest's bathroom.

Price: £30 p.p.

Breakfast: Included – full English.

Meals: Dinner £15 p.p. Lunch from £5 p.p., packed lunch from £3 p.p. on request.

Closed: Never!

A large, handsome 1780's-plus-additions manor quietly rural and with divine Italianate gardens where you will find the added pleasures of tennis court and croquet lawn. So English you can almost smell the cucumber sandwiches and feel the chintz. Smart guest rooms and bathrooms with pretty garden views. There are 6 acres of garden in 100 acres of graping land, plus home-laid eggs and garden fruit for breakfast.

Rooms: 3 doubles, all en suite.

Price: £32.50 p.p.

Breakfast: Included – full English/continental.

Meals: Dinner available locally.

Closed: Christmas & Easter.

From Chingford BR station go down Connaught Avenue, directly opposite. Second turning on left into Eglington Road. Number 25 is third on right.

Map Ref No: 5

Helen & Drummond Clapp
25 Eglington Road
North Chingford
London
E4 7AN
Tel: 0181-5291140
Fax: 0181-5083837

Go west on A319 through Chobham (church on left). Continue towards Knaphill and turn left into Carthouse Lane. Manor signed on right.

Map Ref No: 5

Teresa & Kevin Leeper
Knaphill Manor
Carthouse Lane
Woking
Surrey GU21 4XT
Tel: 01276-857962
Fax: 01276-855503

It is likely that you'll be greeted by the sound of classical music and smell of fresh coffee wafting out as you approach this fairytale 17th-century house. The feeling is rustic, relaxed and rule-free. You wind your way up a dark oak staircase to fresh and delicately finished bedrooms and large bathrooms. People come here again and again as an antidote to stress, helped along by well-cushioned armchairs, lots of books and a heavenly garden – just the sort of place for communing with nature!

Rooms: 1 twin with shared bathroom, 1 double en suite, 1 single with shared bathroom.

Price: £30-£37.50 p.p. doubles, £35 single.

Breakfast: Included – full English/continental.

Meals: Dinner available locally.

Closed: August.

A3 to Milford. From Milford A283 to Petworth. Pickhurst Road is off the green, third house on the left with a large black dovecote.

Map Ref No: 5

Mrs Sheila Marsh
Greenaway
Pickhurst Road
Chiddingfold
Surrey GU8 4TS
Tel: 01428-682920
Fax: 01428-685078

Come to the Old Vicarage and be welcomed into the heart of this charming family whose four young children preclude the slightest possibility of stuffiness! It is a lovely house, built by the Rothschilds in 1865 when they bought the village of Mentmore, with gracious, comfortable rooms. Guests have a choice of sitting rooms and can enjoy Sue Kirchner's delicious recipes in the dining room or al fresco, in a lovingly tended garden overlooking fields. Bedrooms are peaceful and airy (one overlooks the swimming pool) and your children are welcome to join the throng.

Rooms: 1 twin with en suite bathroom, 1 double with en suite shower.

Price: £20 p.p. Children under 12, £10 when sharing.

Breakfast: Included – full English.

Meals: Dinner £15 p.p. Available on request.

Closed: Occasionally.

At Cheddington roundabout left signposted Mentmore. Follow left past gates to Mentmore Towers. Old Vicarage is on right opposite Church.

Map Ref No: 10

Charles & Susie Kirchner
The Old Vicarage
Mentmore
Buckinghamshire
LU7 0QG
Tel: 01296-661227
Fax: 01296-661227

Lutyens built this wonderful house in 1901 for his mother-in-law, the Dowager Lady Lytton, and it is all one would expect of that illustrious architect. Set down a long drive in 6 acres of beautiful gardens and fields, each elevation of the house is different. Architectural peculiarities – such as internal, octagonal windows – abound and Samantha Pollock-Hill has applied her considerable artistic skills to the interior. Unusual colour schemes offset magnificent antiques, tapestries and chinoiserie. The family is happy to share its lovely home with guests and can converse in a clutch of languages.

Rooms: 1 double en suite shower, 1 double with private shower, 1 family suite with bathroom.

Price: £30 p.p. doubles, £40 single.

Breakfast: Included – full English/continental/health foods.

Meals: Dinner £20 p.p.

Closed: 20 December – 3 January.

From Knebworth take B1000 and turn into Station Road which becomes Park Lane. 300m after crossing motorway bridge turn left into Homewood drive. Signposted 'public footpath'.

Map Ref No: 10

Mrs Samantha Pollock-Hill
Homewood
Knebworth
Hertfordshire
SG3 6PP
Tel: 01438-812105

An Elizabethan jewel! Exposed timber ceilings, open fireplaces, a stone courtyard, endless nooks and crannies: this farmhouse trumpets its history at every turn. The garden even has 'old-fashioned' roses and ponds. The Wordsworths (yes, they are related to the poet) are engaging and solicitous people, delighting in their home and guests. Vincent, the pony, is always available to take visitors in a trap around the glorious countryside. Little Brockdale is no longer a working farm but all vegetables are organically homegrown.

Rooms: 1 twin with private bathroom; 2 doubles: 1 with private shower room and 1 with private bathroom.

Price: £27.50-£30 p.p. doubles, £30 single.

Breakfast: Included – full English.

Meals: Dinner £12-£18 p.p.

Closed: Never!

Take B1053 from Saffron Walden to Radwinter. Turn right at church and first left after 1 mile (at grass triangle on sharp right-hand bend). Continue past green sign for Great Brockholds Farm and bear right at end of lane.

Map Ref No: 11

Antony & Anne Wordsworth
Little Brockholds Farm
Radwinter
Saffron Walden
Essex CB10 2TF
Tel: 01799-599458
Fax: 01799-599458

East Anglia

The bedroom interiors in the newly rebuilt stable block are terrific fun: the Oak Room has a 4-poster with red drapes and a Victorian-style bath in the room, the Pine Room is true to its name plus a sunken bath (in the bathroom) and the Brass Room has a brass double bed, beamed ceiling and military prints. The owners, management and staff are all delightful. Tempting menu that doesn't confuse the reader with foodspeak. Much use of local produce. How about staying here instead of going to Stansted Airport?

Rooms: 1 twin, 7 doubles, all with en suite bathrooms.

Price: £45-£52.50 p.p. doubles, £60 singles.

Breakfast: Included – full English/continental.

Meals: Lunch available except Saturdays. Dinner available except Sundays. Dinner £20-£35 p.p.

Closed: First week in January.

From M11 take junction 8 and A120 Colchester road for 8 miles to Great Dunmow. Market Place is off the High Street, the first left turning.

Map Ref No: 11

Brian & Vanessa Jones
Starr Restaurant
Market Place
Great Dunmow
Essex CM6 1AY
Tel: 01371-874321
Fax: 01371-876337

Once you are past the indignant peacock which has dominion over the drive, the welcome to this 17th-century farmhouse is total. Even in summer the smell of wood smoke lingers in the gorgeous, beamed and antiques-filled drawing room. Whether you breakfast in the smart dining room, with its Japanese theme, or outside, you will enjoy views of the surrounding fields through the peep-hole cut in the hedge. The garden itself is landscaped and rambling, full of old-fashioned roses and a miniature vineyard. Life here is unstuffy and relaxed, and – *pace* the peacock! – peace and seclusion are guaranteed. Children over 10 welcome.

Rooms: 1 twin/double en suite shower, 1 twin in large airy attic, sharing bathroom with 1 double.

Price: £20 p.p. shared bathroom & attic room. £25 p.p. en suite. Small supp. for singles.

Breakfast: Included – full English.

Meals: Packed lunch available on request only. Gourmet food locally available.

Closed: 20 December – 2 January.

From Colchester A604 towards Cambridge. Left in Great Yeldham, after White Hart pub, to Toppesfield. Farm is 1.5 miles on left after farmhouse with white railings (on right).

Map Ref No: 11

James & Sue Blackie
Ollivers Farm
Toppesfield
Halstead
Essex CO9 4LS
Tel: 01787-237642
Fax: 01787-237602

An oasis, a 16th-century farmhouse with a big pine kitchen, Aga, log fire and grand piano in the drawing room and an attractive dining room. It is an interesting and comfortable house rather than a smart one, a cornucopia of curiosities: pictures, hats, prints, trays, and lots of plants. The bedrooms are colourful and pretty (patchwork bedspreads) and there are rugs on the wooden floors downstairs. Children over 10 welcome.

Rooms: 2 twins, 1 double, sharing 2 bathrooms.

Price: £20 p.p.

Breakfast: Included – full English/continental/health food.

Meals: Dinner on request, £10-£12.50 p.p.

Closed: Christmas.

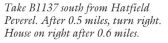

Patricia Mitchell is a knowledgeable guide to the history of this wonderful, Grade 11 listed 14th-century family house. The 'new wing' is 15th-century, and here you have breakfast in front of the log fire. The bedrooms are colourful, cosy and welcoming, with exposed beams, uneven wooden floors and 'museum corners' which enshrine original features of the house. Three pubs within 100 metres or a 2-acre garden providing refuge from the hum of village life, and in the courtyard Patricia's hobby, a second-hand clothes shop, is famous for miles around.

Rooms: 1 family room en suite, 1 twin with own bathroom, 1 single with sep. shower room & wc.

Price: £40-45 family room, with £5 supp. for camp bed. £17.50-£20 p.p. twin, £25 single.

Breakfast: Included – full English.

Meals: No, but locally available.

Closed: Never – except in a crisis!

Take B1137 south from Hatfield Peverel. After 0.5 miles, turn right. House on right after 0.6 miles.

Map Ref No: 11

Mrs Linda Tritton
The Wick
Terling Hall Rd
Hatfield Peverel, Chelmsford
Essex CM3 2EZ
Tel: 01245-380705

On A604, 2.5 miles from A12 junction. House is on left beyond the Cooper's Arms and opposite Queen's Head.

Map Ref No: 11

Patricia & Richard Mitchell
Old House, Fordstreet
Aldham
Colchester
Essex CO6 3PH
Tel: 01206-240456

In a county as crowded as Essex with its dormitory towns and commuter-clogged highways, King's Vineyard is an oasis. The name stems from an ancient plan to plant a vineyard here. It is wonderfully peaceful and in winter there are log fires to make it cosy. There are paths and bridleways to explore, Constable country is close where long-loved pictures leap out at you at every turn. Mrs Tweed is friendly and informative, her rooms softly pastel (one with 1920s maple furniture), her breakfasts in the conservatory have views clear over the Colne valley.

Rooms: 1 twin with shared or private bathroom; 2 doubles: 1 with shared bathroom and 1 with adjoining private shower/bathroom.

Price: £16-£18 p.p. doubles, £20-£23 single.

Breakfast: Included – full English/vegetarian.

Meals: Dinner available locally.

Closed: Never!

From A12 take A604 just before Colchester. Turn right to Fordham & right again at Three Horseshoes pub. Kings Vineyard is signed on left. Continue 1 mile down Fossetts Lane, then farm track. House visible from afar.

Map Ref No: 11

Mrs Inge Tweed
Kings Vineyard, Fossetts Lane
Fordham
Nr. Colchester
Essex CO6 3NY
Tel: 01206-240377
Fax: 01206-240377

There is light and space and air and silence in this lovely 1700s house which has been renovated in Lutyens style. Th traditional drawing room has its grand piano, fireplace and big windows onto the rose garden; croquet on the lawn, midge-swatting by the hidden pond, then Coral's afternoon tea complete the picture of English country life. Bedrooms are bright and well-stocked for midnight feasts, bathrooms have all you could wish for and one of the longest baths we know of.

Rooms: 1 double with private bathroom, 1 twin with private bathroom, 1 single/twin with separate bathroom.

Price: From £20-£30 p.p.

Breakfast: Included – full English.

Meals: Not available.

Closed: Christmas.

From A12 north of Colchester follow A120 towards Harwich for approx 10 m. Turn left to Lt Bromley & follow for 2.9 miles. House set back on right.

Map Ref No: 12

Christopher & Coral McEwen
Aldham's, Bromley Rd
Lawford
Manningtree
Essex CO11 2NE
Tel: 01206-393210
Fax: 01255-870722

Now belonging to the National Trust, this large 17th-century timber-framed house, originally a farmhouse, has been successively transmogrified. Huge and rambling, its furnishings are spartan. One of the many original features is the glorious limed oak staircase with thickly-decorated newel posts – as Mr Pevsner puts it. Bedrooms have their own loo and basin but you journey to the ground floor to use the fairly basic bathroom. Not for those who like their plumbing pristine and it can get chilly in winter, but it is a treat to stay in this lovely historic house.

Rooms: 2 twin/doubles with extra single bed, 1 double, all with basin & private wc. Bathroom shared.

Price: £18 p.p. doubles, £20 single, £5-£10 children under 12.

Breakfast: Included – full English.

Meals: Excellent pubs & restaurants within 3 miles.

Closed: 30 September – Easter.

Romantically-decorated, oak-beamed bedrooms, one with its own ground-floor entrance, another sectioned off. For 'long stayers' a sitting room is also available, with the atmosphere of a gentleman's club. The house itself, dating from the 15th century, is lovely, with a walled garden, 400-year-old tree-lined pond, tennis court, beautiful lawns and – best of all – the River Box meandering through. Kiftsgate roses cascade over the huge and very splendid adjoining barn.

Rooms: 2 doubles en suite, 1 twin en suite, 1 single with private bathroom.

Price: £23 p.p. en suite, £25 single.

Breakfast: Included – full English.

Meals: Available at excellent local pubs.

Closed: Mid-December – 28 February.

Turn west off A12 to Stratford St. Mary and Higham, left in Higham onto B1068. House is in Thorington Street village midway between Stoke and Higham.

Map Ref No: 12

Deirdre Wollaston
Thorington Hall
Stoke-by-Nayland
Suffolk
CO6 4SS
Tel: 01206-337329

3 miles from the A12, on the B1068 between Higham and Stoke-by-Nayland. House on south side of road, 300m east of Thorington Street.

Map Ref No: 12

Patrick & Jennie Jackson
Nether Hall
Thorington Street
Stoke-by-Nayland
Suffolk CO6 4ST
Tel: 01206-337373
Fax: 01206-337373

This Elizabethan marvel is snug beside the equally lovely church. The beautiful drawing room has an open fire for winter but faces south over the water meadows where cattle graze; beyond are the Rivers Brett and Stour flowing lazily. The Parkers will lend you a rowing boat, canoe or punt, or you may fish, play tennis or swim in their pool. Breakfast is at an enormous round table in another open-fired room. This is Suffolk at its most uplifting.

Rooms: 2 triples, 1 twin, each with own sep. bath & wc.

Price: £24-£28 p.p. sharing, £28-£34 single.

Breakfast: Included – full English/continental.

Meals: No but numerous excellent restaurants & pubs within short distance.

Closed: Never!

Ravishing! But I am a soft touch for mediæval Suffolk manor houses. (The name Mary Hall comes from the parish church of St Mary.) Records go back to 1270 and part of the house is 15th-century. Tudor brick floors and Turkish rugs, fine old furniture and touches of luxury. The Morses are keen gardeners but have yielded space to a swimming pool, tennis court and croquet lawn. Katy loves cooking and uses her own vegetables. Fun and well-travelled people in the quietest of lush Suffolk countryside.

Rooms: 1 twin with private bathroom, 1 twin/double en suite, 1 single with private bathroom.

Price: £25-£30 p.p. double, £28 single.

Breakfast: Included – full English.

Meals: Dinner £16 p.p. (book ahead).

Closed: Christmas – New Year.

West off A12 at Stratford St. Mary. House is on left opposite church sign, one mile on Higham road. The house has pink timbers and there is a sign on the wall.

Map Ref No: 12

Meg Parker
The Old Vicarage
Higham
Nr. Colchester
Suffolk CO7 6JY
Tel: 01206-337248

House is 3 miles from Great Yeldham, 5 miles from Sudbury and 1.5 miles from crossroads at Belchamp Walter village in direction of Great Yeldham.

Map Ref No: 11

Mr & Mrs David Morse
St. Mary Hall
Belchamp Walter
Sudbury
Suffolk CO10 7BB
Tel: 01787-237202
Fax: 01787-238302

Real candles burn in the chandeliers above the dining-table. Carved oak headboards retrieved from a church crown some of the beds. The intriguing corners, fresh flowers and graceful comfort within this fine Victorian townhouse instantly retrieve its austere exterior. A pile of books and maps in the sitting-room give every detail about Lavenham. The market place of this 'best-preserved mediæval town in England' is only a few steps away. Efficient and genial, Diana will help with any problem and cook you dinners whose taste will linger.

Rooms: 1 twin en suite, 2 doubles both en suite with either shower or bath.

Price: £22.50 p.p. doubles, £25 single.

Breakfast: Included – full English/continental.

Meals: Dinner £14 p.p. BYO wine.

Closed: Christmas & January, but open New Year.

'A little corner of France in mediæval England' hits the mark. Lavenham is a glorious wool town of timber-framed houses. The Great House itself has a dignified Georgian façade, utterly delightful rooms and a magical patio and walled garden. Safe for children, quiet for newspaper reading, lunches and al fresco dinners are served here whenever possible. Staff are French, rooms are done to a high degree of comfort. The *'cuisine'* is French and, needless to say, *'superbe'*.

Rooms: 4 doubles, all with en suite bathrooms.

Price: £34-£39 p.p. doubles, £50-£75 single.

Breakfast: Included – full English/continental.

Meals: Lunch available except Mondays. Dinner available except Sundays & Mondays. Dinner £16.95-£33.90 p.p.

Closed: First 3 weeks in January.

From Sudbury, take B1115 to Lavenham. Pass Swan Hotel on right, take next right into Market Lane, cross Market Place, turn right, then left. Red House is on right.

Map Ref No: 11

Mrs Diana Schofield
The Red House
29 Bolton Street
Lavenham
Suffolk CO10 9RG
Tel: 01787-248074

From A12 at Colchester A134 towards Bury St. Edmunds. Lavenham is on A1141. In High Street going north, first right after The Swan. In Water Street going east, first left after The Swan up Lady Street into Market Place.

Map Ref No: 11

Régis & Martine Crépy
The Great House
Market Place
Lavenham
Suffolk CO10 9QZ
Tel: 01787-247431
Fax: 01787-248007

If you are looking for peace and quiet, discover secret Nedging! The Old Rectory is near many of the ancient churches, best preserved mediæval towns and villages with lovely colour-washed cottages for which Suffolk is famous. Long Melford is an antique lovers' favourite. The Chetwynds have carefully renovated The Old Rectory, sympathetically adding modern comforts and restoring traditional Georgian features. Rupert loves good food and the excellent three or four-course dinner can be enjoyed in an informal atmosphere 'en famille'.

Rooms: 1 twin with private bathroom, 2 doubles with en suite bathrooms.

Price: £29-£34 p.p. doubles, £34-£40 single.

Breakfast: Included – full English/continental.

Meals: Dinner £19-£23 p.p. 3 or 4 courses.

Closed: Never!

Where have all the vicars and rectors gone? Yet another lovely Suffolk Old Rectory. Pamela is a true professional and as genuine and charming as could be. Enter to a stone floor and then to a grand piano in an alcove, Persian carpets, fine paintings and lovely fabrics, many embroidered by Pamela. Long Italian walnut dining table facing south over the garden and croquet lawn... and perhaps the providers of the free-range eggs. Seize the four-poster if you can.

Rooms: 2 twins/doubles with own private bath, 1 double en suite bath & 4-poster.

Price: £22.50-£27.50 p.p. doubles, £20-30 single.

Breakfast: Included – full English/continental.

Meals: No, but available locally.

Closed: Christmas & New Year.

0.4 miles south of Bildeston, turn left off B1115. The Old Rectory is first house on right just before crest of hill.

Map Ref No: 12

Tess & Rupert Chetwynd
The Old Rectory
Nedging
Nr. Lavenham
Suffolk IP7 7HQ
Tel: 01449-740745
Fax: 01449-740745

Take A14 (once the A45) from Stowmarket and turning to Wetherden. With church on right, follow white line up hill approx. 0.5 mile. House on left with white gate.

Map Ref No: 12

Mrs Pamela Bowden
Wetherden Old Rectory
Wetherden
Stowmarket
Suffolk IP14 3LS
Tel: 01359-240144

Another Suffolk delight for garden lovers and house buffs. There is an orchard, plus a large goldfish pond and a glorious variety of plants and shrubs. Over them looks the Morning Room, staring east, south and west, light-filled and just for guests. Dine in the Tudor dining room at a great round table; breakfast at the scrubbed pine table in a kitchen made cosy by a red Aga. The rooms are big, the decor traditional and very pretty, the duvets and mattresses all one could ask for. Children over 8 welcome.

Rooms: 1 twin with bath & wc., 1 double with sep. shower & wc., 1 single available to share bathroom with twin.

Price: £28 p.p.

Breakfast: Included – full English/continental.

Meals: Dinner £18 p.p., book in advance.

Closed: Christmas, New Year, Easter.

A feast of pleasures both outside and in: a 16th and 17th-century house in four acres of garden with a moat and a pond, seven acres of meadow and woodland, free-range eggs and fresh fruit and veg. from the garden. Inside the delight intensifies: stone fireplaces, brick-floored dining room, bread-oven and copper, a massive roll-topped cast-iron bath, plain walls and gorgeous curtains, oak beams... nothing is missing from the idyll, not even homemade bread. Lovely people, too.

Rooms: 2 doubles, 1 en suite bath, 1 with sep. own bath/shower & wc.

Price: £22.50-£27.50 p.p. doubles, £30-£40 single.

Breakfast: Included – full English/continental.

Meals: Dinner from £12 p.p. on request.

Closed: Christmas – New Year.

From A14 (once A45) take A140 Norwich Road for 4 miles. Right to Mickfield. Right at crossroads in village, last house on right, with white gates.

Map Ref No: 12

Mrs Patricia Currie
The Old Rectory
Mickfield
Stowmarket
Suffolk IP14 5LR
Tel: 01449-711283

B1113 north from Stowmarket for approx. 5 miles. Immediate right after Cotton village sign, right after 0.25 mile and next left. Farm first on right.

Map Ref No: 12

Kim & Claire Grewcock
Hill Farm, Stonham Rd
Cotton
Stowmarket
Suffolk IP14 4RQ
Tel: 01449-780345
Fax: 01449-780345

EAST ANGLIA

I defy anyone to resist either the gentle Raewyn or her voluptuous house. If the bedrooms (wood or stone floors, oriental rugs, ornamental beds, patchwork and chintz) don't get you the orgiastic breakfasts will. Inglenook fireplaces, fallen forests of beams, antiques – nothing mock about this Tudor. Walking, fishing and Suffolk culture all beckon, then dinner in the conservatory... always a languid and imaginative feast. A guesthouse with a special B&B feel to it.

Rooms: 4 doubles, 3 twins, extra singles avail. for families. Some king size/4 posters. 6 have own bath & wc, 1 has own shower & wc.

Price: £22.50-£32.50 p.p. doubles/twins. £17-£32.50 p.p. singles. Children (sharing) £5-£16 depending on age.

Breakfast: Included – full English/continental/health food.

Meals: Dinner £16 p.p. Children (up to 16) £8. Except Sundays.

Closed: Christmas and New Year.

A conversion of a 17th-century stable and barn with real flair. The terracotta tiled floor, scattered with rugs, is a colourful counterpoint to the dramatic beamed and vaulted drawing-room ceiling. On cool evenings a log fire is lit in the enormous chimney. Play the baby grand, billiards or croquet. Remarkable for the care that has gone into providing more thoughtful touches than I could ever think of. Marvellous house and people. Children over 12 are welcome.

Rooms: 2 double/twin en suite in carriage lodge; 1 double 4-poster with en suite shower.

Price: £22-£24 p.p. Single £34-£38.

Breakfast: Full English/continental.

Meals: Dinner £17.50.

Closed: End December to mid-March.

Where A140 joins A14 from Ipswich, take first left at roundabout & follow signs for Pipps Ford.

Map Ref No: 12

Mrs Raewyn Hackett-Jones
Pipps Ford
Needham Market
Ipswich
Suffolk IP6 8LJ
Tel: 01449-760208
Fax: 01449-760561

300 yards north of Otley post-office on right and up a drive.

Map Ref No: 12

Michael & Lise Hilton
Bowerfield House
Helmingham Rd, Otley
Suffolk
IP6 9NR
Tel: 01473-890742
Fax: 01473-890059

Rachel Thomas has thought of everything and the result is an idyllic home in an exquisite setting. Guests have the run of this gorgeous 15th-century home: a warm, light drawing room with a grand piano, oak beams, open fireplace; a sun room to catch the evening light; cosy dining room with Suffolk tiles and inglenook fireplace. The guest bedroom area is self-contained, with a king-size bed and many thoughtful touches. Low leaded windows overlook the peaceful gardens which include a tennis court. Bicycles are available. Rachel is a delight – and a great cook.

Rooms: 1 kingsize double with private bath, shower & wc. (fold-up bed available).

Price: From £50 family room, £22.50 p.p. double, £25 single.

Breakfast: Included – full English/continental.

Meals: Dinner £12 p.p. available on request.

Closed: Christmas & New Year.

Approx. 4 miles between Hadleigh & A12 on country road, 2 miles from Shelley, 1 mile from Polstead and close to Shelley Priory on O.S. map. Ring for details as many approaches possible!

Map Ref No: 12

Rachel & Richard Thomas
Sparrows
Shelley
Ipswich
Suffolk IP7 5RQ
Tel: 01206-337381

A lovingly-restored traditional Suffolk farmhouse blushes pink at the end of a long drive. By the time you reach the front door you have been greeted by grazing ponies and Welsh mountain sheep, peacocks, Belgian chickens and a very heavy Irish wolfhound with more enthusiasm than equilibrium. Guests occupy the 16th-century end of the house, which has all the charm that goes with age (including an original wall-painting and uneven wood floors), coupled with all the comforts of sensitive and imaginative restoration. Steep stairs lead to a luxurious bathroom and cosy bedrooms. An absolute gem!

Rooms: 1 twin, 1 double, sharing bath, shower & wc.

Price: £18-£20 p.p.

Breakfast: Included – full English.

Meals: No, but pubs and restaurants nearby.

Closed: Never!

A12 north from Colchester, left onto B1070, left towards Shelley. House is on right between Shelley and Lower Raydon, 3 miles from A12.

Map Ref No: 12

Mrs Marna Pyman
Spider Hall
Lower Raydon
Ipswich
Suffolk IP7 5QN
Tel: 01473-822585
Fax: 01473-824820

Although not family-owned it is an honest little hotel and Framlingham is a beguiling little town. There is an impressive castle ('a fall'n dismantled pile' wrote a local poet), a fine Perpendicular church and attractive domestic architecture around Market Hill. The hotel rooms are big, spotlessly clean, with plainish carpets, chintz-type curtains and matching bedspreads. Several rooms have beams, there are some ½ tester beds and one superb 4-poster room. No sitting room but the bar is a sociable place.

Rooms: 12 twin/doubles, 1 single, 1 triple – all en suite.

Price: £40-£70 p.p. doubles, £30-£50 single.

Breakfast: Full English £8.50 p.p., continental £5.95 p.p.

Meals: Dinner £15.95 p.p. Lunch available.

Closed: Never!

Grange Farm's mediæval moat reflects Suffolk's wide evening skies and swooping birdlife. The house began in the 13th century and the old beams and sloping floors dignify every room. The style is simple and traditional, unpretentious and very pretty, with log fire and grand piano in the sitting room, an Aga to make the kitchen cosy, lots of books and privacy (or billiards) if you want it. Start the day with breakfast beside the moat, with homemade marmalade and local honey. A remarkable and beautiful place.

Rooms: 2 twin, 1 double. All share bath with wc. Will let as singles.

Price: £18 p.p. double or £18 single. £15 children 10-15.

Breakfast: Included – full English/continental.

Meals: Dinner available on request.

Closed: 13 December – 13 January.

Hotel is at top end of Market Square.

Map Ref No: 12

Sabina Taylor
The Crown Hotel
Framlingham
Woodbridge
Suffolk IP13 9AN
Tel: 01728-723521
Fax: 01728-724274

Take A1120 (Yoxford to Stowmarket) to Dennington. B1116 north for approx. 3 miles. Farm on right 0.9 miles north of Bell pub.

Map Ref No: 12

Mrs Elizabeth Hickson
Grange Farm
Dennington
Woodbridge
Suffolk IP13 8BT
Tel: 01986-798388

Smugglers and travellers alike were always given a warm welcome at this fine Tudor inn. There are comfortable, well-equipped bedrooms and the ones at the back have stunning views across the River Ore, the marshes and sea. The 10 garden rooms are charming, with individual patios – ideal for families or the elderly. Orford is a delightfully unspoilt resort famed for its fish smokeries, Norman Keep and the bird sanctuary of Havergate Island.

Rooms: 12 twins, 7 doubles, 1 single, all with en suite shower and/or bath.

Price: £35 p.p. doubles, £37.50-£50 single.

Breakfast: Included – full English/continental.

Meals: Lunch & dinner available.

Closed: Never!

Meadowland and gardens surround this 16th-century working farm, partly dairy and partly arable, at the end of a half-mile drive. A fine Suffolk house, on a very human scale, unpretentious, cosy yet big enough to swing cats... and ineffably attractive. The rooms are big and comfortable, with plenty of books and pictures and some views over the garden. Dine in a beamed dining-room overlooking a paved patio and lawns, often with home-grown food. An excellent pub a brief walk away; Southwold and the Heritage Coast 8 miles away.

Rooms: 1 double with en suite bathroom; 1 twin with en suite shower; 1 double with private bathroom.

Price: £15-£17 p.p. doubles, £16-£18 single.

Breakfast: Included – full English/continental.

Meals: Dinner available on request.

Closed: Never!

From Ipswich A12 towards Woodbridge; right on A1152 and then B1084 or B1078 to Orford. Hotel is in market square near Orford Castle.

Map Ref No: 12

Sarah & Peter Mann
The Crown & Castle Hotel
Orford
Woodbridge
Suffolk IP12 2LJ
Tel: 01394-450205
Fax: 01394-450176

From A12, take A144 Halesworth road. In Bramfield turn off by Queen's Head. Farm is 0.75 miles on right.

Map Ref No: 12

Mrs Patricia Kemsley
Broad Oak Farm
Bramfield
Halesworth
Suffolk IP19 9AB
Tel: 01986-784232

Up a 400-yard drive and in an acre of cottage garden awaits this beamy Tudor farmhouse plus a complimentary bottle of Wisset wine (the vineyard produces 20,000 bottles a year, a bold and exciting venture). The large drawing room overlooks the garden on three sides, has an open fire and grand piano and is where you breakfast. It is all very charming, with a Pink room and a Peach room, fresh flowers, plain colours, wooden loo-seats and interesting hosts... and fine wine.

Rooms: 3 doubles, 2 en suite, 1 with private bathroom.

Price: £21-£23 p.p. double, £23-£25 single.

Breakfast: Included – full English/continental.

Meals: Not available.

Closed: Christmas & New Year.

Walberswick! A tiny summer-soft winter-bleak Suffolk fishing village central to the 1920s Craft Movement (John Rennie Mackintosh was here), with a ferry operated by the same family for 5 generations across to smart Regency Southwold. Swimming, sailing, crabbing, painting – fun for all the family. The Bell, with its 600 years, ancient beams, flagstones and nice little country-style rooms is also a perfect place for families, bird watchers (Minsmere is here) and East Anglian architecture buffs.

Rooms: 1 triple, 1 twin, 4 doubles, all en suite.

Price: £30 p.p. double, £35 single. Mon-Thurs only.

Breakfast: Included – full English.

Meals: Lunch & dinner.

Closed: Never!

From A144 in Halesworth take Wissett road for 2.5 miles. Once you see the vineyard on the left take the drive for 0.25 miles to the front of the house.

Map Ref No: 12

Jonathan & Janet Craft
Valley Farm
Wissett
Halesworth
Suffolk IP19 0JJ
Tel: 01986-785216
Fax: 01986-785443

From A12 take B1387 to Walberswick. The Bell Inn is on the right, at the far end of the village near the river.

Map Ref No: 12

Mrs Sue Ireland-Cutting
The Bell Inn
Ferry Road
Walberswick, Southwold
Suffolk IP18 6TN
Tel: 01502-723109

You will be treated like a house guest in this 16th-century Yeoman farmhouse. Garden chairs, lots of books, magazines and guides; you can stay around all day if you wish to lap up its tranquillity. Atmospheric with blue-and-white china on the Welsh dresser, a vaulted dining room overlooking the garden and pony-filled paddock, log fires in the sitting room in autumn and winter. Rosemary has encyclopaedic knowledge of surrounding towns, cathedrals etc. and a very warm smile.

Rooms: 1 twin, 1 double with private adjoining bathrooms; 1 twin with basin & wc sharing bathroom.

Price: From £22 doubles, from £22 single.

Breakfast: Included – full English or continental available on request.

Meals: Dinner available locally.

Closed: Christmas week.

From Scole/A140 right onto A143 towards Gt. Yarmouth. After 7 miles right at Harleston onto B1116 to Fressingfield. Pass church and Fox & Goose on left. At top of hill right then left into Priory Road.

Map Ref No: 12

Stephen & Rosemary Willis
Priory House
Priory Road
Fressingfield, Eye
Suffolk IP21 5PH
Tel: 01379-586254

'Olde-worlde' and 'charming' are in fact true of the Batesons' Suffolk-pink farmhouse. A beautiful beamed dining room with refectory table and inglenook fireplace, sitting room for guests – no television but music and lots of books and magazines – and a quarry-tiled floor with Elizabethan-red walls and tapestry hangings on the stairs. The garden is much loved and filled with special plants and trees, including a 14th-century Moss rose. Hearty breakfasts and, on request, light suppers. P.S. Tall people: watch out for low beams.

Rooms: 1 twin, 2 doubles, all sharing guest bathroom.

Price: £17 p.p. doubles, £17-£19 single.

Breakfast: Included – full English/continental.

Meals: Light suppers available on request. Meals also available locally.

Closed: Christmas and New Year.

From A1066 Thetford to Diss road, follow bed signs from east of South Lopham. In Fersfield, right at Fersfield church and next left. Farm first on right.

Map Ref No: 12

David & Pat Bateson
Lodge Farm
Bressingham
Nr. Diss
Norfolk IP22 2BQ
Tel: 01379-687629

Your hostess is an elderly utterly English lady of much character who calls a spade a spade and loves her little terrier. She will regale you with the story of her amazing house, how it was saved from ruin and brought back to life. In 1500 it was a college for priests, conveniently sited next to the church (for practicals...). It has a superb panelled dining room; bedrooms are big, the two en suite bathrooms are ingeniously-converted large cupboards, and have great views. Children over 7 welcome.

Rooms: 1 twin en suite, 1 twin/double en suite, 1 double with adjacent private bath.

Price: £18-£20 p.p.

Breakfast: Included – full English/continental.

Meals: Available nearby.

Closed: Never!

Not only former rectory, but former bishop's residence too. Elegant but not over-grand, big but not overbearing and quite beautifully decorated and furnished with many antiques and old paintings. This immaculate house is owned by a thoroughly human and friendly couple who keep horses (stable room for yours too), a cat and a very large much-loved lurcher. They open their arms to their guests, feed them finely and sleep them in extreme comfort. Children over 5 welcome.

Rooms: 1 twin/double en suite shower & bath; 1 double with en suite shower; 1 twin with private shower & bath.

Price: £28 p.p. doubles, £5 single supp.

Breakfast: Included – full English.

Meals: Dinner £18 p.p. and packed lunch available on request.

Closed: Occasionally.

Take A1075 north towards Watton. After 9 miles turn left to Thompson. After 0.5 miles take second left at red letter box on corner. Turn left again, house is down dead end.

Map Ref No: 11

Mrs Garnier
College Farm
Thompson
Thetford
Norfolk IP24 1QG
Tel: 01953-483318

1 mile S of Norwich on roundabout at junction of A47 & A140 to Ipswich, take exit signposted Caistor St Edmund. After a mile turn left at crossroads and house is on immediate right.

Map Ref No: 12

Kassy & Jonathan Pusey
The Old Rectory
Caistor St. Edmund
Norwich
Norfolk NR14 8QS
Tel: 01508-492490
Fax: 01508-492490

You can see the cathedral from The Beeches and it stands in a 3-acre garden of stunning Victorian design, ornate in its neo-Gothic fountain, elaborate in its Italianate terrace steps and balustrading, woodsy and strollable beyond. The hotel, two old mansion houses plus a modern extension, has large, comfortably but unfussily-furnished rooms, bistro restaurant and bar. A pleasant informal atmosphere is encouraged by the friendly mother and daughter management team.

Rooms: 3 twins, 14 doubles, 8 singles, all with en suite bathrooms.

Price: £65-£75 doubles, £49 singles, per room per night.

Breakfast: Included – full English.

Meals: Dinner from £7 p.p.

Closed: Christmas

Pack your bags and head for the Norfolk Broads. This is the sort of place one can usually only dream of – a lovely old Georgian house. It has everything going for it – looks, position and a mass of luxurious detail inside. The new owners combine a private home feel with impeccable service and food. The bedrooms are mostly large with two charming attic rooms. All are stylishly chintzy and the bathrooms are terrific. The River Bure meanders by and there are rowing boats, or you can dock your own! A country-house feel – more of a home than a hostel, with the family's books and furniture lending the tone.

Rooms: 11 rooms all en suite: 3 twin, 6 double, 2 family.

Price: £32.50 p.p. doubles, £49 single.

Breakfast: Included – full English/continental.

Meals: A la carte – lunch and dinner. Weekly lunch on request.

Closed: Never!

Head for town centre, up hill towards large RC cathedral. B1108/ Earlham Road runs down hill right behind St. Johns RC Cathedral. Hotel is on the left.

Map Ref No: 12

B1150 north to Coltishall. Go over humpback bridge and turn down first right. Turn down drive before church – signed.

Map Ref No: 12

Mr & Mrs K Hill
The Beeches Hotel & Victorian Gardens
4-6 Earlham Road, Norwich
Norfolk NR2 3DB
Tel: 01603-621167
Fax: 01603-620151

Mr & Mrs Fleming
The Norfolk Mead Hotel
Coltishall
Norwich
Norfolk NR12 7DN
Tel: 01603-737531
Fax: 01603-737521

The Winters' is just a laid-back family home on the outskirts of a rural Norfolk village. The house is a fascinating 17th-century rectory with Victorian additions. The huge drawing/dining room, the large kitchen, the 5-acre garden – it is all yours for your stay. You must join in! Children come and go. Dogs and ponies roam. It may seem untidy but the atmosphere is utterly relaxed, the family are good fun and the coast is very close at hand for swimming, sailing and watching the famous Blakeney seals. The rectory is no-smoking except in the dining room.

Rooms: 1 twin with separate, private bath, shower & wc; 1 double en suite bath & wc.

Price: £20 p.p. Discount for children.

Breakfast: Included – full English.

Meals: Dinner £10 p.p. Available on request. BYO wine.

Closed: Christmas.

A splendid 18th-century flint house for family holidays in North Norfolk, half a mile from that much-loved piece of coastline with its swimming, sailing, bird watching and seal watching trips and stately homes for rainy days. The Lacostes have young children of their own so cots and high chairs are available and children's needs easily dealt with. The decoration is simple, the furniture traditional, the paintings by local artists. Pauline is a trained chef and the food is excellent.

Rooms: 1 twin, 2 doubles, 1 family room, all en suite.

Price: £22.50-£25 p.p. doubles, £30 single. Children 4-14 sharing with parents, half-price.

Breakfast: Included – full English/continental.

Meals: Dinner £10-£12.50 p.p. High teas for children also available.

Closed: 14-28 February.

From Fakenham A1067 towards Norwich. At Guist clock tower turn left & take second turning to Wood Norton. House is on right after 100 yards through white gates, over 2 cattle grids.

Map Ref No: 12

Jo & Giles Winter
The Old Rectory
Wood Norton
Norfolk
NR20 5AZ
Tel: 01362-683785

From Holt, leave A148 and go through town centre. Pass 2 garages, turn left after corner following sign to Weybourne 3. Down hill to Weybourne, turn right at T-junction, entrance opposite church and coast road junction.

Map Ref No: 12

Charles & Pauline Lacoste
Rosedale Farm
Holt Road
Weybourne, Holt
Norfolk NR25 7ST
Tel: 01263-588778

An 18th-century windmill with the river lapping the wall beneath. Each room has a different character, with a magnificent round sitting room overlooking the marshes. The best bedrooms look towards the endless seascape – one even has a walk-round balcony. Everything is special about this hotel, from the obvious thrill of staying in a windmill to the great welcome and good coffee at breakfast. You can also have dinner which will probably include caught-that-day fish and the delicious seamarsh vegetable, samphire. Bring your telescope and/or binoculars.

Rooms: 2 twins, 1 en suite, 1 with shared bathroom; 3 doubles, 1 en suite, 2 with private bathroom, 1 single with shared bathroom.

Price: £32.50 p.p. doubles, £32 single.

Breakfast: Included – full English.

Meals: Dinner £14.50-£15 p.p.

Closed: Never!

A largish family hotel in a stunning position beside the quay looking out across the estuary and the salt marshes to Blakeney Point. The rooms vary in size, fittings and price. Some have four-posters, one or two have access to private patios (ideal for dog-owners), some have bunk beds with families in mind; high tea is served at 6pm too. The lobby is bright yellow, the lounge is deep pink, the atmosphere resolutely relaxed and there are masses of things to do (pool, gym, fine gardens).

Rooms: 26 twins, 24 doubles, 10 singles, all with private bathrooms.

Price: From £57-£98 p.p.

Breakfast: Included – full English/continental.

Meals: Lunch & dinner.

Closed: Never!

From Holt take Cley Road through the narrow – and only – street in Cley. There's a sign to the mill on the left. Drive over the bridge to the car park.

Map Ref No: 12

Chris Buisseret
Cley Mill
Cley-next-the-Sea,
Holt
Norfolk NR25 7NN
Tel: 01263-740209
Fax: 01263-740209

Blakeney is located off the A149 Cromer to Kings Lynn road or off the B1156 Blakeney road. The hotel is on the quayside.

Map Ref No: 12

Mr Michael Stannard
The Blakeney Hotel
Blakeney
Nr. Holt
Norfolk NR25 7NE
Tel: 01263-740797
Fax: 01263-740795

Food takes pride of place at Morston Hall – people come from far and wide for Galton Blackiston's divine cooking – but don't forget that you are ½ mile from Morston harbour and trips to Blakeney Point and the seals. The dining room has generous space for all, the furnishing is a good mix of old and new in this renovated Jacobean building, there is a large garden and the bedrooms are big and full of shape and character. Finally, the young proprietors are both relaxed and enthusiastic.

Rooms: 1 twin, 5 doubles, all en suite.

Price: £65-£80 p.p. doubles including dinner, £90-£110 single including dinner.

Breakfast: Included – full English.

Meals: Dinner £26 p.p. Sunday lunch only £15 p.p.

Closed: 1 January – 14 February.

There is room for everyone in this large 19th-century farmhouse. Elizabeth is most friendly, has an excellent sense of humour and seems able to cope with anything. Her working farm house has dogs and geese all over the yard, chicks on the lawn in spring and a thoroughly lived-in feel while guests have their own sitting and dining rooms and large, pleasant bedrooms that give onto the countryside. City-dwellers will feel they have escaped from it all. Children over 12 welcome.

Rooms: 2 twins, 1 double: 1 twin is en suite and 1 shares bath with double.

Price: £20 p.p. en suite, £18 p.p. without. £5 single supp. in season.

Breakfast: Included – full English.

Meals: Dinner from £10.50.

Closed: Christmas & New Year.

Morston Hall is just off A149 Cromer to Kings Lynn coastal road, near Blakeney Point and junction with A1065.

Map Ref No: 12

Tracy & Galton Blackiston & Justin Fraser
Morston Hall
Morston, Holt
Norfolk NR25 7AA
Tel: 01263-741041
Fax: 01263-740419

From Fakenham take B1146 towards East Dereham. After 2 miles turn left to Gt. Ryburgh. In village turn left up Highfield Lane opposite pink cottage. Follow lane for 0.5 miles – house is on right.

Map Ref No: 12

Mrs Elizabeth Savory
Highfield Farm
Great Ryburgh
Fakenham
Norfolk NR21 7AL
Tel: 01328-829249

Lucky Old Rector. Built hexagonally in 1500, modernised in the 1800s...this amazing old building, historic home of the Shelton family, exudes peace. The bedrooms are all different shapes (architectural history showing through), most of them with views over garden and church. The dining room has stone mullioned windows and great oak beams. The restfully informal atmosphere is nurtured by Mrs Scoles's warm smile and practised efficiency. Children by arrangement.

Rooms: 1 twin, 3 doubles/twin, 2 doubles, all en suite bathrooms.

Price: £45 p.p. doubles, £68 single.

Breakfast: Included – full English.

Meals: Dinner from £22 p.p.

Closed: 24-27 December .

Another lovely Norfolk Georgian house, redbrick and with those gateposts that mark its boundary so clearly yet in style. This is the English home at its best, the house that everyone would like to live in. It has the elegant proportions of the late 18th-century country house, the hall, drawing room and dining room are gracious and beautifully-furnished, the big-windowed bedrooms look onto the lovely garden and your hostess is sweet, friendly and most helpful. Children over 10 welcome.

Rooms: 2 twins with shared private bathroom and wc.

Price: £22 p.p. Please book in advance.

Breakfast: Included – full English.

Meals: Dinner £14 p.p. on request.

Closed: Christmas.

Great Snoring is 3 miles NE of Fakenham, off the A148. Old Rectory behind the church on road signposted Barsham from village street. A magnificent beech tree is floodlit by night to guide you.

Map Ref No: 11

Rosamund & William Scoles
The Old Rectory
Barsham Road
Great Snoring, Fakenham
Norfolk NR21 0HP
Tel: 01328-820597
Fax: 01328-820048

From Swaffham take A1065, turn right to Litcham after 5 miles. House is on left as you come into village. Georgian red brick with stone balls on gatepost.

Map Ref No: 11

John & Hermione Birkbeck
Litcham Hall
Litcham
Nr. Kings Lynn
Norfolk PE32 2QQ
Tel: 01328-701389
Fax: 01328-701164

They are a whacky, quirky couple. Jane calls everyone 'darling' and has a heart of gold. She is a good Yorkshire girl, an excellent cook (all her vegetables are home-grown) who used to be a nurse and who loves having guests. Meanwhile, Michael pours the drinks. The house, a converted barn, is eminently and traditionally comfortable, guests may use the large kitchen and the sitting room and also stable their horses. How much more hospitable can one be?

Two of the bedrooms are exceptionally large and have chairs where you can sit and enjoy the peaceful view through the fine long windows. This is a large family farm with plenty of dogs and horses (stabling is available if you bring your own) and delightful hosts of the salt-of-earth race of real farmers, their walls proudly bearing the proofs of their successes at point-to-pointing and showing. Children over 12 by arrangement.

Rooms: 2 twins with adjacent private bathroom & shower room.

Price: £20 p.p.

Breakfast: Included – full English.

Meals: Dinner £10 p.p. Available on request.

Closed: Christmas.

Rooms: 2 doubles, one with en suite shower and one with bath/shower; 1 twin with private bathroom & wc.

Price: £18-£25 p.p. Sing. supp. p.p. £5.

Breakfast: Included – full English.

Meals: Not available.

Closed: Christmas week.

From Fakenham A148 towards Kings Lynn. After 4 miles left opposite garage to Tatterford. At white gates turn left, right and then left. The barn is set back on the right.

Map Ref No: 11

Take A418 N.E. and second of two turnings right to Harpley (no signpost) opposite Houghton Hall sign. After 200 yds crossroads, straight over. House 400 yds on left, white with copper beeches.

Map Ref No: 11

Michael & Jane Davidson-Houston
Manor Farm Barn
Tatterford
Nr. Fakenham
Norfolk NR21 7AZ
Tel: 01485-528393

Mrs Amanda Case
Lower Farm
Harpley
Nr. Kings Lynn
Norfolk PE31 6TU
Tel: 01485-520240

The simple brick face with its delightful fenestration does not prepare you for the outrageously bold festival of designer colours, cushions, canopies, carvings, frills and furbelows that greets you in the drawing rooms and bedchambers (the Scotts met at art school). The peaceful patio garden is in sweet contrast. Strattons is wonderfully different, the owners so obviously enjoy ushering guests into their villa as members of their (large) family. They also love food. An ideal place to restore one's fatigued faculties.

Rooms: 1 twin en suite shower; 5 doubles all en suite (3 with bath, 2 with shower); 1 single en suite shower.

Price: £75-£78 p.p. doubles, £55 single.

Breakfast: Included – full English.

Meals: Dinner £23.50 p.p.

Closed: Never!

Influenced by the Dutch who came to help drain the Fens this wonderful 17th-century gabled house, formerly a merchant's home, has been lovingly added to through the years. A herringbone brick floor gives way to limestone flags in the beautiful 18th-century dining room with its fireplace and hand-printed French wallpaper; the warm, peach-coloured walls of the hall are hung with water colours, prints and portraits and there are restful views over the garden and orchard. Bedrooms are equally lovely and the Bevingtons the most delightful couple.

Rooms: 1 twin, 1 double, each with own bathroom.

Price: £22.50-£28 p.p.

Breakfast: Included – full English.

Meals: Not available.

Closed: 20 December – 5 January.

In central Swaffham, just off the Kings Lynn to Norwich road. North end of market place, entrance between William Brown and Express cleaners.

Map Ref No: 11

Les & Vanessa Scott
Strattons
4 Ash Close
Swaffham
Norfolk PE37 7UH
Tel: 01760-723845
Fax: 01760-720458

From A14 take B1102. Leaving Swaffham Bulbeck, turn left into Commercial End. House (white gates) on left 90 metres after phone box.

Map Ref No: 11

Julia & Loder Bevington
The Merchant's House
Swaffham Bulbeck
Cambridgeshire
CB5 0ND
Tel: 01223-812777
Fax: 01223-812777

EAST ANGLIA

A 1780s Adam-style house tucked away at the edge of the village. The sitting room, with Tudor brick walls, drain-brick floors, fireplace and old velvet sofas is the former coachouse, and Sally adds thoughtful touches to make you feel at home, newspapers and soft drinks among them. The bedrooms are pretty and well-decorated – one with an exceptionally large bed – with flowers and stationery. Sally's cooking is marvellous – she makes her own bread, cures her own salmon – and her menus are mouthwateringly inventive.

Rooms: 2 doubles both en suite.

Price: £25-£30 p.p. doubles, £40 single.

Breakfast: Included – full English.

Meals: Dinner £18 p.p., supper £10-£12.50 p.p. Picnics £10 p.p.

Closed: Never!

Close to the centre of Cambridge, Alice Percival's home is popular with visiting academics and proud parents alike. Despite being off a main road the house is quiet and peaceful with pleasant, comfortable and traditionally-furnished bedrooms. Guests sleep on the ground floor and breakfast upstairs in the dining-room. There is a garden at the back of the building and cat-lovers will be delighted by the company of two delightful Siamese. Non-cat-lovers will find them perfectly discreet.

Rooms: 1 twin, 1 double, both en suite; 1 single with private shower.

Price: £28 p.p. doubles, £35 single.

Breakfast: Included – full English.

Meals: Not available.

Closed: Never!

A14 north of Cambridge take A10 towards Ely. Turn right into Waterbeach. Bear left at village green. House is last at end of high street before left-hand bend. Opposite 2 white houses (look for stone balls). Through white gates.

Map Ref No: 11

Phil & Sally Myburgh
Berry House
High Street
Waterbeach
Cambridgeshire CB5 9JU
Tel: 01223-860702
Fax: 01223-860702

Turn off the M11 at junction 13 or exit B1049 off A14 to Histon turnoff. House is directly on the Huntingdon Road opposite Storeys Way.

Map Ref No: 11

Alice Percival
136 Huntingdon Road
Cambridge
Cambridgeshire
CB3 0HL
Tel: 01223-365285/568305
Fax: 01223-461142

A large, cool 1840 Regency-style house nestles in the bend of a river at the end of the quiet, historic village of Linton. Rooms are elegant and country squire-ish, with glass doors overlooking the gardens. Some have river views. The lovely conservatory, draped with mimosa and with red and black tile floors and park-bench furniture, is for summer breakfasts, whilst in winter one repairs to the dark-green dining-room. Bedrooms are comfortable and well-equipped, and stocked with books. Judith Rossiter looks after all this and two teenage children, and still finds time to be a charming and helpful hostess.

Rooms: 2 doubles – each with own bathroom.

Price: £17.50-£25 p.p.

Breakfast: Included – full English.

Meals: Excellent inn 200 yards away but Judith can cook for those who cannot eat in a pub.

Closed: Never!

The main house appears thrown together in a deliciously random mêlée, a collection of brick and beams that make up a remarkably real watermill on its own quasi-island.... Cross over a wooden bridge into a wild garden with weeping willows and ducks. The interior is just as unexpected and interesting. Charming rooms ramble and meander into each other via angles, shapes and steps of all kinds. All is hidden away at the end of a narrow track that opens out into this haven, well worth making a few wrong turns to find. Our inspector loved it... and the family.

Rooms: 1 family room with private bathroom.

Price: £20 p.p. doubles, £25 single.

Breakfast: Included – full English.

Meals: Not available, but pubs nearby.

Closed: Sunday – Thursday during term-time.

From A1307 Cambridge road left into high street. First right after The Crown (on left) into Horn Lane with tiny Barclays bank on corner. House is on right next to United Reformed chapel and before ford across river.

Map Ref No: 11

Dr Judith Rossiter
Springfield House
14-16 Horn Lane
Linton
Cambridgeshire CB1 6HT
Tel: 01223-891383

Off A1037 between Abington & Linton, and then – good luck! Access is down a tiny gravel lane!

Map Ref No: 11

Lynne & David Hartland
The Watermill
Hildersham
Cambridgeshire
CB1 6BS
Tel: 01223-891520

You can't get much older than this, the oldest inn in England, first recorded as selling liquor in 560AD! Part of the inn's granite floor marks the tomb of a 17-year-old girl who was buried here in 1050 and is said to haunt the place. Old wooden beams divide the interior of the whitewashed and thatched pub into alcoves, while upstairs the bedrooms have been modernised and are cosy, bright and comfortable. A terrace and large garden overlook the River Ouse where you can moor your boat and enjoy the delicious food of this very special inn.

Rooms: 1 twin/double with private bathroom, 4 doubles en suite, two 4-posters with private bathrooms.

Price: £27.25-£36.50 p.p. doubles, £44.50-£54.50 single.

Breakfast: Included – full English.

Meals: Dinner wide selection, variable prices.

Closed: 3-6 p.m. Monday-Saturday & 3-7p.m. Sundays.

From Huntingdon on A1123 to St. Ives. Over 2 sets of traffic lights, along St. Audrey Lane. Pick up Earith/Ely road at next roundabout. Right to Needingworth at roundabout, right to Holywell. Signed Ferryboat 1 mile.

Map Ref No: 11

Shelley Jeffrey
The Old Ferry Boat Inn
Holywell, St. Ives
Huntingdon
Cambridgeshire PE17 3TG
Tel: 01480-463227
Fax: 01480-494885

Go for the room with the view across Rutland Water. The village provides boats for sailing or fishing, or canoes or horses or bikes. This solid stone building was a Victorian coach house and the yard at the back has alcoves of hanging roses with nice garden furniture for lazy summer afternoons; croquet on the lawn, too. Inside, it has high ceilings, stone archways, antique furniture and lots of space. The beds are spread with lacy linen and Cecilie is a delightful hostess and a brilliant cook.

Rooms: 1 twin, 1 double, each with private bathroom.

Price: £25 p.p. doubles, £35 single.

Breakfast: Included – full English.

Meals: Dinner £18 p.p. on request.

Closed: Occasionally.

Middle England

From A1 Stamford by-pass A606 towards Oakham for 3 miles. Fork left for Edith Weston. Passing village sign take first right, Church Lane. Past church right again down hill. Coach House is on right on sharp left bend.

Map Ref No: 10

Tony & Cecilie Ingoldby
Old Hall Coach House
Edith Weston
Oakham
Rutland LE15 8HQ
Tel: 01780-721504
Fax: 01780-721311

The building, originally a farm, dates from 1594. It is now a pretty 'country cottage hotel' in a quiet, unspoilt English village with rooms in the main house and others in converted cottages (with mullioned windows). All are contemporary-cottage decorated with pretty florals, good bedding, matching bathrooms. The well-known restaurant serves 'modern English cuisine' with lots of home-grown vegetables and Neville makes his own brews with walnuts from the garden. You can learn falconry here....

Rooms: 4 twins, 8 doubles, 4 singles, all en suite.

Price: £37.50 p.p. doubles, £65 single.

Breakfast: Included – full English/continental.

Meals: Dinner £19.50 p.p. Lunch & packed lunch also available.

Closed: Never!

A quiet village, a quiet house, a quiet hostess who works for the parish and the lifeboat committee and is a real Bedfordshire buff. Peace at last? Built in the 1600s, the house was Georgianised in the 1800s and conceals a carved coat-of-arms betraying the original owner's royalist leanings in the Parliamentarian stronghold that was Roxton. It is furnished with a mixture of oak and mahogany, old and less old... and the beds are soft. The farm overlooks a country churchyard and there is another church across the road, an architectural oddity, non-conformist in name and nature with its thatched roof and cottage orné style. A rarity... .

Rooms: 1 twin, 1 family room, each with hand basin and sharing bathroom.

Price: From £18 p.p.

Breakfast: Included – full English/continental.

Meals: Not available.

Closed: Never!

From M1 junction 14 to Olney on A509. Left at A428 towards Northampton through Yardley Hastings and right to Castle Ashby.

Map Ref No: 10

Neville Watson
The Falcon Hotel
Castle Ashby
Northamptonshire
NN7 1LF
Tel: 01604-696200
Fax: 01604-696673

Go north on A1 to roundabout of A428. Take first exit to Bedford. Roxton is on left. Follow into High St and over crossroads. House is second on left after parish hall.

Map Ref No: 11

Janet Must
Church Farm
41 High Street
Roxton, Bedford
Bedfordshire MK44 3EB
Tel: 01234-870234
Fax: 01234-871576

A no-nonsense working farm, so don't expect many frills. Arable and sheep farming set the tone and Sue has taken to bee-keeping, producing delicious honey. Chickens drop fresh eggs for breakfast, cats and dogs roam in harmony and a collection of stuffed owls completes the menagerie. Try, if you can, to book the en-suite bedroom with its own entrance up spiral steps for maximum privacy and cosiness: its bathroom wins first prize for 'Best View from the Loo'!

Rooms: 1 double with en suite shower, 1 family room sharing bathroom with owners.

Price: £14-£17 p.p. doubles; supplement for singles.

Breakfast: Included – full English.

Meals: Not available, good local pubs.

Closed: Christmas & New Year.

Tucked beneath the Chilterns in 20 acres of grounds (and lakes) this 16th-century water-mill, a mile from the village, has a very pretty room in the 'Hay-loft'. Most of the chintz-and-antique bedrooms are in a converted stable-block – hotel privacy in a B&B – and you may stay all day, gazing at the lake from the conservatory and victualling yourself from the little kitchen. Rachel is an easy no-rules hostess and can lend you a bike... or offer fly-fishing, tennis, pool and 'ping-pong'.

Rooms: 2 twins, 5 doubles – all en suite.

Price: £25-£32.50 p.p., children £7.50.

Breakfast: Included – full English.

Meals: Dinner from £12.50 p.p.

Closed: Never!

Turn off the A1198 at Longstowe. The house is exactly 3 miles along the B1046, between Little Gransden and Longstowe.

Map Ref No: 11

Mrs Sue Barlow
Model Farm
Little Gransden
Sandy
Bedfordshire SG19 3EA
Tel: 01767-677361
Fax: 01767-677361

From Dunstable SW on B489. Right at roundabout by Plough pub. Bellows Mill 3rd on right.

Map Ref No: 10

Rachael Hodge
Bellows Mill
Eaton Bray
Dunstable
Bedfordshire LU6 1QZ
Tel: 01525-220548
Fax: 01525-222754

Low ceilings, exposed beams and stone fireplaces and the bedrooms, perched above their own staircases like crows' nests, are delightful. The barn room has its own entrance. All rooms are unusual and characterful; the family's history and travels are evident all over. Your hosts will occasionally dine with guests. They are amusing and utterly friendly, as is Ulysses, their large soppy golden retriever. You may not want to leave.

Rooms: 1 double en suite bath & wc; 1 double/twin en suite bath, shower & wc; 1 double/twin private bathroom.

Price: £24-£27 doubles/twin, supp. £8 single.

Breakfast: Included – full English.

Meals: Dinner £18.50 p.p.

Closed: Never!

The Caves, who will have converted their farm to exclusively organic produce by 1998, give their guests a proper farmhouse welcome. They hope to encourage you to leave your hectic habits behind, slow down and enjoy the peace of their surroundings and the healthy organic food they provide. Their one guestroom is pastel and floral with beams, two windows, old pine furniture and a power shower and triangular corner bath. Black pudding for breakfast if you choose.

Rooms: 1 family/twin/double with own bath, shower & wc.

Price: £18.50 p.p.

Breakfast: Included – full English, continental by arrangement.

Meals: No, but locally available.

Closed: Never!

From Banbury exit 11 on M40 onto A422. Right at Farthinghoe for Charlton, first left after Rose & Crown pub.

Map Ref No: 10

Col & Mrs Grove-White
Home Farmhouse
Charlton
Nr Banbury
Oxfordshire OX17 3DR
Tel: 01295-811683
Fax: 01295-811683

B4525 N.E. from Banbury for 4 miles. Follow signs to Sulgrave Manor. First right into Park Lane. Farm entrance is approx. 170 metres on right.

Map Ref No: 10

Steven & Libby Cave
Wemyss Farm
Sulgrave
Banbury
Oxfordshire OX17 2RX
Tel: 01295-760323

Parts of this fine stone house are 400 years old; it has nary a straight wall or a right angle and betrays its organic growth in its many level changes, so the garden is naturally built on three fascinatingly different terraces too (the Parrotia Persia Pendula is spectacular). The guestrooms are large, light and furnished in manorial style, the breakfasts are feasts of fishcakes or kedgeree and there is a priesthole under the dining room. The Willses are most welcoming hosts – they really seem to enjoy it all.

Rooms: 1 twin with private bath & shower, 1 twin/double en suite bathroom, 1 double with private bath & shower.

Price: £24-£28 p.p. doubles.

Breakfast: Included – full English.

Meals: £17.50-£20 p.p. by arrangement. Good local pubs and restaurants.

Closed: Christmas & New Year.

The Feathers, a classy inn close to Blenheim Palace, was once four 17th-century houses and still has four winding staircases (tough on the elderly). The staff are young and welcoming, the bar snacks excellent, the food delicious, the garden tiny. The luxurious bedrooms (quieter ones at back) are decorated with lovely fabrics and wallpapers, antiques and original prints and the bathrooms are marble. Pricey but both service and breakfast are top-class, the new owner actually likes children and there's not a trouser-press in sight. Mountain bikes free for guests.

Rooms: 3 suites; 6 twins with en suite bathrms; 7 doubles with en suite bathrms; 1 double with private bathrm.

Price: From £50-£75 p.p. Suites: £92.50-£97.50.

Breakfast: Included – continental/ health food. £7.85 full English.

Meals: Dinner from £15 p.p.

Closed: Never!

Culworth is off B4525 Northampton Road. Follow signs for Thorpe Mandeville/Culworth. Turn up along Culworth village green. Fulford House is 30 yards beyond on left.

Map Ref No: 10

From A44 Oxford go past main gates of Blenheim Palace, approx 200 yards, turn left into Market Street.

Map Ref No: 10

Mr & Mrs Stephen Wills
Fulford House
The Green
Culworth, Nr. Banbury
Oxfordshire OX17 2BB
Tel: 01295-760355
Fax: 01295-768304

Tom Lewis
The Feathers Hotel
Market Street
Woodstock
Oxfordshire OX20 1SX
Tel: 01993-812291
Fax: 01993-813158

MIDDLE ENGLAND

A haven in the middle of Oxford. Clever use of design detail and materials have kept the old-house feel and intimacy of a private club. All redecorated in 1991, the splendid bedrooms, in smart florals and checks – some with fireplaces and panelling – have glorious marble bathrooms. Entrance hall with bar and winter fire, paintings and prints everywhere, leather chairs in the Parsonage Bar dining room. Hotel guests have exclusive use of first floor roof garden, lush with plants, for tea or sundowner. First class service and a morning newspaper.

Rooms: 6 twins, 19 doubles, 4 suites, 1 single, all en suite.

Price: £75 p.p. doubles, from £115 single.

Breakfast: Included – full English/continental.

Meals: Lunch & dinner available.

Closed: 24-27 December.

"What a welcome! She's really chatty, no hang-ups, I felt completely at home and wanted to stay longer", wrote a captivated inspector. It is an idyllic spot, a 17th-century house in a small hamlet with 14th-century church, surrounded by orchards and a nature reserve. The river Thames runs through the village. Beams, uneven floors, period furniture, open fire in inglenook, oak doors, local or home-grown food (even local milk). Attractive and comfortable without any pretension at all.

Rooms: 1 double en suite, 1 double with private bathroom.

Price: £19-£22 p.p. doubles, £25 single.

Breakfast: Included – full English/continental.

Meals: Available locally. Packed lunch available on request.

Closed: Never!

From A40 ring road south at Banbury Road roundabout to Summertown and towards city centre. Hotel on right next to St. Giles's church.

Map Ref No: 10

Jeremy Mogford
Old Parsonage Hotel
No. 1 Banbury Road
Oxford
Oxfordshire OX2 6NN
Tel: 01865-310210
Fax: 01865-311262

Turn right at the T-junction in Little Wittenham. Rooks Orchard is the fifth building on the right behind a long hedge. Turn right into second gate.

Map Ref No: 4

Jonathan & Deborah Welfare
Rooks Orchard
Little Wittenham
Abingdon
Oxfordshire OX14 4QY
Tel: 01865-407765

Refreshingly original as well as ravishingly beautiful and the owners are fun, too. They are well-travelled and as laid-back as they are efficient... unusually for owners of houses like this. The decor is oak floors, white walls, wood, antique and contemporary simplicity (no chintz), with more than a touch of Mexico. The drawing room has a vast fireplace for winter. To add icing to the cake they have put a swimming pool in the old Victorian vine-house.

Rooms: 1 twin en suite, 1 double en suite, 1 double with private bathroom.

Price: £35 p.p.

Breakfast: Included – full English/contintental.

Meals: Dinner £25 p.p. By arrangement.

Closed: Christmas.

All you'll hear are the birds, so quiet is this little spot beside the village green with, blessedly, no through road... a place to renew your love of the English countryside and village. The houses are 16th and 17th-century, built for the staff of nearby Grey's Court (now National Trust). It is a lovely house: a big sitting room full of Persian rugs, a fireplace, grand piano and backgammon. There are 8 acres of grounds with all-round views and free-range hens.

Rooms: 2 twin/doubles en suite, 1 double with private bathroom, 1 single with private shower & wc.

Price: £20-£25 p.p. doubles, £24-£34 single.

Breakfast: Included – full English/contintental etc.

Meals: Not available.

Closed: Christmas week.

From M40 exits 7 or 8, A329 towards Wallingford. In Stadhampton take lane immed. after mini roundabout to left across village green. The Manor is stone house straight ahead at end of lane.

Map Ref No: 4

Anthea & Stephen Savage
The Manor
Stadhampton
Oxfordshire
OX44 7UL
Tel: 01865-891999
Fax: 01865-891640

Go NW on Peppard Road from Henley for 3 miles, then right for Shepherds Green. House is on right after 0.3 miles. Please phone to advise time of arrival.

Map Ref No: 5

Mrs Sue Fulford-Dobson
Shepherds
Shepherds Green
Rotherfield Greys, Henley-on-Thames
Oxfordshire RG9 4QL
Tel: 01491-628413

The same family has lived here for five generations. From the spectacular panelled hall with its piano and fireplace, you ramble into the heart of the house. Equally lovely, with family portraits throughout, it has an elegant and lived-in dining room, huge romantic double bedrooms (especially the 4-poster), lovingly equipped bathrooms (hangover cures and other essentials). Mrs Ovey is a character – great fun, no nonsense (smoking definitely unwelcome!), buzzing with energy. A sense of space and peace prevails. Not to be missed.

Rooms: 1 twin en suite, 2 doubles (1 with 4-poster en suite; 1 with queen boat bed & own separate bathroom).

Price: £37.50 p.p. 4-poster, £35 p.p. double/twin, £45.50 single.

Breakfast: Included – full English. Continental on request.

Meals: No, but good pub food and fine restaurants within 1 mile.

Closed: December – mid-January.

In Henley centre take Duke St. After 170 metres go right into Grey's Rd. After almost 2 miles (as you leave 30 m.p.h. zone) drive in where you see sign on right – 'Hernes Estate. Private Drive'.

Map Ref No: 5

Richard & Gillian Ovey
Hernes
Henley-on-Thames
Oxfordshire
RG9 4NT
Tel: 01491-573245
Fax: 01491-574645

If you want something old, and lived-in, this cosy Georgian house is the place to be – creaky floorboards and all! Candles are brought out for dinner on a small table beneath the painted gaze of Inigo Jones – a forebear of Mr. Wallace. Weather permitting, breakfast and an inspired dinner will be served in the garden under the vines. The atmosphere is simple and unpretentious and the Wallaces are a charming couple.

Rooms: 2 twin/doubles, 1 en suite bath, 1 en suite shower, 1 single with adj. bathroom.

Price: £25 p.p. doubles, £20 single.

Breakfast: Included – full English.

Meals: Dinner £14 p.p.

Closed: Never!

From A40 Junction 5. Through Stokechurch, right to Lane End and to Frieth. In Frieth follow through village & on towards Hambleden and Henley. House is 0.75 miles along on right.

Map Ref No: 5

Wynyard & Julia Wallace
Little Parmoor
Frieth
Henley-on-Thames
Oxfordshire RG9 6NL
Tel: 01494-881447
Fax: 01494-883012

Holmwood is a huge Georgian manor, but don't be daunted; it is very welcoming and relaxing, too. Since their three children grew up and went their own ways, Brian and Wendy have turned their massive bedrooms into very dignified guest rooms with good, modern bathrooms. The interior is immaculate and exactly right for its period. There are distant views over the Thames valley, acres of garden and woodland to explore, tennis and croquet to play. No surprise that the house lends itself to holding special events.

Rooms: 2 twins, 2 doubles, 1 single, all with en suite shower & bath.

Price: £25 p.p. doubles, £30 single.

Breakfast: Included – full English.

Meals: Available locally.

Closed: Christmas

Spellbindingly placed almost on the Ridgeway ('the oldest road in Europe', a prehistoric M4, well-loved by riders, walkers and cyclists), the Reids' is an all-grass organic beef farm plus a family cow for milk, hens for eggs, loads of homegrown veg. and horses for competent riders. The walking is exceptional, the prehistoric sights fascinating, the bedrooms cosy but not cushy, and Penny's enthusiasm for all things equine and all things 'green' could be catching.

Rooms: 2 twins, 1 en suite, 1 sharing bathroom with owner.

Price: £18 p.p. doubles, £25 single.

Breakfast: Included – full English/continental.

Meals: Dinner £12-£15 p.p.

Closed: Christmas.

From Henley-on-Thames A4155 towards Reading. After 2.5 miles Shiplake College on left and Plouden Arms on right. Before pub turn into Plough Lane, becomes Shiplake Row. Past pub up hill on left.

Map Ref No: 5

Brian & Wendy Talfourd-Cook
Holmwood
Shiplake Row
Binfield Heath, Henley
Oxfordshire RG9 4DP
Tel: 0118-9478747
Fax: 0118-9478637

Between Lambourn, Berks & Wantage, Oxon, 0.25 miles south of Ridgeway Path off Lambourn/Kingstone Lisle road. Take track on right at corner by muck heap. You will see 2 green barns & orange house in distance.

Map Ref No: 4

Mrs Penny Reid
Down Barn Farm
Sparsholt Down
Wantage
Oxfordshire OX12 9XD
Tel: 01367-820272

The 12th-century church is known as 'the little cathedral in the Vale'. A rose-filled garden surrounds this old country cottage full of rich colours, stencilling and original paintings. Power shower, fluffy cotton towels, Egyptian cotton sheets, Victorian iron and brass bedsteads, firm new mattresses and fresh flowers, oak beams and a log fire are enough for most. But let me add: home-baked bread, juice from the orange, eggs from their hens, organic sausages... plus 3 adored border collies and a few sheep.

Rooms: 1 twin, 1 double, both en suite; 1 single with private bathroom.

Price: £25 p.p.

Breakfast: Included – full English/continental.

Meals: Dinner £19 p.p. Available at weekends by arrangement.

Closed: Never!

In the village made famous by Edward Thomas's poem, the Warricks designed and built their house themselves using soft-coloured local stone and fine hardwoods. It is solid, unpretentious, no-nonsense-decorated and most welcoming. Bob and Margaret are warm, kindly hosts. At the bottom of the delightful garden there is a little brook and the beehives whence comes the honey for your breakfast. You can also have homemade rolls and continental meats and cheeses. Children over 8 welcome.

Rooms: 1 twin/double with en suite bathroom; 1 double with washbasin & en suite wc & private shower.

Price: £18.50-£20 p.p. doubles, £22-£24 single.

Breakfast: Included – full English/continental.

Meals: Dinner available locally. Packed lunch available on request.

Closed: December & January.

From A420 at Faringdon follow brown tourist signs for Uffington White Horse. Continue until village of Uffington. Shotover is the last house on the right leaving the village on road to White Horse.

Map Ref No: 4

Elizabeth Shaw
Shotover House
Uffington
Oxfordshire
SN7 7RH
Tel: 01367-820351

From Stow A436 to Chipping Norton. After 3 miles left to Adlestrop. After 0.25 miles right at T-junction. In village right at triangular flower bed. Cottage signed second on right.

Map Ref No: 10

Bob & Margaret Warrick
Honeybrook Cottage
Main Street
Adlestrop, Moreton-in-Marsh
Gloucestershire GL56 0YN
Tel: 01608-658884
Fax: 01608-658884

The owners call it 'a townhouse in the country'. It is a Victorian manor whose Englishness is lightly spiced with a North American touch in the decor. Two of the bedrooms look across the wide Dikler valley, green as far as the eye can see. You can walk for miles and come back for a sauna. The house is renowned for its home-baked bread and the Simonettis also organise personally-guided tours of famous local gardens. They will clearly go to great lengths to meet your needs. Children over 12 welcome.

Rooms: 1 twin en suite shower/bath; 3 doubles, all en suite (1 with shower, 1 with shower & bath, 1 with bath).

Price: £34 -£44 p.p.

Breakfast: Included – full English/continental/health food.

Meals: Dinner £22-£25 p.p.

Closed: January.

This is high quality on a tiny scale. Jane's snug little cottage was a relief after a day inspecting grander places; I unwound immediately. We chatted over homemade cake and tea and warmed each other's nostalgia for our teaching days in front of the fire. Jane is the perfect hostess: intelligent, sensitive and open-minded. She drives the community bus and gives walkers a special welcome. Oddington too, is worth coming for; it is a real working Cotswold village. Children over 5 welcome.

Rooms: 1 twin en suite shower room & wc., 1 double with adj. bathroom & wc.

Price: £18-£20 p.p. doubles, £22-£24 single.

Breakfast: Included – full English & substantial continental.

Meals: Dinner £12.50-£14.50 p.p.

Closed: December, January, February.

From Stow take B4068 to Lower Swell. House is on left, driveway entrance opposite Unicorn Hotel.

Map Ref No: 10

Take A436 from Stow towards Chipping Norton. Right fork to Kingham, follow 0.5 miles. The Oddington turn is at end of double bend on hill. Back Lane first turn on left. Gate to cottage is first on right.

Map Ref No: 10

Frank Simonetti
Crestow House
Lower Swell
Stow-on-the-Wold
Gloucestershire GL54 1JX
Tel: 01451-830969
Fax: 01451-832129

Jane Beynon
Orchard Cottage
Back Lane
Upper Oddington
Gloucestershire GL56 0XL
Tel: 01451-830785

The Lamb's qualifications are many: beside the village green, about 350 years old, local stone, old beams and a focal point for locals. Some of the guestrooms are in outbuildings but the core still has the traditional feel of the wayside inn. It has warmth, good food cooked to order and a resident ghost who seems so friendly that some guests come back in the hope of meeting her again. Richard and Kate are relaxed, efficient innkeepers with lots of energy to put at your service.

Rooms: 5 suites (2 garden with king size beds) all en suite bath, 1 suite with 4-poster, 8 doubles en suite bath or shower.

Price: £22-£37.50 p.p.

Breakfast: Included – full English/continental.

Meals: Dinner from £15 p.p.

Closed: Christmas & Boxing Day.

On the village green in the village of Great Rissington between Burford and Cheltenham off the A40.

Map Ref No: 10

Richard & Kate Cleverly
The Lamb Inn
Great Rissington
Nr. Bourton-on-the-Water
Gloucestershire GL54 2LP
Tel: 01451-820388
Fax: 01451-820724

By dint of sheer determination the Barrys have worked a builder's miracle. It is hard to believe their 'before' pictures of ruinous walls partly covered with corrugated iron. The 'after' is a long stone house with lovely high windows in the central part, a shape that caresses the natural ground and, maturing nicely, a fine garden. Inside, the decor is fresh – so are the flowers – the furniture and books old, the delightful owners happy and proud to have you in their house. Children over 12 welcome.

Rooms: 1 twin with en suite bath & wc; 1 twin & 1 double sharing bath, shower & wc.

Price: £25-£28 p.p. £10 single supplement.

Breakfast: Included – full English/continental.

Meals: Dinner available locally.

Closed: Christmas, New Year & Easter.

From Cirencester A417 towards Fairford/Lechlade. At Meysey Hampton crossroads left to Sun Hill. After 1 mile left at cottage. Hampton Fields is 400 yards down drive.

Map Ref No: 4

Richard & Jill Barry
Hampton Fields
Meysey Hampton
Cirencester
Gloucestershire GL7 5JL
Tel: 01285-850070

Steep honey-coloured gables, mullioned windows and weathered stone tiles enfold this lovely 17th-century house on a quiet village lane. It is English to the core – and to the bottom of its lovely garden (the house sits in six acres). Caroline is a warm and competent hostess who has a cool, gentle manner and a talent for understated high-class interior decor. The two ample, airy guestrooms are furnished with antiques and the bathrooms are modern.

Rooms: 1 twin en suite bath, 1 double en suite shower/bath.

Price: £22.50-£30 p.p.

Breakfast: Included – full English/continental.

Meals: Excellent pub nearby.

Closed: December & January

Any tree-lover will relish the prospect of a mere stroll from the farm to the famous Westonbirt Arboretum. And if you are easy and understanding you will enjoy the honest value of this B&B. Peel back the modern paraphernalia and farmhouse furniture and you can see the yeoman farmhouse beneath. Sonja is an engaging hostess, utterly without pretension; no frills, a hard-working husband and son, a typical modern farmyard happily out of view. Come for simple good value and a walk among those trees.

Rooms: 1 twin en suite shower, 1 double en suite shower, 3 separate wcs.

Price: £17.50 p.p.

Breakfast: Included – full English.

Meals: No, but locally available.

Closed: Never!

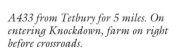

South through village from A417. Turn right after Masons Arms. House is 200m on left.

Map Ref No: 4

Roger & Caroline Carne
The Old Rectory
Meysey Hampton
Near Cirencester
Gloucestershire GL7 5OX
Tel: 01285-851200
Fax: 01285-851200

A433 from Tetbury for 5 miles. On entering Knockdown, farm on right before crossroads.

Map Ref No: 4

Sonja King
Avenue Farm
Knockdown
Tetbury
Gloucestershire GL8 8QY
Tel: 01454-238207
Fax: 01666-840191

400 years ago this was a wool merchant's house and a wealthy man he must have been. Now a small and very smart hotel, it is sumptuously decorated without being ostentatious and has a touch of informality. Some rooms have four-posters, some are larger than others, all are attractive and immaculate and there is a nice policy of giving you a better room for no extra charge in slack periods. The hotel is on a busy road (a very pretty town, by the way) but most rooms face the garden. Children under 12 have high tea not dinner.

Rooms: 1 twin, 11 doubles (3 with 4-posters), all en suite with either bath and/or shower.

Price: £42.50-£100 p.p. From £90 single.

Breakfast: Included – full English/continental.

Meals: Lunch and dinner available. Dinner from £25 p.p.

Closed: Never!

There is no moat now, but what an astonishingly lovely place! Gillie has restored this old house to more than its former glory. She has the eye of an interior designer and it has penetrated every corner with a rare perfection. She has also managed to avoid traditional English country-house style, creating a flawless interior full of surprises and interest. Note the way she has squeezed one particular bathroom in among the beams. Try the 'Giggle Suite' or the 4-poster room. The attic rooms are simple but attractive. Gillie's food is as thoughtful as her design.

Rooms: 2 twins, 3 doubles, one 4-poster, all en suite.

Price: £35 p.p. doubles, £45 single.

Breakfast: Included – full English.

Meals: Dinner £17.50 p.p. By prior arrangement.

Closed: Never!

In the centre of Tetbury, just past the mini-roundabout on Market Square.

Map Ref No: 4

Manager: Jonathan Dawson
The Close Hotel
Long Street
Tetbury
Gloucestershire GL8 8AQ
Tel: 01666-502272
Fax: 01666-504401

M4 junct.18 into Pucklechurch. Turn right into Parkfield Road opposite church. The Moat House is at bottom, straight ahead.

Map Ref No: 3

Gillie Edwards
The Moat House
Kings Lane
Pucklechurch
Gloucestershire BS17 3PS
Tel: 0117-9372283
Fax: 0117-9372539

A treat: utterly delightful people of exquisite manners and wide-ranging interests (ex-British Council and college lecturing; arts, travel, gardening...) in a manor-type house full of beautiful furniture. The house was born of the Arts and Crafts movement and remains fascinating: green-wood panelled and log-fired drawing-room for guests, quarry tiles on window-sills, handsome old furniture, comfortable proportions... elegant but human. The garden's massive clipped hedges and great lawn are impressive, as is the whole place. Refined but easy.

Rooms: 2 twins, 1 double: 1 with private bathroom/shower and 2 with shared bathroom.

Price: £25 p.p. doubles, £30 single.

Breakfast: Included – full English.

Meals: Dinner £17.50 p.p. Can bring own wine.

Closed: November – March.

Frampton is special, its elongated village green (the longest in England?) flanked by a goodly lesson in English architecture through the ages, duck ponds and a tiny cricket patch. The Old School House is built of warm Frampton brick and Carol's welcome is just as warm. The large rooms are pleasing to look at, the garden is full of colour, the world outside consists of fields and footpaths. A restful stay is guaranteed. Children over 10 welcome.

Rooms: 2 twins, 1 en suite, 1 with sep. private bath & wc.

Price: £20 p.p.

Breakfast: Included – full English.

Meals: No, but locally available.

Closed: 21 December – 1 January.

Take B4060 from Stinchcombe to Wotton-under-Edge. Go up long hill, house is at top on left – the gateway is marked.

Map Ref No: 4

Hugh & Crystal St John Mildmay
Drakestone House
Stinchcombe
Dursley
Gloucestershire GL11 6AS
Tel: 01453-542140

From A38 turn W onto B4071. Take first left, drive the length of village green. 300 yards after it finishes turn right into Whittles Lane. The Old Schoolhouse is the last on the right.

Map Ref No: 9

Carol Alexander
The Old School House
Whittles Lane
Frampton-on-Severn
Gloucestershire GL2 7EB
Tel: 01452 740457
Fax: 01452 740 457

A superb Grade 1 listed house, utterly without pretension to modern luxury, in a most interesting village. The family has lived at Frampton since the 12th century. The house speaks the elegant language of Vanburgh, is beautifully crafted (do study the stonework outside, the carving and panelling inside), finely furnished (your big bedroom has antiques, wall hangings and hand-embroidered bedcovers) and has a Strawberry Hill Gothic orangery (now let for self-catering). Dutch ornamental canal, water lilies, superb views....

Rooms: 1 double en suite, 2 singles with shared bathroom.

Price: £35 p.p. doubles, £45-£50 single.

Breakfast: Included – full English/continental/other.

Meals: Available locally.

Closed: Never!

Anne Boleyn may well have planted the vast oak but history begins here with the 14th century. Four footpaths (almost) cross the front garden and the Cotswold Way is nearby. This is a real working farm so the milk, lamb and veg. are real too – as are the jams, eggs and welcome. The bedrooms and bathrooms are comfortable enough – big and farm-housey – but the memories are made by the authentic and homely farm atmosphere. You can come and go all day, a rare treat in B&B.

Rooms: 1 twin, 1 double, both with shared bathroom, 1 family room en suite shower.

Price: £18.50-£21.50 p.p. doubles, £25 single.

Breakfast: Included – full English/continental.

Meals: Dinner £15 p.p. By prior arrangement (24 hours).

Closed: December & January.

From M5 junction 13 west, then B4071. Turn left through village green. Entrance (imposing stone gate posts) is between two large chestnut trees on left, behind long brick wall.

Map Ref No: 9

Mrs Henriette Clifford
Frampton Court
Frampton-on-Severn
Gloucestershire
GL2 7EX
Tel: 01452-740267

From Stroud A46 towards Cheltenham. Through Painswick. Turn right towards Sheepscombe. Pass Damsels Lodge on right. Continue for 1 mile to bottom of hill. Farm entrance on left. Long mud track.

Map Ref No: 9

Michele Burdett
Damsels Farm
Painswick
Gloucestershire
GL6 6UD
Tel: 01452-812148

The children have flown the nest but the atmosphere is still that of a family home. The big kitchen is where things happen; Petrina is a keen cook and loves the bustle and conversation of those who congregate there. They are new to B&B so the house is still sparkling fresh and clean with big, airy rooms, plain colour schemes and big beds – rare in the UK. There is a large garden with sweeping views. An attractive and elegant house.

Rooms: 2 king-size/twin, 1 en suite (sep. shower & wc), 1 with adjoining bathroom shared with 1 double – good for family use.

Price: £25 p.p.

Breakfast: Choice.

Meals: Dinner £17.50 p.p., gourmet £22.50 p.p.

Closed: Never!

Unusual; this self-catering flat is in the oldest (18th-century) part of the old vicarage. Lynda keeps an organic garden (you can pick herbs for your own pot) and provides the ingredients, many homemade, for an ecologically-sound breakfast every morning. You will be surrounded by daffodils in spring, bluebells in May, chromatic festivals in autumn. The Forest of Dean is all about, the River Wye only a mile down the path. Ideal for a family holiday and the road is quiet at night.

Rooms: Self-contained flat: 1 double, 1 bunk-bed, 1 single, 1 shower & wc.

Price: £38 for whole flat per night, sleeps 2-5.

Breakfast: Included – health food.

Meals: Dinner available locally.

Closed: Never!

Take A40 from Gloucester towards Ross-on-Wye, then B4215 towards Highnam. 2 miles on left is Whitehall Lane. House is approx. 0.5 miles down lane on right behind laurel hedge.

Map Ref No: 9

James & Petrina Pugh
Whitelands
Whitehall Lane
Rudford
Gloucestershire GL2 8ED
Tel: 01452-790406
Fax: 01452-790676

From Gloucester A40 to Ross on Wye. At Huntley left to Monmouth A4136. At '5 acres' right at crossroads into Park Road. At end turn right. House is next to church.

Map Ref No: 9

Lynda Steiner
The Old Vicarage
Christchurch
Nr. Coleford
Gloucestershire GL16 7NS
Tel: 01594-835330
Fax: 01594-837555

Darryl Gregory has taken his obsession with authenticity as far as antique loos and telephones. Cheltenham must have been emptied of antiques the year he furnished his 'gent's res'. He is also passionate about perfect service – and it shows. The dining room is crisply, elegantly Regency-striped and its menus are amazing. The bedrooms are stunningly handsome and have fantastic yet lighthearted bathrooms (a yellow duck in each). And, moreover, he has a huge sense of humour. Children over 8 welcome.

Rooms: 4 twins, 6 doubles, 1 suite with 4-poster, 1 junior suite – all en suite.

Price: £45.75-£74.75 p.p. doubles/suites/four-poster, from £74.50 single occupancy.

Breakfast: Full English £8.25 p.p. Continental £6 p.p.

Meals: Dinner £21.50-£26 p.p. Lunch à la carte.

Closed: Never!

From town centre, join one-way system and exit at signpost to Evesham. Continue down Evesham Road until you see the hotel signed on the left.

Map Ref No: 9

Mr Darryl Gregory
Hotel on the Park
Evesham Road
Cheltenham
Gloucestershire GL52 2AH
Tel: 01242-518898
Fax: 01242-511526

Kemerton is one of several pretty and ancient villages on Bredon Hill. Anglo-Saxons and Romans enjoyed it and the site of the water mill was recorded in the Domesday Book. The house is a magnificent Georgian manor in 15 acres of grounds, a delightful marriage of the formal and the wild, with mill, lake and dovecote. Life here is elegant and luxurious; the antique-dealer owners have filled the house with gorgeous things. To cap it all it is just a short stroll to the village.

Rooms: Four 4-posters en suite; 1 twin en suite; 1 twin/double en suite.

Price: £37.50-£42.50 p.p. doubles, £15 single supp.

Breakfast: Included – full English.

Meals: Dinner from £25 p.p. for 4 persons or more.

Closed: Christmas.

A435 north from Cheltenham, then B4079. About 1 mile after A438 crossroads, sign to Kemerton on right. Leave road at war memorial. House is behind parish church.

Map Ref No: 9

Bill & Diana Herford
Upper Court
Kemerton
Tewkesbury
Gloucestershire GL20 7HY
Tel: 01386-725351
Fax: 01386-725472

The converted barn has had a chequered history as village wash house, pig stye and a thatch store. It now has 3 modern bedrooms and bathrooms plus a living room where guests can either be self-catering (booking the whole annex) or B&B guests. A neat set-up whereby you leave your breakfast order form out for collection but also have the bonus of a drink-stocked fridge in your room. If you play tennis 'Mattie' the dog will return stray balls if you say "dead".

Rooms: 1 twin en suite, 2 doubles both en suite.

Price: £25-£30 p.p. doubles, £35-£40 single.

Breakfast: Included – à la carte breakfast menu.

Meals: Excellent local pub/restaurants nearby.

Closed: Christmas.

The great old kitchen is the hub of the house at Marston and Kim is a darling, making her guests feel thoroughly at home among her lively, bubbly family. You will be offered tea on arrival, or even a walk round the village with the dogs. Hers is a large 1900s country house with tennis court, terrace, fine garden, croquet lawn and homemade jams. The rooms are large, soft, supremely comfortable and have carpeted bathrooms. A good place.

Rooms: 1 twin, 1 double, each with separate private bathroom.

Price: £22-£25 per person, doubles and singles.

Breakfast: Included – full English/continental.

Meals: Dinner £17.50 p.p. on request.

Closed: Never!

From Stratford A46 towards Evesham. After 4 miles left to Binton. Fork left at Blue Boar. House 350m down hill on right. Turn into tarmac drive, house on left.

Map Ref No: 10

Denise & Guy Belchambers
Gravelside Barn
Binton
Stratford-Upon-Avon
Warwshire CV37 9TU
Tel: 01789-750502
Fax: 01789-298056

From Banbury A 361 north. At Byfield village sign left into Twistle Lane, straight on into Priors Marston. House is white, fifth on left with cattle grid, just after S-bend.

Map Ref No: 10

Kim & John Mahon
Marston House
Priors Marston
Rugby
Warwickshire CV23 8RP
Tel: 01327-260297
Fax: 01327-262846

Two intelligent, active, grandmothers (formerly a solicitor and a special school head) welcome family and guests of all ages to their big friendly Georgian rectory on the edge of the Forest of Dean. Your children may share the swings and sandpit but guests have their own piece of garden. This lively home is furnished with a mix of old and less old, has pictures and books, sensible bathrooms, wholesome bedrooms and an annual Garden Opera performed by young musicians in the 2.5-acre garden.

Rooms: 1 twin with private bath, shower & wc; 2 doubles sharing bathroom, shower & wc.

Price: £18.50 p.p.

Breakfast: Included – full English/continental/health food.

Meals: Not available.

Closed: Never.

Welsh Borders

East on A40 to Ross on Wye. Turn right to Hope Mansell & Pontshill. Take third lane on left. After 1 mile enter village. House is on left between lane sign-posted 'village hall & church'.

Map Ref No: 9

Mrs Carol Ouvry & Mrs Valerie Godson
The Old Rectory
Hope Mansell, Ross-on-Wye
Herefordshire HR9 5TL
Tel: 01989-750382
Fax: 01989-750382

Garway Church, a Norman gem, belonged to the Knights Templar and then the Knights of St John. The house is late Victorian and throbs with warmth and charm. There is a real fire to sit by and a long plank table at which to eat delicious Aga breakfasts and dinners. The herb garden is a step away from the kitchen and from the rose garden there are lovely views across the Malverns. Somehow the tranquillity and simplicity of the church have communicated themselves to this house.

Rooms: 1 double four-poster, 1 twin/double, both with handbasins. Shared bathroom, separate shower/cloakroom & wc.

Price: £17.50-£20.p.p., doubles, £5-£6 single supp.

Breakfast: Included – full English.

Meals: Dinner £15 p.p. by prior arrangement.

Closed: December – March.

Devoted restoration over 20 years has breathed new life into this Hereford manor (rather grander than typical) complete with stone barn, clapboard cow byre and puddleduck pond. Martin and Daphne are rightly proud of their work and greet guests like visiting friends. The bedrooms, named after birds, have immense character, the best fabrics, antiques, nice pine. Upstairs views to hills, downstairs French doors onto a pretty garden. Magnificent cruck hall with gallery and fire. Nearly totally organic food, served with panache. A heavenly experience.

Rooms: 3 twins all en suite, 9 doubles all en suite, 2 four-posters en suite, 1 family room en suite.

Price: £36.25-£46.25 p.p. doubles, £51.25-£61.25 single.

Breakfast: Included – full English/continental.

Meals: Dinner from £25 p.p.

Closed: January.

Take B4521 from near Hereford to Abergavenny. Cross A466 to Broad Oak. Turn right to Garway. First right past school signposted Garway Hill. Old Rectory is 150 metres on right.

Map Ref No: 9

Caroline Ailesbury
The Old Rectory
Garway
Herefordshire
HR2 8RH
Tel: 01600-750363
Fax: 01600-750364

Off A44 Leominster to Kington road, 1 mile east of Kington on the right. Hotel is signposted 200m down a smooth track.

Map Ref No: 9

Martin Griffiths & Daphne Lambert
Penrhos Court Hotel
Kington
Herefordshire
HR5 3LH
Tel: 01544-230720
Fax: 01544-230754

This lovely wisteria-clad Georgian house has all the advantages of being in a small town, with a rural atmosphere thrown in. One side overlooks a church, whilst the other faces a large garden which disappears into rolling hills. Andrew hires out mountain bikes. He and Lis are delightful (Lis is an opera singer, Andrew a wine merchant) with three exuberant young children and treat you as a guest in their beautiful yet comfortable home. Crisp cotton sheets, fresh flowers, homemade jams – service comes with a large smile and a decidedly personal touch.

Rooms: 1 twin with handbasin, 1 double with shared bathroom.

Price: From £17.50-£20 p.p.

Breakfast: Included – full English.

Meals: Dinner available locally. Packed lunch available on request.

Closed: Christmas.

Truly, madly, deeply in the middle of nowhere, this is an unpretentious modernised mill house. Rooms are small and cosy, with exposed beams and slate window sills, and only the old mill itself interrupts the view of the surrounding greenness. Best of all, though, is sinking into downy sleep to the sound of the Arrow River burbling away – a real tonic for frazzled city-dwellers. Grace is chatty and informal and though guests have the run of the cottage the cosy kitchen tends to be the gravitational centre of this home. Children over 5 welcome.

Rooms: 1 double with en suite shower, 1 double shares bathroom & wc with 1 twin.

Price: £16-£18 p.p., half price children 5-12.

Breakfast: Included.

Meals: Dinner £10, snack £6.

Closed: From end October – beginning April.

From Hereford take A438. Right before Willersley onto A4112 and bear left onto A4111 straight to Kington. Through centre of town and up hill to St. Mary's Church. House is clearly named on left opposite church.

Map Ref No: 9

Andrew & Lis Darwin
Church House
Church Road
Kington
Herefordshire HR5 3AG
Tel: 01544-230534
Fax: 01544-231100

Take A438 from Hereford. After Winforton turn right for Brilley. Straight over crossroads for 2 miles. Right at T-junction, immed. left to Huntingdon. Pass phone box, next right, cont. 0.5 mile, right into 'no through road' and first right.

Map Ref No: 9

Grace Watson
Hall's Mill House
Huntingdon
Kington
Herefordshire HR5 3QA
Tel: 01497-831409

You rattle up a drive past grazing sheep to arrive at a Grade 11 star listed farmhouse nestling modestly behind outbuildings. The most striking features about this lovely house are the stone floors and fireplaces and the 16th/17th-century oak panelling and exposed beams. There are a breakfast room and elegant dining room for 4-course dinners of home-grown produce. An excellent retreat for those looking for rural tranquillity, long walks, and riparian pursuits on the nearby River Wye. (Stabling facilities are also available.)

Rooms: 1 double en suite, 1 twin or double with private bathroom.

Price: £28 p.p.

Breakfast: Included – full English.

Meals: Dinner £18.

Closed: Christmas & New Year.

This large welcoming family loves other people's children (really). The Domesday-mentioned farm and former cider mill has its own stream and lake, pretty ducks, aimiable dogs and cat. Inside, there are high beamed ceilings to its big pleasant rooms, antique and modern farmhouse furniture (one bedroom has a fine half-tester), and fine views. The Youngs will happily drive you to nearby restaurants for dinner and collect you by 11pm, then serve you delicious breakfast next morning. Service indeed.

Rooms: 1 triple, 2 doubles, all with separate private bathrooms.

Price: £20 p.p. doubles, £20 single.

Breakfast: Included – full English/continental.

Meals: No, but available locally.

Closed: Never!

From A438 Hereford/Brecon road turn right in Clyro and follow signs for Newchurch. After 4 miles farm is on right hand side.

Map Ref No: 9

Glyn & Anne Williams
Dolbedwyn
Newchurch
Kington
Herefordshire HR5 3QQ
Tel: 01497-851202

Going north on A4172, pass Little Marcle church. Sign for house is on right, as is house. Priors Court is up a long drive (about 0.25 mile) just after Newbridge Farm Park on left.

Map Ref No: 9

Roger & Judy Young
Priors Court
Aylton
Nr. Ledbury
Herefordshire HR8 2QE
Tel: 01531-670748
Fax: 01531-670860

Part of a former 18th-century coaching inn, this red-brick cottage on a quiet road has delightful minimalist white paint and country furniture inside, a well-equipped kitchen with original terracotta tiles and fine views, an uncluttered sitting room with its old range, books, games and nice textiles, one big, one tiny bedroom up very steep stairs. You are welcomed by the artist/weaver couple who live and work next door. The cider orchard and stream are yours. Babies and children over 10 welcome.

Rooms: Self contained cottage: 1 double sharing bathroom with 1 single.

Price: £180-£290 per week.

Breakfast: Self-catering.

Meals: Self-catering.

Closed: Never.

Wisteria wraps itself around the brick-and-timbered manor house, sheep bleat behind the stable, a pond shimmers in the lower garden...and you can walk the Malvern Hills. Half-timbered bedrooms with window-seats, massive carved canopied beds, dark Jacobean panelling, fireplaces and an upstairs sitting room. Eat garden asparagus, potatoes, rhubarb and berries at the massive dining table and enjoy old-fashioned hospitality in a magnificent house.

Rooms: 3 doubles, 2 four-posters, 1 twin, all with private bathrooms.

Price: £32 p.p. double, £47 single. Small children free.

Breakfast: Included – full English.

Meals: Dinner £20 p.p.

Closed: Christmas and New Year.

2 miles on A438 from Ledbury, on left enter yard of 'Roger Oates Design Country Weavers'. Main door on road. Parking at back in yard.

Map Ref No: 9

Roger & Fay Morgan Oates
Somers Arms House
Eastnor
Ledbury
Herefordshire HR81EL
Tel: 01531-631622
Fax: 01531-631361

Leave M50 at Junction 2, towards Ledbury. Take first left to Bromsberrow Heath. Turn right by post office in village and go up hill. Grove House is on right.

Map Ref No: 9

Michael & Ellen Ross
The Grove House
Bromsberrow Heath
Ledbury
Herefordshire HR8 1PE
Tel: 01531-650584

In a magnificent setting overlooking the River Wye, Old Court is a mediæval manor house dating from 1350. The large central hall – the sitting and dining room for guests – has a 15-foot-high stone fireplace which provides a small inferno during winter. Both bedrooms have modern 4-poster beds and are attractively and simply furnished, comfortable and cosy – particularly the 'granary room', with its own entrance up stone steps. This is a working farm, so there are no frills, but Sue is a Cordon Bleu cook and supper can be heard bleating succulently outside....

Rooms: 2 four-poster doubles with en suite showers, 1 family room with private bathroom.

Price: £20 p.p.

Breakfast: Included – full English/continental/other.

Meals: Dinner £14. Half price for children under 10.

Closed: Christmas.

A focal point in the tiny hamlet of Bredwardine, this straightforward country inn has larger-than-expected rooms and good bathrooms. The place you should stay if you want to catch your salmon! There are 8 miles of the River Wye on which to do it, so you should be rewarded. Alternatively, you can spend many hours in the famous old bookshops of Hay-on-Wye, play on one of the many golf courses, go canoeing or cycling (thigh-challenging hills about!). Nicely presented, wholesome food using a lot of local produce.

Rooms: 5 twins, 2 doubles, 1 single, 2 triples, all en suite.

Price: £25-£31 p.p. doubles, £32-£38 single.

Breakfast: Included – full English/continental.

Meals: Lunch & dinner.

Closed: Christmas Day.

Take A438 from Hereford, turn left onto B4352. House is over the bridge and first on the right.

Map Ref No: 9

Turn left off A438 Hereford/Brecon road onto B4352. The hotel is in Bredwardine village.

Map Ref No: 9

Mrs Sue Whitall
Old Court
Bredwardine
Herefordshire
HR3 6BT
Tel: 01981-500375

Mike & Lynn Taylor
The Red Lion Hotel
Bredwardine
Herefordshire
HR3 6BU
Tel: 01981-500303
Fax: 01981-500400

WELSH BORDERS

Such an unusual place, miles from nowhere on the Welsh borders. Built in the 17th century as a grain barn, lovingly renovated with weatherboarding and stone tiling, it has a vast open threshing bay which frames the woods and hills like an old-time idyll of rural England. The double-aspect dining room is above this bay. The cattle byres round the yard, perfect in their ancient curviness, house the conservatory/greenhouse where guests can sit. The bedrooms have simple modern furniture and share a small shower-room. Superb views to the Black mountains.

Rooms: 1 family room, 1 single – both with shared shower & wc.

Price: £16 p.p. Children under12: £12.

Breakfast: Included – full English.

Meals: Dinner £12 p.p. Packed lunch also available.

Closed: October – Easter.

This half-timbered 16th-century building served as the court house during the Civil War where the notorious Judge Jeffries passed sentence. The present owner, a more benign presence, has transformed the place into a welcoming home. Bedrooms are pretty with oak beams and four-posters, the dining room boasts a large stone fireplace and, as well as a log-fired drawing room, guests can use a small library. Near a fairly major road, but one is scarcely aware of it – particularly in the walled courtyard and gardens.

Rooms: 1 double en suite, 1 four-poster with private bathroom.

Price: £21 p.p. en suite. £22 for 4-poster. £5 supp. for singles.

Breakfast: Included – full English.

Meals: No, but locally available.

Closed: Never!

Take B4350 from Hay to Clifford. Pass Castle & turn right to Bredwardine. Take third left at top of hill. Pass between chapel & small football ground. Castleton Barn is ahead on right.

Map Ref No: 9

Ann & Ron Tong
Castleton Barn
Clifford
Nr. Hay-on-Wye
Herefordshire HR3 5HF
Tel: 01497-831690

On A438 half way between Hereford and Brecon. In centre of Winforton village, not far from The Sun Inn, signposted.

Map Ref No: 9

Jackie Kingdon
Winforton Court
Winforton
Herefordshire
HR3 6EA
Tel: 01544-328498

The gorgeous gardens are the real seduction of this rambling 17th-century house. Guests in one bedroom can step out of the door and straight into them. From the conservatory views of the distant Black Mountains frame the heavenly garden scene. The grounds of Darkley lead in every direction to wildflower meadows, cider orchards and picturesque villages. Bedrooms are to be found in the converted barn, duck house and stables. A wonderful place for oak beam enthusiasts.

Rooms: 1 twin en suite; 1 triple en suite shower; 2 doubles (one private bath, one private shower); 2 doubles with shared bathroom and sitting room.

Price: £20 p.p. Minimum 2 nights stay.

Breakfast: Included – full English.

Meals: Dinner £14 p.p.

Closed: Christmas.

Super people with humour and most hospitable instincts, the Daltons call their house 'rambling, romantic, ancient, silent'. A big old manor with gardens and croquet lawn just beside the lovely 12th-century church. You may breakfast beside the great log fire in the Tudor dining room on chilly mornings or under the spreading chestnut tree on warmer days; relax after dinner in the oak-panelled sitting room. Rooms are big, family-style, with books, flowers, fruit and garden views.

Rooms: 2 twins, 1 double, all with shared bathroom.

Price: £17.50-£20 p.p. doubles, £20 single.

Breakfast: Included – full English/continental.

Meals: Dinner £14 p.p. Available on request, as is a packed lunch.

Closed: Never!

Take A480 from Hereford. At Norton Canon take lane to Norton Wood & Hurstley. Follow through disused railway arch, sharp bend, past cottages on right. Single track driveway is on left.

Map Ref No: 9

Jill & Malcolm Ainslie
Darkley House
Norton Canon
Herefordshire
HR4 7BT
Tel: 01544-318121

From A417 left to Ullingswick. Continue through village. Turn left then right at signs to Ullingswick church. Court drive is on right before church lychgate.

Map Ref No: 9

Christopher & Susan Dalton
Upper Court
Ullingswick
Herefordshire
HR1 3JG
Tel: 01432-820295

Possibly one of the best views in Herefordshire? The house is grand, the estate huge, the gardens splendid and the peacocks haughty – but Mike and Anne are immensely likeable, informal and fun. The atmosphere in the house is warm and relaxed too. It was built in 1950 with the stone from the 'Victorian monstrosity' that stood there previously but the original 1850s courtyard and clocktower still stand – a pleasing group. Tennis too. Children over 10 welcome.

Rooms: 2 twins: 1 en suite bath, 1 with private bath; 1 double with private bath.

Price: £30-£35 p.p., £10 single supp.

Breakfast: Included – full English/continental.

Meals: Dinner available on request £18.

Closed: Christmas, New Year & February.

From Leominster take A44 Brecon. After 8 miles just past the Weobley turn off, turn right, marked to Broxwood/Pembridge. Straight over crossroads. After 200m turn left over cattlegrid. Drive through courtyard.

Map Ref No: 9

Mike & Anne Allen
Broxwood Court
Broxwood
Leominster
Herefordshire HR6 9TJ
Tel: 01544-340245
Fax: 01544-340573

A 15th-century house that was subsequently Georgianised, Welland Court has a fine garden, a trout-stacked lake (guests may fish here) and stands at the foot of the Malverns with stupendous views. Inside, it boasts a dazzling black-and-white floored hall, antique-filled dining and drawing rooms and florally-decorated bedrooms (where the house scotch awaits you). Cordon Bleu dinners at the beautifully-set mahogany dining table.

Rooms: 2 twins, 1 double, all en suite.

Price: £30 p.p. doubles, £40 p.p. singles.

Breakfast: Included – full English/continental.

Meals: Dinner £30 p.p. incl. drinks & wine. Available on request.

Closed: Open all year.

West on A4104 to Upton-upon-Severn. Once there, cross river, turn left up main street until you see old telephone kiosk on left. Turn left at sign and take left fork.

Map Ref No: 9

Philip & Elizabeth Archer
Welland Court
Upton-upon-Severn
Worcestershire
WR8 0ST
Tel: 01684-594426
Fax: 01684-594426

No. 28 is on a beautiful Georgian street of listed and restored buildings, just outside the town walls and only 85 metres from the river (the ducks take their morning stroll past the house). The house is a gem, every detail thought through. The welcome and hospitality are generous and genuine. The rooms are full of books and the walls covered with paintings, antique prints and plates... just like home without the washing up... and in one of the finest of Georgian towns.

Rooms: 1 twin en suite bath, shower; 1 double en suite shower. Cottage: 1 family, 1 double – both en suite bath and shower.

Price: £25-£27.50 p.p. doubles, £10 single supp.

Breakfast: Included – full English/health food.

Meals: Dinner £17.50 p.p. by arrangement.

Closed: Never!

The stupendous site and generous size of this house denote the status of the ancestor who built it here on the Welsh border in 1740. The present-day Salweys are farmers and Hermione's scrumptious fare is based on home-grown meat and vegetables. The large softly-furnished bedrooms have antique chairs and modern bedding while the whole house is a gallery of family portraits down the centuries. The Salweys are lovely, interesting people and the estate even boasts a Georgian bath house near the trout lake.

Rooms: 1 twin, 2 doubles (1 with Louis XV bed). All with private bathrooms.

Price: £35 p.p. double, £40 single.

Breakfast: Included – full English.

Meals: Dinner £16 p.p., £20 p.p. with wine.

Closed: 31 October – 1 April. Please book at least 24 hours in advance.

House at bottom of Broad Street, between Broadgate and Ludford Bridge. Under AA sign.

Map Ref No: 9

Patricia & Philip Ross
Number Twenty Eight
28 Lower Broad Street
Ludlow
Shropshire SY8 1PQ
Tel: 01584-876996
Fax: 01584-876996

From Ludlow over River Teme by traffic lights, 2nd right to Presteigne & Richard's Castle on B4361. After about 100 yards, drive is first right by a stone wall and unmarked gatehouse.

Map Ref No: 9

Humphrey & Hermione Salwey
The Lodge
Ludlow
Shropshire
SY8 4DU
Tel: 01584-872103
Fax: 01584-876126

Admire the typical Georgian window proportions and valley roof of this eminently gracious house in its many acres of Welsh border country. It has a millstream and a weir, a motte and a heronry, a point-to-point course and a ha-ha... and Yvonne is a qualified cook! All this before tasting the delights of the world beyond the gate. Good-sized bedrooms, fine furniture and long green views complete the picture, though you must climb steep stairs to get there.

Rooms: 1 double en suite shower; 2 twins/doubles with private bath; 1 single sharing bathroom.

Price: £25 p.p. all rooms.

Breakfast: Included – full English.

Meals: Dinner £18 p.p. – book in advance.

Closed: Never!

Leintwardine was once a Roman garrison; it is still in one of England's last unspoilt areas. This handsome former farmhouse is part 17th-century, off a country lane so quiet that buzzards and deer are often seen close by. Log fires and beams, a communal dining table, a large garden and orchard, welcoming hosts, modern comforts plus a certain elegance... all this amidst a rare plethora of castles and historic towns.

Rooms: 1 double en suite shower; 1 double private bathroom; 2 twin en suite shower.

Price: £22-£24 p.p., children 10-12 years £11-£12. No single supplements.

Breakfast: Included – full English.

Meals: Dinner £16 p.p.

Closed: Christmas.

From Ludlow A49 to Shrewsbury. At Bromfield A4113. Right in Walford for Buckton, continue until second farm on left. Look for large sign on building.

Map Ref No: 9

Hayden & Yvonne Lloyd
Upper Buckton
Leintwardine
Craven Arms
Shropshire SY7 0JU
Tel: 01547-540634

From Leintwardine, cross river, take first right signposted Knighton, first left signposted Hereford, first right up narrow unmarked lane. Lower House is 300 yards on left.

Map Ref No: 9

Hildegard & Graham Cutler
Lower House
Adforton
Leintwardine
Shropshire SY7 0NF
Tel: 01568-770223
Fax: 01568-770592

A hillside retreat offering lavish hedonism. Your host owns four elegant London restaurants. Outside, this is a grey stone Borders farmhouse, inside it is gloriously stylish with stone-flagged floors, wood-burning stoves, polished tables, antiques blended with naive textiles, vast and luxurious bathrooms, pure cotton on the beds and amazing electronics in each bedroom to delight professional musicians and baffle the over-50s. An unstinting welcome, sophisticated comfort, unequalled value.

Rooms: 1 twin, 1 double, both en suite.

Price: £25-£30 doubles, £35 singles.

Breakfast: Included – full English/continental.

Meals: Dinner from £15 p.p., available on request.

Closed: Open all year.

Take B4368 W to Clun. Left at fork towards Knighton on A488. Over bridge. Cockford is 1 mile from bridge, signed on left and house on right up long steep drive.

Map Ref No: 9

Roger Wren
Cockford Hall
Clun
Shropshire
SY7 8LR
Tel: 01588-640327
Fax: 01588-640881

The name of this charming 18th-century house is utterly right. Carol and Bryan are kind, attentive hosts, thinking of everything for their guests. The house has been lovingly restored; beams, thick walls, a high-ceilinged drawing room with tall windows and ornate plasterwork. The largest bedroom has a half-tester bed; other rooms are smaller and cottagey – sprigged wallpaper, antique towel rails, pretty china. Orchard and garden at the back of the house. Dinner, taken around one table, sometimes includes Bryan's catch of the day.

Rooms: 1 twin, 1 double, 1 single, all sharing 2 bathrooms.

Price: £16 p.p.

Breakfast: Included – full English.

Meals: Dinner £8.50 p.p. Available on request.

Closed: February.

From Llanymynech B4398 signed to Knockin. Pass village hall and playing fields on left. Over hump-back bridge, house fourth on left.

Map Ref No: 9

Mrs Carol Fahey
Hospitality
Vyrnwy Bank
Llanymynech
Shropshire SY22 6LG
Tel: 01691-830427

WELSH BORDERS

Staggeringly beautiful scenery surrounds this c.1845 rectory hotel. Easy-going atmosphere and unpretentious comfort: the entrance hall doubles as a bar in the evenings and the dining room has a curtained-off sitting area with plump chairs and a fire. A nice touch is having mineral water, fruit and chocolates laid out on the sideboard for anyone to help themselves. Bedrooms are not large but are thoughtfully decorated and nearly all have spectacular views. Great food to suit all tastes. People come again and again.

Rooms: 4 twins, 3 doubles, 1 family room – all en suite.

Price: £33-£35 p.p. doubles, £42-£46 single.

Breakfast: Included – full English/continental.

Meals: Dinner £14.50 p.p. Lunch available.

Closed: Christmas & 1 – 14 January.

Quiet Maria and charismatic Bjorn took seven years to restore their 1580s manor to its authentic splendour. Now you can have log fires in your four-poster bedroom, delicious 17th-century food (Maria is a passionate searcher after olde foode) sitting at a candlelit communal table wearing the appropriate costume! (extensive wardrobe to choose from); most fruit, veg. and herbs come from their garden. There is also a knot garden. People arrive warily then never want to leave. Children over 12 welcome.

Rooms: Five 4-posters en suite; 1 twin sharing bathroom with a 4-poster.

Price: £35-£87.50 p.p. doubles, singles negotiable.

Breakfast: Included – continental/full English.

Meals: Lunch available on request. Dinner £25-£36 p.p.

Closed: Never!

From A5 head into Oswestry. Leave town on B4580 signed Llansilin. Hotel on left just before Rhydycroesau.

Map Ref No: 9

Miles & Audrey Hunter
Pen-Y-Dyffryn Country Hotel
Rhydycroesau
Nr. Oswestry
Shropshire SY10 7JD
Tel: 01691-653700
Fax: 01691-653700

Colehurst is about 1 mile off the A41 clearly signed, or 1 mile south of Tern Hill roundabout, again clearly marked.

Map Ref No: 9

Bjorn & Maria Teksnes
Old Colehurst Manor
Colehurst
Market Drayton
Shropshire TF9 2JB
Tel: 01630-638833
Fax: 01630-638647

Nothing ordinary here! Ten self-catering cottages in a haven of 850 years of English history. The estate has a 12th-century abbey, a vast Jacobean stableblock, the biggest privately-owned natural lake in Britain and a unique fruit-tree maze. Visitors include Wellington, Charles II, Sam Johnson. Each cottage in the converted stableblock is individually designer-decorated and has a real sitting room. A breakfast pack and a list of ready-made meals await you. Sounds good? It's even better for real.

Rooms: 10 cottages with 2 or 3 bedrooms. All bathrooms with basins, wc, baths with shower attachments.

Price: From £80 per night (2 nights minimum Sept – June, 3 nights June, July, Aug) per cottage.

Breakfast: Self-catering.

Meals: Home-cooked frozen meals available.

Closed: Never!

Ducks quack on the pond and perhaps by the front door, but the only other sounds are from sheep, goats and birds. Anthea bubbles with energy and effusive welcome. This is a fine old farmhouse with an enormous fireplace in the kitchen, a formal dining room with beautiful table... traditional but not quaint. One of the bedrooms is a 'suite' with kitchen, a treat if you want to stay in and eat simply. One big room has easy access for the less able. Gardens are fairly new but promising.

Rooms: 2 twins, 1 double, 2 singles, all en suite.

Price: £27.50 p.p. doubles, £40 single, £15 for extra person in twin.

Breakfast: Included – full English.

Meals: Dinner £20 p.p. by arrangement. £7.50 p.p. cold light supper.

Closed: Never!

From Whitchurch A525 towards Nantwich. 100 yds past junction A525/A530 towards Nantwich. Entrance on left through stone pillars with falcons.

Map Ref No: 9

Mrs Sarah Callander Beckett
Combermere Abbey
Whitchurch
Shropshire
SY13 4AJ
Tel: 01948-871637
Fax: 01948-871293

From Malpas B5069 towards Bangor-on-Dee for 1 mile. First right for 1 mile to Chorlton. At phone kiosk turn right. After 0.25 mile you will see sign on light for Laurel Farm on right.

Map Ref No: 9

Mrs Anthea Few
Laurel Farm
Chorlton Lane
Malpas
Cheshire SY14 7ES
Tel: 01948-860291
Fax: 01948-860291

We welcome this farm, perfect for easy-going adults and children who won't fall in the canal. There are geese, hens, guinea-fowl and a pony to play with and an old-fashioned farmhouse-friendly atmosphere. The decor (red and green dralon, patterned carpets, rose-flowered curtains, nylon lace) is brightly-coloured and cheerful. This is a real working farm with unassuming folk and well-equipped practical rooms...plus two self-catering cottages. Hearty breakfasts too.

Rooms: 1 twin, 2 doubles, 1 family room, 1 four-poster – all with en suite bath and/or shower.

Price: £17.50-£25 p.p. doubles, £20-£25 singles.

Breakfast: Included – full English/continental.

Meals: Packed lunches only.

Closed: Never!

As you arrive you quickly get the feel of Roughlow, planted as it is in the very hillside – it is simple, solid, authentic, and greatly loved. The cobbled entrance yard is a treasure box of carefully-nurtured natural textures and materials, flowering trees and shrubs; the terrace looks out over the Welsh border (40 miles on a clear day); there's a tennis court and a field of cows. Bedrooms are big and simply-furnished, the suite is vast and Sally is delightful.

Rooms: 3 twins: all with private bathroms and 1 with sitting room.

Price: £25-£30 p.p. £5 single supplement.

Breakfast: Included – full English.

Meals: Dinner £15 p.p. on request for minimum of 4 people. Good pubs and hotels nearby.

Closed: Never!

Take A51 north, by-passing Nantwich. At crossroads, take right to Chester Road heading north. 2 miles past Hurleston waterworks, B+B sign opposite village sign. Follow B+B signs to farm.

Map Ref No: 9

A51 from Chester. Cross roundabout at Tarvin & take A54 to Manchester (not Tarporley). Pass Elf garage. Take second right & follow signs to Oscroft. Straight over crossroads & up Chapel Lane, up hill. Farm on right with sign.

Map Ref No: 9

Mrs Georgina West
Stoke Grange Farm
Chester Road
Nantwich
Cheshire CW5 6BT
Tel: 01270-625525
Fax: 01270-625525

Mrs Sally Sutcliffe
Roughlow Farm
Willington
Tarporley
Cheshire CW6 0PG
Tel: 01829-751199
Fax: 01829-751199

'Our guests seem to oversleep'. This is peace indeed. A haven for garden buffs, walkers, birdwatchers – Britain at its best with rare trees planted in 1860, flowers everywhere, a pond and a passionate owner/gardener. Mrs Major also embroiders her own designs. The house is furnished in country house style with a gracious drawing room, big high-ceilinged dining room, two large light bedrooms and one smaller cosy one. Your hosts like to treat their visitors as guests of the family. Children over 12 welcome.

Rooms: 2 twins, both with private bathrooms and 1 with shower; 1 double en suite.

Price: £19-£22 doubles, £25 single.

Breakfast: Included – full English/continental.

Meals: Lunch & dinner on request. Dinner £14 p.p. BYO wine. Good village pubs.

Closed: Christmas week – 3 January.

A neat little guest house on the quietest country lane with the village pub at the end of the drive and Dunham Massey Deer Park 5 minutes walk away, and all just 6 miles from Manchester. The rooms are good, modern and almost luxurious (television and video sets hidden in wooden cabinets) and have great country views. One bed has 9 pillows. Janice is a trained cook, specialising in vegetable dishes. Children over 12 welcome. Great value so close to the city yet so rural.

Rooms: 1 twin/double en suite; 2 doubles: 1 en suite, 1 with private shower & bath.

Price: £25-£31 p.p. doubles, £38-£45 single.

Breakfast: Included – full English.

Meals: Dinner from £12. Private dinner parties available on request.

Closed: Christmas & New Year.

From Chester, A55 west. Then A5104 to Broughton, left at roundabout to Pennyffordd on A5104. Through Broughton and over A55. First left to Kinnerton down Lesters Lane. Only house on right.

Map Ref No: 9

Take A556 NE to Manchester, then left on A56 towards Lymm. At first pub turn right down Park Lane. House is next to The Swan with Two Necks.

Map Ref No: 14

Jonathan & Rachel Major
The Mount
Higher Kinnerton
Chester
Cheshire CH4 9BQ
Tel: 01244-660275

David & Janice Taylor
Ash Farm Country Guest House
Park Lane, Little Bollington
Near Altrincham
Cheshire WA14 4TJ
Tel: 0161-9299290

Our inspector was so impressed with Denstone that she popped back for a riding lesson. 'Blissful', she wrote. It is gorgeous riding country with vast views and noisy bird-life, plus dogs, cats and the ubiquitous horses. The Staffordshire Way is ½ mile away. All you might dream of from a B&B: a real 'working' home, dining room with Welsh dresser and grandfather clock overlooking the garden, a kitchen with Aga and pine table, fruit from the garden and homemade jams.

Rooms: 1 twin with en suite bath, 2 doubles sharing private bathroom.

Price: £20 p.p.

Breakfast: Included – full English.

Meals: Dinner £6.50/£9.50. Pubs & restaurants available locally.

Closed: Christmas Day.

The North East

In village, follow signs to Denstone College and enter grounds. In front of College buildings turn left. Continue for 300 yards to stud.

Map Ref No: 9

Mrs Phyl Price
Denstone Stud and Riding Centre
Hall Riddings
Denstone
Staffordshire ST14 5HW
Tel: 01889-591472

Guardhouse, moat, portcullis, turrets: a pink, crenellated castle c.1270 awaits you. The interior is Jacobean with vast, oak-panelled drawing and dining rooms, all with massive carved fireplaces. Upstairs, billiards and pool in an immense room; everything here is on a superlative scale. Bedrooms are panelled and romantic, bathrooms excellent. There is an indoor swimming pool for summer, two lakes and two self-catering turrets. An experience! Children and unquarrelsome dogs welcome.

Rooms: Three 4-posters, all en suite, 2 self-catering turrets for 2/4 persons.

Price: £30-£40 p.p. doubles, £50 single. Turrets £60 a day, £300 a week.

Breakfast: Included – full English/continental.

Meals: Dinner available locally.

Closed: 1 November – February.

M6 junct. 14 onto A34 to Stone. A520 towards Leek to Weston Coyney. Right there for 1 mile. Cross moat between two churches for castle entrance.

Map Ref No: 9

Yvonne Sargent
Caverswall Castle
Caverswall
Staffordshire
ST11 9EA
Tel: 01782-393239
Fax: 01782-394590

This Grade II listed Georgian house (actually in Leicestershire) with its massive chimney stacks and quirky level-changes is a blend of 18th-century elegance and natural country kitchen charm. The fantastic 4.5-acre garden has great old trees, a canal, a swimming pool and a fine conservatory. It has bags of charm, comfort and space. Robin and Jenny are gracious friendly people, the bedrooms (two in the stable block) are big designer-cum-trad decorated with nearby separate bathrooms. Last but not least, they pay proper homage to food and wine.

Rooms: 1 twin with sep., private bathroom, 2 singles with shared bathroom, all in main house; 2 doubles en suite in stable block.

Price: £22.50 p.p. doubles, £27.50 single.

Breakfast: Included – full English/continental.

Meals: Dinner available on request.

Closed: Never!

Located on B4116 between Twycross and Measham. Almost opposite Snareston village church.

Map Ref No: 10

Robin & Jenny Gregson-Brown
Snareston Lodge
Snareston
Via Swadlincote
Derbyshire DE12 7DA
Tel: 01530-270535
Fax: 01530-273801

Gateposts topped with stone pineapples, symbols of hospitality, and huge copper beeches lead to a glorious Georgian house set in 50 acres with grass terraces leading to the River Dove. Sophisticated interiors with silk brocade chairs and gleaming mahogany; one bedroom has a 4-poster with golden coverlet from another 'fin de siècle'. French beds and pale peach walls. Your hostess can serve formal dinners or earlier meals for foot-sore walkers; your host is a keen country sportsman and can arrange fly-fishing.

Rooms: 1 twin, 1 double 4-poster, both with separate private bathrooms.

Price: £30 p.p.

Breakfast: Included – full English/continental.

Meals: Dinner available nearby.

Closed: 1 December – 1 January.

There are panoramic views over the Dove valley towards Alton Towers (a comfortable 5 miles away!) and the house is up a tiny country lane in a fine garden. An ancestor of Peter's was Lord Mayor of London... hence the memorabilia. Cynthia is Australian; is that why they are such a delightful and friendly couple? Although elegant the house is not a 'show home' and guests really are treated as friends. The hall sets the tone beautifully: bare boards, Indian rugs, wood-burning stove and fine paintings.

Rooms: 2 doubles, 1 en suite and 1 with private bathroom.

Price: £20 p.p.

Breakfast: Included – full English.

Meals: Not available.

Closed: Christmas.

In Ashbourne A515 north. At top of hill left at Bowling Green pub; first right to Mappleton; through village towards Thorpe. After last cottage, house is on right with white gates.

Map Ref No: 10

Mr & Mrs Cedric Stevenson
Hinchley Wood
Mappleton
Ashbourne
Derbyshire DE6 2AB
Tel: 01335-350219
Fax: 01335-350219

From Ashbourne take A515 Lichfield road. After 4 miles, right onto B5033. After 1 mile right past Queen Adelaide Inn (set back in field). Rose Cottage is about ½ mile on right (cream coloured).

Map Ref No: 10

Mrs Cynthia Moore
Rose Cottage
Snelston
Ashbourne
Derbyshire DE6 2DL
Tel: 01335-324230
Fax: 01335-324230

Le Patron races vintage cars, Madame cooks beautifully, both are gracious and supremely welcoming hosts. Their splendid Georgian mansion was 'improved' in 1850 with some pillars and later with a High Victorian conservatory where breakfast is 'mandatory'. The house has the elegance of Georgian proportions and shutters, plain colour-wash walls, antique furniture and fine country or garden views. The bedrooms are in keeping, with excellent bathrooms. Children over 14 welcome.

Rooms: 1 twin en suite, 2 doubles – both en suite.

Price: £22.50-£25 p.p. doubles, £30 single.

Breakfast: Included – full English/continental.

Meals: Dinner £16 p.p., available on request.

Closed: Christmas week.

People come to Biggin to treat insomnia and asthma, such are the ambient peace and purity. Surrounded by an organically organised group of local-stone farm buildings, Biggin Hall has mullioned and leaded lights, a great fireplace, roof timbers (visible in the Master Suite, for example) and space. Whether you sleep in the Hall or in a converted outbuilding you will enjoy the resident chef's breakfast (a speciality) or farmhouse dinner in the simple dining room. Children over 12 welcome.

Rooms: 1 family/twin and 1 twin sharing bath, shower & wc.

Price: £19.50-£37.50 p.p. doubles. Supp. for singles.

Breakfast: Included – full English/continental.

Meals: Dinner £10 residents.

Closed: Never!

From A514 Swadlincote to Derby road, turn off towards Melbourne. In Melbourne – Ashby Rd.

Map Ref No: 10

Robert & Patricia Heelis
Shaw House
Robinsons Hill
Melbourne
Derbyshire DE73 1DJ
Tel: 01332-863827

From A515 take turning to Biggin between Ashbourne and Buxton. Turn right just after Waterloo pub up drive to Biggin Hall.

Map Ref No: 10

James Moffett
Biggin Hall
Biggin by Hartington
Buxton
Derbyshire SK17 0DH
Tel: 01298-84451
Fax: 01298-84681

A beautiful 17th-century stone house restored with intelligence and individuality, it is a real 'home' with everyone mucking in; a very special atmosphere. Bedrooms are lovely, one of them in a huge and stunning old barn, 18 x 30 feet with own access. The sitting room has a large stone fireplace, deep 'dirty pink' walls and rush matting. Antiques mix well with country furniture, stone floors and exposed beams. Wonderful and inventive food, warm and interesting people.

Rooms: 1 twin, 1 double, 1 single, each with private wc and shared bathroom.

Price: £20 p.p. doubles, £18 single.

Breakfast: Included – full English/other.

Meals: Available on request.

Closed: December & January.

Set in the heart of the Peak National Park, the Lathkil's panoramic view is hard to beat. This country pub welcomes locals, tourists, walkers and 'relaxers' with a bar buffet at lunchtime, hearty home-cooked dinners (or sandwiches) in the evening plus a wide choice of draught beers and wines. The guestrooms are compact but well-designed, two of them with that spectacular view. The walls are hung with art exhibitions and the atmosphere is informal and welcoming.

Rooms: 2 double/twins, 1 double, 1 single/double, all with en suite shower or bath & wc.

Price: £35 p.p.

Breakfast: Included – full English/contintental.

Meals: 3-course dinner £10.50.

Closed: Never!

Great Hucklow is 2.5 miles north east of Tideswell and signed from A623. Follow signs to village, pass Queen Anne pub on right and continue for 300m. Hall is last house on left of village (converted barn next door).

Map Ref No: 15

John & Angela Whatley
Hucklow Hall
Great Hucklow
Buxton
Derbyshire SK17 8RG
Tel: 01298-871175
Fax: 01298-871175

Leave Bakewell on B5055, take left to Over Haddon. Hotel is in the east of the village.

Map Ref No: 10

Robert & Helen Grigor-Taylor
The Lathkil Hotel
Over Haddon
Nr. Bakewell
Derbyshire DE45 1JE
Tel: 01629-812501
Fax: 01629-812501

A sturdy 18th-century house in the middle of the Peak National Park, so take your walking boots. Or you can watch trout in the gin-clear waters of the twin rivers running by. Otherwise good for Chatsworth, Hardwick Hall, Calke Abbey and others. Jan and Bryan Statham, having travelled widely, know from experience how to please guests. If you arrive in time you will be served tea in the stone-flagged hall-sitting room, beside the fire if chilly. Jan bakes bran muffins for breakfast, a different flavour daily.

Rooms: 2 twins, 1 with en suite shower and separate wc, 1 with private bathroom; 1 double with private bathroom.

Price: £20 p.p.

Breakfast: Included – full English/continental.

Meals: Not available.

Closed: Never!

A6 E of Bakewell, right onto B5056 to Ashbourne. Follow signs to Youlgrave and Alport, 1.75 miles. House is first on right in hamlet; sign at gateway.

Map Ref No: 10

Mrs Jan Statham
Rock House
Alport
Bakewell
Derbyshire DE45 1LG
Tel: 01629-636736

Sir Anthony Babington rode vainly from here to rescue Mary Queen of Scots from Wingfield Castle. This is a handsome grit stone farm house with 200 acres for sheep in the loveliest setting which makes this house so special. The hamlet has but three farms and a 13th-century church. Mrs G. has a magnificent kitchen with a great stone fireplace. She gives you the run of the place and makes her own jams; the bees make their honey, the hens lay their eggs and you use linen napkins at table. Perfectly placed for forays to Chatsworth, Haddon, Keddlestone and Hardwick.

Rooms: 2 doubles with en suite showers; 1 twin/double with shared bathroom and use of private sitting room.

Price: From £23 p.p.

Breakfast: Included – full English/continental served at 8.30.

Meals: Not available.

Closed: Christmas.

From M1 leave jnct. 28. A38 then A615 following Matlock signs all the way. Left 3 miles before Matlock where it says Dethick Lane. Down lane 1 mile.

Map Ref No: 10

Harold and Ruth Groom
The Manor Farm House
Dethick
Matlock
Derbyshire DE4 5GG
Tel: 01629-534246

If you love gardens you'll wallow in this one; it is Margaret's passion. There are stone troughs, herbaceous beds, a lily-pool and a lovely terraced garden of stone walls, hidden patios and streams...exquisitely planned and unfussy. The house is easy-going and relaxed (a tone set by the cocker spaniel), full of country furniture and soft colours. The huge wood-burning stove in the dining room warms your cockles as you tuck into organic eggs, homemade jams and garden fruit. Glorious setting...and place.

Rooms: 1 double en suite bath & shower; 1 family and 1 twin sharing bathroom & wc.

Price: £19-£21 p.p., £8 children 5-10, £10 children 10-14.

Breakfast: Included – full English.

Meals: Not available.

Closed: 23 December – 4 January.

'A room with a view'. People come from miles away for the glory of the countryside and the magic of this lovingly restored farmhouse. Welcoming and atmospheric from the flagstoned yellow-walled hall with ticking grandfather clock to the pretty drawing room with sky-blue walls and clouds of cream damask at the windows. Flowers everywhere, dark oak furniture, lots of rugs, fine ancestral bits and pieces. The terraced garden will delight gardeners. Lovely, welcoming owners.

Rooms: 1 double en suite, one 4-poster en suite.

Price: £22.50-£25 p.p. doubles, £30 single.

Breakfast: Included – full English/continental.

Meals: Dinner available locally.

Closed: Christmas.

Take A621 from Sheffield, turn onto B6051 to Chesterfield. Take first main turn left towards Holmesfield. The House is on left soon after the turning.

Map Ref No: 15

Mrs Margaret Ford
Horsleygate Hall
Horsleygate Lane
Holmesfield
Derbyshire SI8 5WD
Tel: 0114-289 0333

A625 from Sheffield into Hathersage. Right into School Lane. After 100m left fork up church bank. 50m on, right fork, then 0.5 mile. Over cattle grid. Signed.

Map Ref No: 15

Mary Bailey
Carrhead Farm
Hathersage
Nr. Sheffield
Derbyshire S30 1BR
Tel: 01433-650383

You name it, it's organic! Breakfast is entirely 'happy' meat, cereals, milk and tea from Di Shouls's organic shop, served in English china and glass. She is a wonderful grandmother who loves children (she has cots, stair gate, play shed, sand pit and hay barn for them). She designed, built and cherishes this house-by-the-fields with its airy upstairs sitting room, beams and sloping ceilings, soothing colours, pine furniture and dried flowers. Lovely person, lovely place.

Rooms: 2 twins, 1 family room, 1 single, all sharing 2 bathrooms.

Price: £15.50 p.p.

Breakfast: Included – full English/continental.

Meals: Dinner available locally. Packed lunch available on request.

Closed: Never!

Southwell's lovely Minster is 'the most rural cathedral in England' and can be seen, occasionally floodlit, from some of the Old Forge's bedrooms. The whole house has a cottagey feel with a pink front, brick back, garden and pond beyond. It is furnished with a mix of antique and modern, the rooms are not huge but pretty in their pastels and Hilary's breakfasts (in the conservatory or beside the pond in summer) are famous. She advises well on things to discover in this little-known area.

Rooms: 3 twins; 2 en suite, 1 with separate private bathroom; 3 doubles all en suite.

Price: £22-£24 p.p. doubles, £7-£10 single supplement.

Breakfast: Included – full English/continental.

Meals: Light dinner available on request. Otherwise available nearby.

Closed: Never!

From A46 towards Newark to East Bridgford. At village crossroads right into Kneeton Road. 20-30m after Reindeer pub left up track and drive to end.

Map Ref No: 10

Mrs Di Shouls
Barn Farm Cottage
Kneeton Road
East Bridgford
Nottinghamshire NG13 8PJ
Tel: 01949-20196

From Nottingham A612 to Southwell. Turn right past Minster. Pink house opposite library.

Map Ref No: 10

Hilary Marston
The Old Forge
Burgage Lane
Southwell
Nottinghamshire NG25 0ER
Tel: 01636-812809
Fax: 01636-816302

THE NORTH EAST

The Walmsleys think of everything to make things welcoming, homely and comfortable: they love having people and showing them around the cottages personally. These are adorable, with masses of extras: fresh flowers and plants, lots of pictures and candles; logs for the open fires, a welcome bottle of wine, linen provided, well-equipped kitchen and all possible goodies in the bathrooms – better than the best hotel. Pretty little gardens and then the view over Rutland Water.

Rooms: 4 self-catering cottages sleeping 2-4 people.

Price: £175-£400 per week, £95-£235 for 3-night break.

Breakfast: Self-catering.

Meals: Self-catering.

Closed: Never!

This is indeed a cottage, 300 years old with a narrow old staircase, sloping bedroom ceilings, a garden full of flowers and an utterly delightful elderly gentleman who decided to share his beloved house with others when he found himself alone four years ago. It is a privilege to join him and his two well-groomed gentle retrievers in their lucky spot. His hospitality is natural, he will greet you with tea – or sherry if it is that time of day – and provide a hearty breakfast in the morning.

Rooms: 2 doubles with handbasins in rooms & shared bathroom.

Price: £16 p.p. doubles, £18 single.

Breakfast: Included – full English.

Meals: Available locally.

Closed: Christmas.

From A1 take A606 Oakham road for 3 miles. Turn left to Edith Weston and on for 2 miles into village. Cottages are in Edith Weston itself.

Map Ref No: 10

Tim & Kitty Walmsley
Rutland Water Cottages
Dormer Cottage
Ryhall, Stamford
Lincolnshire PE9 4JA
Tel: 01780-64001
Fax: 01780-482808

On A6121 from Stamford to Bourne/Sleaford. Ryhall is 2 miles from Stamford. Cottage is in village opposite church.

Map Ref No: 10

William Clifford
St. John's Cottage
Church Street
Ryhall, Nr. Stamford
Lincolnshire PE9 4HR
Tel: 01780-63175

THE NORTH EAST

Stamford (the BBC's 'Middlemarch' set) has been called 'the finest stone town in England' – St George's is its church and Kim is its vicar. He and Penelope live with their children in a big Victorian rectory opposite the 15th-century church where the Knights of the Garter first worshipped. There are beams, original floor tiles, fireplaces and plasterwork. Penelope is quiet and softspoken and gives stewed fruit, local honey and homemade jam for breakfast. Lots of books and a real family atmosphere.

Rooms: 2 twins with choice of 2 large separate bathrooms.

Price: £15-£17.50 p.p. doubles, £20-£22.50 single.

Breakfast: Included – full English.

Meals: Dinner available locally. Packed lunch available on request.

Closed: Never!

From A1 take B1081 signed to Stamford. After 1 mile through lights over bridge and up hill. Turn right onto St. Mary Street. At T-junct. right into St. George's Square. No. 16 on right with steps up to front door.

Map Ref No: 10

Mrs Penelope Swithinbank
St. George's
16 St. George's Square
Stamford
Lincolnshire PE9 2BN
Tel: 01780-482099
Fax: 01780-63351

This 16th, 17th and 18th-century house, first built as a mediaeval hall, is very special. The guestrooms are all in the Georgian wing so have high ceilings, original panelling and shutters. Moya paints (300 of her works hang in the house), decorates (the drapescreens are hers) and she and John welcome you with exceptional warmth. There are seats beside the river at the bottom of the garden that the Actons have totally recreated from wilderness. The menus are mouthwatering.

Rooms: 1 twin/double, 2 doubles, all with en suite bath, shower & wc.

Price: £37.50 p.p. doubles, £55 single.

Breakfast: Included – full English.

Meals: Dinner £16.50-£19.50 p.p. Light snacks & packed lunches available.

Closed: 23 December – 2 January.

From A1 take A6121 to Ketton. Turn into Church Road towards Ketton Station & Collyweston. Turn into The Priory opposite the churchyard.

Map Ref No: 10

John & Moya Acton
The Priory
Church Road
Ketton, Stamford
Lincolnshire PE9 3RD
Tel: 01780-720215
Fax: 01780-721881

A fascinating great house, still very much as it was built in 1900 in a mixture of styles (Late Victorian Medieval Eclectic?), with a pure 'Arts & Crafts' galleried staircase and panelled dining room, ancient gargoyles and lions and big rooms. The bedrooms have just been refurbished with bright coordinated colours and new bathrooms and have views of the landscaped garden or onto the lovely stoney Stamford. The family is welcoming and most knowledgeable about local history and art.

Rooms: 1 twin/double en suite, 1 double en suite, 1 double with separate private bathroom.

Price: From £20-£22.50 p.p. doubles, £2.50-£12.50 single supplement.

Breakfast: Included – full English.

Meals: Dinner available locally.

Closed: 24-28 December.

The family has farmed here and lived in the redbrick farmhouse for three generations. The sense of durability is compounded by uninterrupted views across gently rolling hills with the Roman road to the west and a fine Norman manor house at Boothby Pagnell where 'Ivanhoe' was filmed (Sue can arrange for you to visit). Bedrooms are all big, warmly furnished, prettily decorated with pastels, florals and pictures. A friendly family with a piano, two dogs and a rabbit. Children over 12 welcome.

Rooms: 1 twin en suite, 1 double en suite, 1 double with private bathroom.

Price: £20 p.p. doubles, £25 single.

Breakfast: Included – full English.

Meals: Dinner available locally. Packed lunch available on request.

Closed: December – February.

From A1 take A606 to Stamford. 1 mile and when road slopes downhill count 4 houses on left. Look for stone gateposts & sign of Rock Lodge on left. Park on driveway.

Map Ref No: 10

Angela & Timothy Lee
Rock Lodge
1 Empingham Road
Stamford
Lincolnshire PE9 2RH
Tel: 01780-64211
Fax: 01780-482442

3 miles east of A1 turn off B6403 to Bassingthorpe. After 1.5 miles left to Lower Bassingthorpe. House at end of village on left.

Map Ref No: 10

Sue & Philip Robinson
Sycamore Farm
Bassingthorpe
Grantham
Lincolnshire NG33 4ED
Tel: 01476-585274

Cawthorpe lies in a bed of roses, 3.5 acres of them: Ozric makes the only genuine English rose oil and water, sold in pretty blue glass bottles. The house has some intriguing features: two boat-shaped windows; a vast studio/sitting room built in the 1900s by Gardner of the R.A. and filled with paintings and African carvings; some fearsome fish on the Portuguese tiles round the claw-footed bath. Ozric and Chantal are lovely people who will make you very welcome.

Rooms: 1 twin with basin, wc & shared shower, 1 double en suite, 1 single with shared bathroom & wc.

Price: £25 p.p.

Breakfast: Included – full English/continental.

Meals: Dinner available locally. Packed lunch available on request.

Closed: Christmas & New Year.

Rawene, a severe-faced Grade II listed early Victorian house, is hugely welcoming inside. Karen is a warm-hearted Irishwoman, they have a baby girl and enjoy families. The big, light-filled guestroom, which has just been redecorated, has a sofabed as well as the new pine bed. The house is on the high street but, as in all provincial towns, traffic is quiet at night. A ghost is said to pass through but they haven't met him yet. 'No other word but fantastic' (a guest).

Rooms: 1 double/family room with private bathroom.

Price: £15 p.p. double, £20 single.

Breakfast: Included – full English/continental/or to order.

Meals: Packed lunch available on request as is a light evening snack.

Closed: Never!

Leaving Bourne on A15 north towards Sleaford, first hamlet on left signed to Cawthorpe. The house last on right before road becomes a track.

Map Ref No: 11

Ozric & Chantal Armstrong
Cawthorpe Hall
Bourne
Lincolnshire
PE10 0AB
Tel: 01778-423830
Fax: 01778-426620

From A17/A15 roundabout to Sleaford. House is on the right-hand side in town just past Tescos entrance.

Map Ref No: 11

Karen & Mark Jordan
Rawene
41 Northgate
Sleaford
Lincolnshire NG34 7BS
Tel: 01529-302942

Another lovely symphony in simple brick nestling beneath the village church. Penny is a keen gardener, Roger a classic car enthusiast and they are a cheerful and engaging couple. The family room has bare, 300-year-old floorboards and all rooms have firm beds and old furniture. There is a huge choice for breakfast; the house is warm and friendly. The area is fascinating: Boston was England's second port in the Middle Ages whence the Pilgrim Fathers first tried to sail but were thrown in gaol.

Rooms: 1 double, 1 family room, 1 single, all en suite.

Price: £15-£18 p.p.

Breakfast: Included – full English.

Meals: Dinner £7 p.p. Available on request as is a packed lunch.

Closed: Never!

This impressive listed Queen Anne vicarage was built with local hand-made bricks which have mellowed charmingly. It has a remarkable painted and wall-to-wall, floor-to-ceiling panelled sitting room and a red pine staircase leads out of the typical square Lincolnshire hall where panelling and stone flags vie for admiration. Michael (ex-Navy, ex-MP) and Julia both love cooking and have a huge fruit and vegetable garden. Bedrooms and bathrooms are perfectly comfortable.

Rooms: 1 twin – 1 double, both with private bathroom.

Price: £22.50 p.p. doubles, £30 single.

Breakfast: Included – full English.

Meals: Dinner £15 p.p. Packed lunch also available.

Closed: Never!

From A16 turning to Sutterton at roundabout, between Boston and Spalding. House just before church with spire, on the right in centre of village.

Map Ref No: 11

Roger & Penny Fountain
Georgian House
Station Road
Sutterton Boston
Lincolnshire PE20 2JH
Tel: 01205-460048
Fax: 01205-460048

A52 to Skegness. Wrangle 9 miles from Boston, 15 from Skegness. Follow signs to Angel Inn. The Old Vicarage opposite church by war memorial.

Map Ref No: 11

Michael & Julia Brotherton
The Old Vicarage
Wrangle
Boston
Lincolnshire PE22 9EP
Tel: 01205-870688
Fax: 01205-870688

If you're lucky rabbits and squirrels will play for you on the croquet lawn while you breakfast. The fine, unusually asymmetrical 18th-century manor is enclosed in a walled garden that seems to cut it off from the bustle outside. Delightful Jill will proffer homemade cake when you arrive and set you up for the day with a 'jolly good breakfast', including her own marmalade. The rooms are of generous proportions with garden views, pale paint and floral curtains. Children over 10 welcome.

Rooms: 2 twins: 1 with en suite bath/shower, 1 with separate private bathroom; 1 double with en suite shower.

Price: £20 p.p. doubles, £25 single.

Breakfast: Included – full English.

Meals: Dinner available nearby.

Closed: Christmas & New Year.

From Lincoln A15 south. Once in Bracebridge Heath, Manor House is last house on left hidden among trees with walled garden.

Map Ref No: 10

Jill & Michael Scoley
The Manor House
Sleaford Road
Bracebridge Heath
Lincoln LN4 2HW
Tel: 01522-520825
Fax: 01522-542418

The Hillcrest is just 5 minutes from the cathedral yet its pesticide-free, insect-friendly, hedgehog-run garden is like a rural haven. This successful town guesthouse was a Victorian rectory and still feels more like a house than a hotel. There are candlelit conservatory dinners, traditional bedding, unfussy furniture and a warm welcome from Jennifer Bennett, her staff, Yorkshire terriers and Grey Lady the ghost.

Rooms: 1 twin, 6 doubles, 4 family rooms, 6 singles, all en suite.

Price: From £30 p.p. doubles, from £45 single. Children 2-14 £5 when sharing with parents.

Breakfast: Included – full English/continental/vegetarian.

Meals: Dinner £12-£14 p.p. Lunch & packed lunch also available.

Closed: 22 December – 6 January.

Pass Lincoln Cathedral on your right and at next T-junction, pub in front of you, turn left. Immediately right into Upper Lindum Street. Left at end.

Map Ref No: 10

Jennifer Bennett
Hillcrest Hotel
15 Lindum Terrace
Lincoln
Lincolnshire LN2 5RT
Tel: 01522-510182
Fax: 01522-510182

Only the tennis net separates the lovely garden from the herd of handsome red cows (calving is Jan-April). Once a famous stud (the 1875 Derby winner was bred here), Baumber is a large farm whose interesting owners, a botanist and an ornithologist, are very conservation-aware. The old horse-watering pond is now a wildlife haven and a home hive gives breakfast honey. The back of the house is beautifully 18th-century, the front was Victorianised; the guestroom is big and full of character.

Rooms: 1 twin with shared bathroom (private basin and w.c.); 1 small single.

Price: £17.50 p.p.

Breakfast: Included – full English.

Meals: Dinner available locally. Packed lunch available on request.

Closed: Christmas & New Year.

This is a well-designed long low modern house with lots of interest in the roofline and great picture windows onto stunning views of rolling fields. It is one of the warmest, most generous, best-decorated houses we have seen – no wonder people who stay with the Stamps never want to go anywhere else. Anne is a writer and both she and Richard love doing B&B – one cannot but feel relaxed here. They offer you space and light, beautiful rooms, divine food and are committed to conservation on their farm. Children over 8 welcome.

Rooms: 1 twin, 1 double, both en suite.

Price: From £20 p.p. doubles. Sing. supp. payable.

Breakfast: Included – full English.

Meals: Dinner £13.50 p.p. by arrangement, also available locally.

Closed: Christmas & New Year

From Horncastle A158 west for 4 miles. Turn towards Bardney on A158 south. In Baumber the farm is 0.25 miles down road towards Baumber Park.

Map Ref No: 11

Michael & Clare Harrison
Baumber Park
Baumber
Nr. Horncastle
Lincolnshire LN9 5NE
Tel: 01507-578235
Fax: 01507-578417

Turn off A157 in East Barkwith at War Memorial into Torrington Lane. Bodkin Lodge is last property on the right on edge of village.

Map Ref No: 16

Anne & Richard Stamp
Bodkin Lodge
Torrington Lane
East Barkwith
Lincoln LN3 5RY
Tel: 01673-858249

The farmhouse is 200 years old, the farm is down the road from the house, there is a large lake nearby and Christine Ramsay is one of the most welcoming and helpful people we have met – she also cooks a delicious cake. The flower-filled garden is lush and lovely, log fires warm you indoors, the bedrooms are most attractive, the 14th-century church boasts John Wycliffe as former rector. Guests keep coming back.

Rooms: 1 twin with shared bathroom, 1 double en suite, 1 single with shared bathroom.

Price: £15-£17.50 p.p. doubles, £5-£7.50 single supplement.

Breakfast: Included – full English.

Meals: Dinner £11 p.p. High tea £7.50 p.p. Lunch & packed lunch available on request.

Closed: Christmas & New Year.

From Lincoln A15 north. Second left after Scampton RAF station signed to Fillingham & Ingham. First right onto B1398. Second left to Fillingham. First house at bottom of hill on right.

Map Ref No: 16

Christine & Bill Ramsay
Church Farm
Fillingham
Gainsborough
Lincolnshire DN21 5BS
Tel: 01427-668279
Fax: 01427-668025

A fine double-fronted Victorian terrace house in York's only residential square, this is a sophisticated base whence to venture forth each morning and tease every secret out of historic York. It is graciously proportioned with wide staircases, antiques, fresh flowers alongside paintings by the owners' son and a gorgeous kitchen. Anne has created a lovely secluded garden at the back and is a cultivated, interesting and attentive hostess.

Rooms: 1 twin with private shower; 2 doubles: 1 with en suite shower, 1 with en suite bath.

Price: £30 p.p. doubles, £10 single supp.

Breakfast: Included – full English/continental.

Meals: No, but available nearby.

Closed: Occasionally.

The North

In the south-west side of the city just off the Holgate road, which is part of the A59 from York to Harrogate.

Map Ref No: 15

Mike & Anne Beaufoy
18, St. Pauls Square
York
North Yorkshire
YO2 4BD
Tel: 01904-629884

Mid-way between London and Edinburgh, on the banks of the River Swale, lie the twin villages of Brafferton and Helperby – of Saxon and Viking origins respectively. In a quiet corner, you will find Brafferton Hall, a 1720 Dower House owned by the affable Whites who will probably greet you with tea and gingerbread after a long journey and make you feel thoroughly at home. Surrounded by the moors and dales of 'Herriot Country' where there are many walks and lovely houses to explore.

Rooms: 3 doubles: 2 en suite, 1 with private adjacent bathroom; 1 single en suite.

Price: £30 p.p.

Breakfast: Included – full English.

Meals: Dinner £18.50 p.p. available on request as are lunch & packed lunches.

Closed: Never!

The façade of this superbly solid Georgian house is a lesson in architectural hierarchy – the lower the grander. The big, floral-and-wood bedrooms have lots of books, old chests, window seats and a warmly enfolding atmosphere; one has a four-poster. There are horses – riding can be arranged for guests – sheep, black ducks on the pond, coarse fishing if wanted, a hard tennis court, croquet and a fine welcome from the relaxed and amusing Keys. Very central for many Yorkshire delights.

Rooms: 1 twin en suite shower & wc; 2 doubles: 1 with en suite bath, 1 with private bathroom.

Price: £23-£25 p.p.

Breakfast: Included – full English/continental.

Meals: Available by arrangement or nearby.

Closed: Never!

From A1 take Boroughbridge exit. North side of Boroughbridge follow Easingwold & Helperby signs for 4 miles. In village right at T-junct. and right again up Hall Lane. Hall on left opp. school.

Map Ref No: 15

John & Sue White
Brafferton Hall
Brafferton/Helperby
York
North Yorkshire YO6 2NZ
Tel: 01423-360352
Fax: 01423-360352

From A1 at Boroughbridge take Easingwold road to Helperby . Turn right at The Oak Tree pub. Take next right, go 300m, turn left into Hall Lane. Laurel Manor Farm is straight ahead.

Map Ref No: 15

Sam & Annie Key
Laurel Manor Farm
Brafferton
Helperby
North Yorkshire YO6 2NZ
Tel: 01423-360436
Fax: 01423-360436

An early Georgian granary, across the yard from Halfway house, makes a neat conversion from its former agricultural use. It now has two lovely double bedrooms: the Upper has its own outside staircase, the Lower has a four-poster bed. Pretty lace and pine furniture. Jo Hilling admits she hates cooking but will happily serve continental breakfast in your room – in bed if it's that sort of day. The more eager will be up and away to the Yorkshire Dales and moors, or to glorious York City.

Rooms: 1 double en suite, one 4-poster with private bathroom.

Price: £20-£22.50 p.p.

Breakfast: Included – continental served in bedroom.

Meals: Not available.

Closed: Christmas – New Year.

An elegantly understated Georgian exterior in sharp contrast to its very comfortable, plush and pelmeted inside. There are antiques, open fires, high ceilings and those wonderful shutters; most of the big rooms overlook the garden with its wealth of great old trees (only two guestrooms give onto the road – busy in the day, quiet at night). Friendly, artistic Pat decorates, grows her own organic veg and serves mouthwatering menus. Children over 10 welcome.

Rooms: 3 twins, 1 twin/double, 4 doubles, all en suite. (5 with bath, 3 with shower.)

Price: £29.50-£34.50 p.p. for 2/3 nights. Less for longer stay, more for 1 night stay.

Breakfast: Included – full English/continental.

Meals: Dinner £13.50-£15.95 p.p.

Closed: Mid-November – mid-February.

A19 York to Thirsk road. In Easingwold right signed to Crayke. Half way up, right into lane opposite red post box. House immediately on right.

Map Ref No: 15

Phillip & Jo Hilling
Halfway House
Crayke
York
North Yorkshire YO6 4TJ
Tel: 01347-822614
Fax: 01347-822614

From Malton & Norton follow signs to Beverley. Hotel on B1248, 0.5 mile beyond last houses, at junction with road to Setherington. Look out for small sign on stone entrance pillar.

Map Ref No: 16

Paul & Pat Williams
Newstead Grange
Beverley Road
Norton-on-Derwent, Malton
North Yorkshire YO17 9PJ
Tel: 01653-692502
Fax: 01653-696951

The Worsley family is Hovingham – the Hall, the hotel, the village are all part of the estate, all steeped in aristocratic and architectural history. The small, intimate 1840s hotel on the village green – cricket is played here – has a solid Yorkshire stone face and a gentle English garden. It is furnished in traditional chintz-and-pelmet style, has good big rooms and a personal, informal touch. Also baby-sitting and listening, minors' meals, bedboards for lower back sufferers... all very thoughtful.

Rooms: 12 twins/doubles, 5 doubles, 2 singles, all with en suite bathrooms.

Price: £37.50 p.p. doubles, £55 single.

Breakfast: Included – full Yorkshire.

Meals: Dinner £24 p.p.

Closed: Never!

Take A64 to Malton, then B1257 to Helmsley. Hovingham is 8 miles from Malton. Hotel is in centre of village, 3 miles form Castle Howard.

Map Ref No: 15

Euan & Debbi Rodger
The Worsley Arms Hotel
Hovingham
York
YO6 4LA
Tel: 01653-628234
Fax: 01653-628130

A c.1770 Grade 11 listed house, an adjacent deer park and an interior decorator and wine buff in residence must be a recipe for something wonderful. No disappointment then to arrive at this exquisite home where everything you see is suited to its surroundings and period. Just two beautifully decorated bedrooms and bathrooms which will make you want to take up permanent residence. The house is almost at the gates of Studley Royal Deer Park and Fountains Abbey; golf, riding and clay pigeon shooting can be arranged.

Rooms: 2 twins both with en suite bathrooms.

Price: £38 p.p. doubles, £48 single.

Breakfast: Included – full English/continental.

Meals: Dinner £20 p.p. by prior arrangement.

Closed: Christmas – New Year.

Of A1 to Ripon. Take B6265/Pateley Bridge road for 2 miles. Left into Studley Roger. Lawrence House last on right.

Map Ref No: 15

John & Harriet Highley
Lawrence House
Studley Roger
Ripon
North Yorkshire HG4 3AY
Tel: 01765-600947
Fax: 01765-609297

A solid early Victorian Yorkshire house set in farmland and woods with fine views to the south. The ground floor has a 'circular' plan, formal dining room (one large table laid with pretty things) leading to comfy sitting room, all furnished with old family possessions. The Orrs are happy here and seek kindred spirits to share their delight. They are cultivated, curious, enjoy good conversation and serve delicious country-house meals. Ideal for the treasures of Yorkshire, cultural and physical.

Rooms: 2 twin/doubles en suite, 1 single with sep. private bath.

Price: £20-£24 p.p.

Breakfast: Included – full English/continental.

Meals: Dinner £17.50 p.p.

Closed: Never!

The Parsonage where the Brontë family lived is now a museum and only steps away from cobbled West Lane and Weavers, a restaurant with rooms. The Rushworths have run this very popular restaurant for nineteen years and grow their own herbs, soft fruits and vegetables. The bedrooms are largely furnished with old furniture, collected specially. Four former weavers' cottages gave the restaurant its name and there is an interesting collection of weaving paraphernalia in the entrance.

Rooms: 1 twin, 1 double, 1 single: all with private bathrooms.

Price: £37.50 p.p. doubles, £50 single.

Breakfast: Included – full English/continental.

Meals: Dinner from £12.50 p.p. Packed lunch available on request.

Closed: Christmas – New Year & Sundays.

From A170 between Kirkbymoorside and Pickering turn into Sinnington. On village green keep river on your left, fork right between cottages. Turn up lane bearing right uphill, past church. It's signed.

Map Ref No: 15

From A629 take B6142 to Haworth. Follow Brontë Parsonage Museum signs. Use their car park as Weavers backs onto it!

Map Ref No: 15

John & Jane Orr
Hunters Hill
Sinnington
York
North Yorkshire YO6 6SF
Tel: 01751-431196
Fax: 01751-43

Colin & Jane Rushworth
Weavers
15 West Lane
Haworth
West Yorkshire BD22 8DU
Tel: 01535-643822
Fax: 01535-644832

A stream runs through the garden and dozens of greedy ducks wander freely round the garden. It is all utterly peacefully rural (no telly in your room to destroy that peace) yet only a mile from Harrogate. The house is 200 years old, has oak beams and an old stone arch that used to be the dairy and is now the breakfast corner. Peter and Marion are quiet hosts, their only concern being your rest and recuperation. There is a lovely little library as well as a guest sitting room. Children over 12 welcome.

Rooms: 2 twins: 1 with en suite shower, 1 with private bath/shower; 1 double en suite shower.

Price: £20 p.p.

Breakfast: Included – full English.

Meals: Not available.

Closed: Christmas & New Year.

What a lovely house with its mullioned windows, triple gable and perfectly restored and furnished interior. What a welcome from a kind and generous hostess. Drink before dinner in the oak-panelled log-fired drawing room with fellow guests and Fudge the dog. Breakfast in the sun and plant-filled conservatory whence you fall into the stunning garden. Admire the herd of pedigree Aberdeen Angus beef cattle. Fine bedrooms and big bathrooms too. Children over 12 welcome.

Rooms: 2 twins both with en suite shower & bath; 1 double with private shower & bath.

Price: £31 p.p. doubles, £4 single supp.

Breakfast: Included – full English/continental.

Meals: Dinner available on request, £17 p.p.

Closed: Christmas.

Off the A61 north of Harrogate, signed on the road.

Map Ref No: 15

Peter & Marion Thomson
Knox Mill House
Knox Mill Lane
Harrogate
North Yorkshire HG3 2AE
Tel: 01423-560650
Fax: 01423-560650

Off B6451 4 miles south of Pateley Bridge. Stone entrance to Low Hall is between Dacre Banks & hilltop hamlet of Dacre. Look for 'Dacreherd' sign.

Map Ref No: 15

Pamela Holliday
Low Hall
Dacre
Near Harrogate
North Yorkshire HG3 4AA
Tel: 01423-780230

Built in 1908 on the sunny side of the hill the Stone House presides proudly over its lovely dale. It is a family-run hotel with the air and decoration of an elegant family home, albeit a large one. It has an old red telephone box in the courtyard, an oak-panelled, log-fired drawing room, a billiard room and serves good honest Yorkshire food. The bedrooms are all different, some with four-posters. The tennis/croquet lawn and the curious collections help maintain that inimitable family feel.

Rooms: 19 rooms: 1 family, 7 twins, 10 doubles (3 with 4-poster), 1 single. All en suite except 1 of the doubles.

Price: £27.50-£39 p.p. doubles, single supp. according to season.

Breakfast: Included – full Yorkshire/continental.

Meals: Dinner £16.50 p.p.

Closed: January

High Green is a small Georgian house beside the village green of a quiet little Yorkshire village where the great air of the Dales will lift any city stuffiness from your lungs. Pat cooks splendid traditional Yorkshire meals (local lamb and veg.) and will greet you with a sherry. They both enjoy a good chat after dinner. The rooms are restfully plain and unfussy, one is fully equipped for handicapped guests and a log fire is lit on chilly evenings.

Rooms: 1 twin en suite bath & shower; 2 doubles: 1 with en suite shower and 1 with private bath & shower.

Price: £24- £27.50 p.p. doubles, £10 single supp. Small children free, £5-£10 up to 12, normal rate over 12.

Breakfast: Included – full English/continental.

Meals: Dinner £15.50 p.p. except Tuesdays.

Closed: 31 October – April/Easter.

From Leyburn take A684 to Hawes. Follow signs to Muker for about 0.5 miles. At T-junction turn right towards Askrigg. House is on left and signed.

Map Ref No: 15

The Taplin Family
Stone House Hotel
Sedbusk, Nr. Hawes
Wensleydale
North Yorkshire DL8 3PT
Tel: 01969-667571
Fax: 01969-667720

From Leyburn take A684 to Aysgarth. Turn left into Thoralby. House is on the right next door to post office overlooking village green.

Map Ref No: 15

Pat & Ted Hesketh
High Green House
Thoralby
Nr. Leyburn
North Yorkshire DL8 3SU
Tel: 01969-663420

Breakfasts fit for a king! You would have to stay a month in this supremely alive, welcoming house (a 'restaurant with rooms') to try them all. Everyl is a darling and a brilliant cook; her house is cluttered with antiques, herbs and sounds of music and flows with wine. The bedrooms, one with a four-poster, offer fresh fruit, sherry, smellies of all sorts and more. The house-guest atmosphere is complete. Once you are utterly seduced you can be married here.

Rooms: 1 twin en suite shower & bath, 4 doubles (2 with 4-poster): 2 en suite shower & bath, 1 en suite shower, 1 private bath & shower.

Price: £30-£40 p.p.

Breakfast: Included – full English.

Meals: Dinner from £19.50 p.p.

Closed: Never!

Sumptuous English elegance – each outsize Georgian window a triumph of glass over glazing bar – in an informal continental way. Oriella is an easy-going, fun-loving, arty hostess who will happily sit and chat with you and her Irish wolfhound. The furnishings are richly warm, the hall a treasure trove of English and oriental pieces; the bedrooms are big, chintzy/paisley (one has a 7-foot bed), the breakfast room is sunny, the evening snug has an open fire. The garden... enough. Over 16's welcome.

Rooms: 2 doubles, 1 twin: 2 with en suite bath & shower, 1 en suite bath.

Price: £35-£40 p.p., suite £45.

Breakfast: Included – full English.

Meals: Dinner £20 p.p.

Closed: Never!

Northbound from A1 take the Thirsk, Masham turning to Middleham, B6267. House is off the village square on same road.

Map Ref No: 15

Everyl & Brian Madell
Waterford House
19 Kirkgate
Middleham
North Yorkshire DL8 4PG
Tel: 01969-622090
Fax: 01969-624020

Turn off A694 to Newton-Le-Willows. Turn right at T-junction, left at Wheatsheaf pub, then immediate right through high gates.

Map Ref No: 15

Oriella Featherstone
The Hall
Newton-Le-Willows
Bedale
North Yorkshire DL8 1SW
Tel: 01677-450210
Fax: 01677-450014

Along a quiet country lane, in the heart of Herriot Country (he was in fact their vet), Siân's lovely 17th-century farmhouse with its fine outbuildings is a genuinely friendly place to lay your head. She is a happy, chatty, outgoing soul who will ply you with homemade flapjacks – and black pudding for breakfast. The house is simply furnished, there are family photographs galore, the bedrooms are small and cosy and there is a delicious walled garden. What is more, Silton church is close by and to be seen. Excellent value.

Rooms: 1 double, 2 singles all sharing bathroom with shower & wc.

Price: £12.50 p.p.

Breakfast: Included – full English/continental.

Meals: Dinner £5.50 p.p.

Closed: Never!

These are the nicest and most genuine farming folk imaginable. Even in the middle of lambing they will greet you with twinkling eyes, a warm handshake, tea and homemade biscuits. The rooms, three in converted outbuildings, one in the main house, are equally unpretentious, mostly pine-furnished with country textiles, garden views and modern shower rooms. Some have old oak beams. And always the Pearsons' delightful, straightforward manner.

Rooms: 1 family, 1 twin, 1 double, 1 single, all with en suite shower.

Price: £17-£25 p.p.

Breakfast: Included – full English/continental.

Meals: Dinner £10 p.p.

Closed: 1 December – 28 February.

Take road off A19 to Over Silton. Go into village, turn left then bear right, farm is next to Manor House on left.

Map Ref No: 15

Mrs Siân Goodwin
Moorfields Farm
Over Silton
Thirsk
North Yorkshire YO7 2LJ
Tel: 01609-883351

From Northallerton, take A167 for 4 miles. House is on right-hand side and signed.

Map Ref No: 15

John & Mary Pearson
Lovesome Hill Farm
Lovesome Hill
Northallerton
North Yorkshire DL6 2PB
Tel: 01609-772311

'The only house beyond the stream', Darnholm is reached through a ford. It nestles in its wooded moorland fold, sheep graze safely, the steam railway passes in the distance – a charming scene from earlier days. Linzi is warm and welcoming, 'a real brick' who glories in her new home with its warm terracotta colours, its chequered career written all over its architecture, its incomparably peaceful setting – and all within striking distance of Goathland.

Rooms: 2 twin/doubles, 1 double, all with en suite shower.

Price: £22.50-£25.00 p.p.

Breakfast: Included – full English/continental.

Meals: Dinner by prior arrangement, £12.50-£15 p.p.

Closed: Dec 20 – Jan 4.

From its spectacular cliff-top position the Cliffemount looks down onto the old fishing village, where local fishermen still bring in lobster, crab and fish of the day (often evident on the hotel's menus), and across Runswick Bay with its ideal family beach. All but two guestrooms have sea views. Furnishings are modern/trad with padded headboards, good lights, pretty curtains and cushions. The pleasant lounge has an open fire and young, energetic Ashley Goodrum is genuinely friendly.

Rooms: 2 twins, 8 doubles, 1 single: all with en suite facilities.

Price: £24-£33.75 p.p. doubles, £24-£35 single.

Breakfast: Included – full English/continental.

Meals: Dinner approx. £15 p.p. Lunch & packed lunches also available.

Closed: 25 & 26 December.

From A169 Pickering to Whitby, turn towards Goathland. In village road past car park to Darnholm. At crossroads, turn right, down hill, over ford, up private drive.

Map Ref No: 16

Linzi & Colin Ward
Darnholm Grange
Darnholm
Goathland, Whitby
North Yorkshire YO22 5LN
Tel: 01947-896271

From A171 NW of Whitby take B1266 then A174 north and turn off to Runswick Bay and Cliffemount Hotel (red brick building).

Map Ref No: 15

Mrs Ashley Goodrum
Cliffemount Hotel
Runswick Bay
Whitby
North Yorkshire TS13 5HU
Tel: 01947-840103
Fax: 01947-841025

You will be godmothered but not smothered in this bay-windowed farmhouse (Anne's son is the farmer). A peaceful, informal spirit prevails. The carpets are thick and soft, the colours pale and fresh, the books interesting and the views, of course, will grab you and hold you for long moments. Go out and walk among those views! You are spoiled for fresh air and space, Anne's home cooking is delicious and you will find every inducement to sleep well. Children over 12 welcome.

Rooms: 1 twin with private bathroom; 1 twin/double with private bathroom & bidet.

Price: £30. Sing. supp. £10

Breakfast: Included – full English/contintental.

Meals: Dinner £19 p.p.

Closed: December & January.

Going north on A172 pass sign on right to Carlton & Busby. House is 0.5 mile further on the left. Tree-lined drive.

Map Ref No: 15

Mrs Anne Gloag
Busby House
Stokesley
North Yorkshire
TS9 5LB
Tel: 01642-710425
Fax: 01642-713838

Potto Grange, a serene Grade II listed Georgian house, originally dating from 1750, has belonged to the same family for 250 years and sits at the end of a long drive, amongst parkland where Scotch Blackface sheep and white Galloway cattle graze. The guests' beautifully furnished drawing room has a grand piano which may be played, and the peaceful garden with croquet lawn, tennis court and table tennis for children is there to be enjoyed. There is plenty to visit in the area – ancient abbeys, moors and dales, the great cities of York and Durham, and Herriot Country is just down the road. The entire area is excellent walking country.

Rooms: 1 twin with private separate bathroom, 2 doubles both en suite.

Price: £25 p.p. doubles, £30 single.

Breakfast: Included – full English/continental/health food.

Meals: Dinner £15 p.p.

Closed: 1 December – 30 April.

From A19 take A172 towards Stokesley for 3 miles. Turn left, go straight over crossroads. House is 0.25 mile ahead on right.

Map Ref No: 15

Major & Mrs Julian Kynge
Potto Grange
Nr. Northallerton
North Yorkshire
DL6 3HH
Tel: 01642-700212
Fax: 01642-700212

Delightful Ann is mad about salerooms and will go miles for a Staffordshire dog. She has two real dogs and likes people too: guests are offered tea or a drink before dining at one of the excellent local pubs. A lovely house on the village green, it has a moulded-ceilinged, marble-fireplaced, antique-furnished, great-bayed drawing room looking onto an enchanting garden. Bedrooms are big, prettily furnished with lovely patchwork quilts and good bathrooms. Not suitable for children.

Rooms: 1 twin en suite, 1 double with private adjacent bathroom.

Price: £30 p.p. doubles, £30 single.

Breakfast: Included – full English/continental.

Meals: Available locally.

Closed: 20 December – 3 January & Easter.

Gail and Ann run a very special place; they bake their own bread, make jams and marmalade and squeeze oranges. Their dinners are delicious and utterly real: Lancashire tart, for example, lots of spices with fresh produce. This is a cosy, traditional Victorian house with marvellous views, right at the head of Wensleydale (the local cheese factory has been bought by the locals) and in the heart of the Yorkshire Dales National Park. Not luxurious but very comfortable, and who cares when the beds are mahogany and oak four-posters.

Rooms: 1 twin, 3 doubles, (two 4-posters) all with handbasins sharing a bathroom and a shower-room.

Price: £17-£18 p.p. doubles, £8 single supp.

Breakfast: Included – full English/health food.

Meals: Dinner £11 p.p. book in advance, except Thursdays.

Closed: 31 October – 31 January.

From A1 at Scotch Corner roundabout right to Middleton Tyas. Continue 1 mile. Pass the Shoulder of Mutton. House is on village green on right with white gate.

Map Ref No: 15

David & Ann Murray
Foresters Hall
Middleton Tyas
Richmond
North Yorkshire DL10 6QY
Tel: 01325-377722

The house is approx. 320 metres off the A684 on the road north out of Hawes, signposted Muker and Hardraw.

Map Ref No: 15

Ann Macdonald
Brandymires
Muker Road
Hawes
North Yorkshire DL8 3PR
Tel: 01969-667482

The Varleys run this small characterful family hotel with care and efficiency. It is their own house and they know and love it well with its fine cantilevered staircase, tongue-and-ball ceiling moulding and grandfather clock in the hall. The furniture is warmly worn, the open fires most welcoming, the very adequate bedrooms (two in a converted cottage) are done in country style, the food is good. Altogether 'a good place to be snowbound'. No under 5s in the restaurant.

Rooms: 4 twins, 5 doubles, one 4-poster, 2 family rooms – all en suite.

Price: £40-£53 p.p. doubles including dinner, £48-£61 p.p. single including dinner.

Breakfast: Included – full English.

Meals: Lunch available on request. Dinner £15.50-£19.50 p.p.

Closed: 2-26 January

There are nine (up to 30 guests at once) cleverly-converted, country-furnished, fully-fitted cottages round the courtyard plus, on dinner nights there, the drawing and dining rooms in the main house where the family and their dogs have their space. On other lazy days you can have dinner delivered to your door by Robert who cooks tempting dishes with home-grown vegetables and herbs. The walled garden (for guests' use) with its fountain is a haven in this moorland setting.

Rooms: 9 self-catering cottages sleeping between 2 and 6.

Price: £190-£790 per cottage per week.

Breakfast: Champagne breakfast available by arrangement.

Meals: Dinner in restaurant £21 p.p., in cottages £12-£19 p.p. Available on request.

Closed: Never!

Leave A590 (M6 – Barrow Carriageway) at top of Lindale Hill. Follow signs to Cartmel. Aynsome Manor on right 3 miles from A590 (sign in field).

Map Ref No: 14

Take A590 to Barrow. 1 mile past Lindale roundabout and up steep hill, left to Cartmel. Left at crossroads and left at next junction past Longlands Farm. House second drive on left.

Map Ref No: 14

Mr & Mrs Tony Varley
Aynsome Manor Hotel
Cartmel
Cumbria
LA11 6HH
Tel: 015395-36653
Fax: 015395-36016

Robert & Judy Johnson
Longlands at Cartmel
Cartmel
Cumbria
LA11 6HG
Tel: 015395-36475
Fax: 015395-36172

An attractive remnant of a 15th-century hamlet. Roam the walled gardens, feed the ducks or savour a drink in the courtyard. Guests dine in informal dinner-party style at a large oak table beneath the lofty beams of a Great Hall. Prepare yourself for tasty home-grown food and a succession of wines. The rooms are mostly furnished with antiques. The Emily and Charlotte Brontë suites are tucked away in the cosy courtyard cottage. A house with some style but Ian and Jos could not be more easy-going. Children over 12 welcome.

Rooms: 2 twins, 3 doubles – all en suite; 2 cottage suites.

Price: £42 p.p. doubles, £69 single, £47 p.p. cottage apartments.

Breakfast: Included – full English.

Meals: Dinner £23 p.p.

Closed: December – February.

Coniston Water's mirrored depths provide the backdrop to this 17th/19th-century farmhouse beside the main road in a 3-acre woodland garden. Traditional chintzy bedrooms with matching wallpaper have glorious views. A log fire warms the lounge; the dining room ceiling is supported by massive ship's timbers; admire the ancient oak settle, highly polished from centuries of shifting occupancy. Breakfast on Staffordshire oat cakes, Cumberland sausage and black pudding but work your appetite up for a special dinner too. A friendly, helpful and professional welcome awaits.

Rooms: 5 doubles: 3 en suite, 2 with handbasins & shared bathrooms; 2 singles with handbasins & shared bathrooms.

Price: £20.50-£27.50 p.p. doubles, £30.50-£37.50 single.

Breakfast: Included – full English/continental.

Meals: Dinner £16 p.p. or £17.50 for non-residents.

Closed: Christmas – January; 1 week in July; Sundays (not bank holidays).

Leave M6 at junction 36 and follow A65 past Kirkby Lonsdale. House is on left 8.5 miles from M6 junction 36.

Map Ref No: 14

Ian Bryant & Jocelyn Ruffle
Hipping Hall
Cowan Bridge
Kirkby Lonsdale
Cumbria LA6 2JJ
Tel: 015242-71187
Fax: 015242-72452

From M6 south take A590 then A5092 to Lowick. A5084 to Water Yeat (about 3 miles). House signed on the left.

Map Ref No: 14

Jill & Pierre Labat
Water Yeat Country Guest House
Water Yeat
Ulverston
Cumbria LA12 8DJ
Tel: 01229-885306

Naturally you will be packing your walking boots to visit this Mecca for active admirers of England's most majestic landscapes, not least to work up a hearty appetite for your hosts' bountiful hospitality. Everything is homemade from the banana bread served for tea to breakfast's spacious rooms. A typically solid Lakeland country house with big unpretentious rooms. Dany Brown and her husband, Robin, breed Highland cattle and sheep on their 36 acres – so you can start walking from the front door.

Rooms: 2 twins, 1 with en suite shower & wc, 1 with separate private bath, 1 double en suite.

Price: £22.50-£30 p.p.

Breakfast: Included – full English/continental/health food.

Meals: Dinner £15 p.p.

Closed: Christmas & New Year.

Exit 36 off M6, A591 NW. B5284 through Crook village. After 3 miles Sun Inn on right. Up hill past village hall. 0.5 miles on right after church turn right up hill. Entrance ahead 90 metres.

Map Ref No: 14

Robin & Dany Brown
Birksey Brown
Crook
Cumbria
LA8 8LQ
Tel: 015394-43380

Although newish the cottage is imbued with homeliness. Guests are immediately wrapped in the Midwinters' cheerful enthusiasm, just as Low Jock Scar itself is folded into the comforting slopes of the valley. From the conservatory you are lured out to ramble in the flourishing gardens, the pride of your green-fingered hosts. Listen out for the burbling beck and rest on its banks in the evening to recover from the 5-course feast at dinner.

Rooms: 2 twins and 2 doubles, all en suite; 1 twin and 1 double sharing bathroom.

Price: £21.50-£26.50 p.p. doubles, £8 single supp.

Breakfast: Included – full English.

Meals: Dinner £15 p.p.

Closed: 1 March – 31 October.

Leave Kendal on A6 to Penrith. In 5 miles you see the Plough Inn on left. Turn into lane on left in 1 mile.

Map Ref No: 14

Alison & Philip Midwinter
Low Jock Scar
Selside
Kendal
Cumbria LA8 9LE
Tel: 01539-823259
Fax: 01539-823259

Very near Bowness – the honeypot of the Lake District – and all things rural and cultural, this is a superb country house hotel in a glorious site. Its style is deeply restful, smart, 'lived-in' and humorous too, with rich tapestry materials, kilims, antiques, log fires and specials, eg. bath robes, fly fishing on site and a dog kennel in the summer house! Drag yourself away from Mike Bevans – a most congenial host – and explore the great outdoors before returning to mouth-watering food at whatever time of day.

Rooms: 4 twins, 12 doubles, 1 suite, 1 single, all with en suite bath & shower.

Price: £65-£90 p.p. doubles, from £90 single.

Breakfast: Included – full English.

Meals: Dinner £29.50 p.p. Lunch also available, on Sundays £14 p.p.

Closed: Never!

An oasis in a crowded village, this old stone guest house has a tiny 'entrance' garden, a cosy sitting room with good books, and pine-tabled dining room (separate tables). Lots of style, too. The bedrooms are snug, with Victorian patchwork quilts, the bathrooms minuscule but the comfort generous; two of them look over the town to the hills. There are prints on the walls, an open fireplace, antiques and fresh flowers and food prepared with flair and imagination (and organic ingredients if possible).

Rooms: 2 twins, 2 doubles, all en suite.

Price: £22-£27 p.p. doubles.

Breakfast: Included – full English/continental.

Meals: Dinner £12.50 p.p.

Closed: 2 weeks mid-January.

From M6 junction 36 take A591 for Windermere. Turn onto B5284/Crook Road. Hotel is 1 mile past Windermere Golf Club on left.

Map Ref No: 14

Entering Windermere village from the A591 the Archway is on College Road, first right off Elleray Road.

Map Ref No: 14

Mike Bevans
Linthwaite House Hotel & Restaurant
Crook Road
Windermere
Cumbria LA23 3JA
Tel: 015394-88600
Fax: 015394-88601

Anthony & Aurea Greenhalgh
The Archway
College Rd
Windermere
Cumbria LA23 1BU
Tel: 015394-45613

Floors, doors, beams, panels, stairs and furniture are all old oak – the 17th century reigns still. It has left the stone fireplace and bread oven and an unusual spice cupboard over a writing bureau; there are fascinating 19th-century wall-tiles picturing Aesop's fables; and lots more. Janet will communicate her love for her Westmoreland farmhouse and country twixt Lake and Dale, the Pennines visible in the distance. Utter peace. Superb walking too. Children over 8 welcome.

Magnificent scenery, echoes of history and literature, hiking, biking, boating on Lake Windermere, fishing.... Whatever you've come to the Lake District to find, start here. This handsome and roomy Gentleman's Residence will reveal its share of historical and cultural links and provide a nourishing buffet breakfast, local information, maps and a clothes-drying room. Bustling Ambleside is only a short walk away but the pastel and chintz bedrooms are recommended for their oh-so-romantic views of river and award-winning garden.

Rooms: 1 twin, 1 double, 1 single all with shared bathroom.

Price: £17 p.p.

Breakfast: Included – full English/continental.

Meals: Dinner £11 p.p. Packed lunch available on request.

Closed: 31 October – 1 March.

Rooms: 1 family, 1 twin, 3 doubles, all en suite.

Price: £20-£29 p.p. No singles.

Breakfast: Included – full English.

Meals: No.

Closed: Never!

From Ambleside A593 Coniston road to Rothay Bridge (approx 500 yards). Cross bridge and turn immediately into Riverside lodge entrance.

Map Ref No: 14

Take A685 towards Kirkby Stephen. After 5.5 miles left to Kelleth/Great Asby. Immediately left again. House third on left with yew trees in front.

Map Ref No: 14

Alan & Gillian Rhone
Riverside Lodge
Nr. Rothay Bridge
Ambleside
Cumbria LA22 OEH
Tel: 015394-34208
Fax: 015394-31884

Janet & Graham Paxman
Low Lane House
Newbiggin-on-Lune
Kirkby Stephen
Cumbria CA17 4NB
Tel: 015396-23269

Described as the best B&B in the country (and it may be so) it began life as a farmhouse in 1650. Dani and David exposed the oak timbers and slate floors and battled to retain the vernacular features as a backdrop for their astonishing hospitality and very pretty bedrooms. Lace bedspreads on big iron-frame beds, whirlpool baths and views to dream of. All done with real affection and originality, as is the food. A stunning place. There is also a gorgeous cottage to rent, overlooking the lake.

Successive owners of this 200 to 300-year-old house have scratched their names in the glass in the sitting room. Your architect and solicitor hosts are talented renovators and decorators. They have kept the original panelling but used designer colour schemes and soft furnishings. The bedrooms are 'four-poster mediaeval' and 'brass-bed Mediterranean' respectively. All the good points have been teased out and enhanced. Delicious meals too, if you wish.

Rooms: 4 doubles en suite.

Price: £36.50 p.p.

Breakfast: Included – full English/continental/vegetarian.

Meals: Dinner £21.50 p.p., picnic lunch £4.50 p.p.

Closed: Mid-November – mid-March.

Rooms: 1 twin with en suite shower, one 4-poster with en suite shower.

Price: £20 p.p. doubles, £24 single.

Breakfast: Included – full English/continental.

Meals: Dinner (£10 p.p.) and packed lunches available on request.

Closed: Christmas & New Year.

In Kirkby Stephen 100m north of main square, left to Soulby/Crosby Garrett. After 3 miles left to Crosby Garrett. After 0.75 miles left again. In village, left at church and left through gates into rectory.

A66 from Keswick towards Cockermouth. Left onto B5292 through Lorton towards Buttermere. Left fork after about 2 miles onto B5289. Entrance is on right after 0.3 miles.

Map Ref No: 14

Map Ref No: 14

Mrs Anne McCrickard
The Old Rectory
Crosby Garrett
Kirkby Stephen
Cumbria CA17 4PW
Tel: 017683-72074

Dani & David Edwards
Pickett Howe
Buttermere Valley
Cumbria
CA13 9UY
Tel: 01900-85444
Fax: 01900-85209

Melbreak Cottage is a rarity – the perfect retreat with creature comforts. A long track leads to this stylishly refurbished 17th-century cottage and its welcome basket of locally-made delicacies. You will also find such goodies as music centre, games, maps, a better-than-average kitchen – and a whirlpool bath! Breathtaking scenery of mountains and water – and absolute silence except for birdsong and humming bees. Hit the hills, take a 15-minute lakeside walk to the pub or fall asleep in the hammock!

Rooms: 1 double en suite with 4-poster; 1 twin and 1 double/twin sharing bathroom, shower room, wc.

Price: £360-£670 per week. Low season only: 3-night weekend break/4-night mid-week break, 60% of weekly rate.

Breakfast: Self-catering.

Meals: Self-catering.

Closed: Mid-November – mid-February. Open Christmas and New Year.

A66 from Keswick towards Cockermouth. Left onto B5292 through Lorton towards Buttermere. Left fork after about 2 miles onto B5289. Entrance is on right after 0.3 miles.

Map Ref No: 14

Mrs Dani Edwards
Melbreak Cottage
c/o Pickett Howe
Buttermere Valley
Cumbria CA13 9UY
Tel: 01900-85444
Fax: 01900-85209

A glorious confection of comfort, decoration and sumptuous food in this wedding cake of a Victorian residence enhanced by unbeatable views over water and mountains. Except for one vibrant bedroom, all are classily dressed in muted tones with bathrooms of equal merit. Public rooms are swagged and bowed in 19th-century manner with log fires for winter. Pauline and Derek own and manage Underscar Manor with tireless enthusiasm and are informative about the roe deer, badgers, guinea-fowl and rare red squirrels in their grounds.

Rooms: 11 doubles, all en suite.

Price: From £75 p.p. doubles including dinner, £95 p.p. single including dinner.

Breakfast: Included – full English.

Meals: Dinner £29.50 p.p. non-residents, £30-35 p.p. à la carte. Lunch available.

Closed: Never!

From M6 junction 40, take A66, by-passing Keswick. At roundabout A591 exit towards Carlisle. Immediately right. Follow lane for approx. 1 mile. Entrance to hotel is on right.

Map Ref No: 14

Pauline & Derek Harrison
Underscar Manor
Applethwaite
Nr. Keswick
Cumbria CA12 4PH
Tel: 017687-75000
Fax: 017687-74904

The atmospheric, even idiosyncratic, decorative style starts in the Garden Room entrance with Chris's artistic display of gardening/farming implements. In the bedrooms you will find exquisite antique linen, patchwork quilts and dried flowers plus original beams, wooden floor-boards and cast-iron tubs. Add views of Skiddaw (England's 4th highest mountain), grazing livestock, a walker's-size breakfast including home-laid eggs. Throw a packed lunch over your shoulder and take to the hills or go for culture in the nearby haunts of John Peel, Wordsworth, Coleridge et al.

Rooms: 1 double with en suite bath, 1 twin with en suite cast-iron bath.

Price: £18 p.p.

Breakfast: Included – full English/health food.

Meals: Only breakfast.

Closed: 22-27 December.

A true working farm where breakfast is served in Wedgwood china on a linen cloth and you can watch the dogs working the 500 sheep. It is a lovely old farmhouse with a 'developing' garden (Marjorie works hard in it), an inviting sitting room and playroom with snooker. Bedrooms all have endless views of rolling Border Country, modern decor, nice 'country charm' touches and a basket of goodies in each shower room. There is a sauna and a warmly welcoming family.

Rooms: 1 twin, 2 doubles, all with en suite showers.

Price: £18-£20 p.p./£22.50-£25 p.p. doubles, £30 single.

Breakfast: Included – full English.

Meals: Dinner available locally.

Closed: Christmas.

A591 form Keswick to Carlisle (approx 6.5 miles). Right at Bassenthwaite Chapel into village (0.5 mile). Straight on at village green for 170 metres.

Map Ref No: 14

Roy & Chris Beaty
Willow Cottage
Bassenthwaite
Keswick
Cumbria CA12 4QP
Tel: 017687-76440

From Brampton A6071 road to Longtown for 2 miles. After bridge with traffic lights, right to Walton-Roadhead. At Kirkcambeck, over bridge then look for B&B sign. Cracrop 12 miles on right.

Map Ref No: 19

Marjorie Stobart
Cracrop Farm
Kirkcambeck
Brampton
Cumbria CA8 2BW
Tel: 016977-48245
Fax: 016977-48333

Pauline is a qualified archaeologist and knows a great deal about the Roman Wall. The 'Longest Breakfast Menu in the World', a morning Roman orgy, is here (133 items), in a secluded farmhouse built with stones from Hadrian's Wall; delicious (no-choice) dinners too. The house is thoroughly off the beaten track (through fields and ford); guestrooms are comfortable but unremarkable with ingeniously squeezed-in shower rooms. The area is facinating and teems with wildlife. (Wheel-chair access all year in self-catering, Nov-March for B&B).

Rooms: 4 twin/double, all with en suite showers.

Price: £23-£24 p.p. doubles, £33-£34 single. Children sharing £16.50 p.p.

Breakfast: Included – full English/Scandinavian buffet/health foods.

Meals: Dinner £17 p.p., available on request.

Closed: 18 December – 18 January.

In Greenhead village, off A69, take track between YHA and 'Ye Old Forge Tearooms'. Go over narrow bridge and through 2 fields and 2 gates to reach farm situated below ruined castle. About 0.5 miles.

Map Ref No: 19

Brian & Pauline Staff
Holmhead Farm
Hadrian's Wall,
Greenhead-in-Northumberland
Via Carlisle CA6 7HY
Tel: 016977-47402
Fax: 016977-47402

David is a horsebreeder and will give guided tours of the stables at evening feed time. Susan collects Limoges porcelain boxes and also runs cookery courses. She produces magnificent meals, of course, served at a polished table in lovely china and silverware. The large house is very finely furnished, the sitting room has a log fire, the guestrooms are in country-house chintz and-lace style and one of them is very big indeed. Three have fine country views.

Rooms: 2 twins, 1 en suite, 1 sharing bathroom; 2 doubles en suite.

Price: £22.50-£27 p.p., from £30 single.

Breakfast: Included – full English/continental.

Meals: Dinner £17.50 p.p., available on request.

Closed: Never!

From Hexham take B6306 south. First right to Witley Chapel to top of hill and into dip. Tree on right with sign to farm. Right down track for 0.75 miles.

Map Ref No: 19

David & Susan Carr
East Peterelfield Farm
Hexham
Northumberland
NE46 2JT
Tel: 01434-607209
Fax: 01434-601753

(The address is correct!) Mrs Elliott specialises in interior wall finishes, her renovation work is superb, she even had the front door made especially in Georgian style to fit the original frame and fanlight. The house stands on a fairly main road between the church and the convent and used to be the Catholic Presbytery. Until St Mary's was built the top floor was the chapel. She is a fount of information and her guestrooms are big, sunny and beautifully decorated. Children over 10 welcome.

Rooms: 1 twin en suite; 1 twin sharing bathroom with 1 triple; one 4-poster double one with en suite shower.

Price: £20-25 p.p. doubles, from £25 single.

Breakfast: Included – full English.

Meals: Dinner available locally.

Closed: Never!

Nothing is too much trouble for the Minchins. They are solid, genuine Northern folk who clearly enjoy looking after people. David has a good sense of humour and June is a midwife in her spare time. Their late Victorian house has big rooms – the sitting room is very big – with a rich style of decoration using swags, drapes, lace, voile and velvet. Breakfast can include raspberries, cream and Drambuie (in season) and dinner is good English cooking.

Rooms: 1 family room with shower; 2 twins: 1 en suite and 1 sharing bathroom with 1 double; one 4-poster with en suite shower.

Price: £19-£26 doubles. Price on application for singles.

Breakfast: Included – full English.

Meals: Dinner £14.50 p.p., available on request.

Closed: Never!

Hexham is 1 mile south of A69. Middlemarch is in Hencotes next to St Mary's Catholic Church. Turn off main road and into driveway.

Map Ref No: 19

Mrs Eileen Elliott
Middlemarch
Hencotes
Hexham
Northumberland NE46 2EB
Tel: 01434-605003

Take B6320 north to Bellingham. Cross bridge. House is first on left opposite fire station.

Map Ref No: 19

David & June Minchin
Westfield House
Bellingham
Nr. Hexham
Northumberland NE48 2DP
Tel: 01434-220340
Fax: 01434-220340

These are hard-working farmers – a beef herd and 399 acres of cereals surround the house – who still find the time to greet, advise and get to know their guests. They are never happier than if people are still chatting round the table at 10 o'clock at night: 'Getting on is what it's all about'. The views across the fields to the sea are stunning, the coast is beautiful, the rooms are large, light and colourful, breakfast a feast and the whole family are easy to talk to and laugh with.

Rooms: 3 doubles, all with en suite shower. Bathroom also available.

Price: £21 p.p.

Breakfast: Included – full English.

Meals: Dinner £11 p.p. Available on request.

Closed: Mid-October – Easter.

From Alnwick take A1068 to Alnmouth. At Hipsburn roundabout follow signs to railway station and cross bridge. Straight on to Bilton Barns down first left-hand lane, about 0.5 mile from road.

Map Ref No: 20

Brian & Dorothy Jackson
Bilton Barns
Alnmouth
Alnwick
Northumberland NE66 2TB
Tel: 01665-830427
Fax: 01665-830063

This Scottish manse is such a happy house. The owners have lived here for years and it is full of memories of their long lives. The dining table is a family antique, the paintings were done by your hostess's grandfather during his World Tour in the 1800s, the lace bedcover in the single room was embroidered by her governess. You have stepped into a bygone age. The welcome is so genuine, the garden so well-tended that you thoroughly like the slightly worn old-fashioned interior too.

Rooms: 2 twins, 1 single, sharing bathroom. One family/party only.

Price: £20-£25 p.p.

Breakfast: Included – full English.

Meals: Dinner £15 p.p., available on request.

Closed: Never!

Scotland

From A74M take junction 20 onto B722 to Eaglesfield. Turn left after 350 metres towards Middlebie. In Middlebie house and gate are next to church, up the drive.

Map Ref No: 19

Jock & Rosemary Milne-Home
Kirkside of Middlebie
Lockerbie
Dumfries and Galloway
DG11 3JW
Tel: 01576-300204

The list of virtues is long: a small fishing loch, 20 acres of rhododendrons and woods, a turf and gravel maze, a croquet lawn, a full-size Victorian billiard table, roaring log fires, lots of books and some fine paintings and sculpture – no ordinary old shooting lodge this. Christopher, a vintage car enthusiast and keen gardener, lives mostly on his lawn mower. Mary is an excellent cook (with a big veg. garden), both are warm hosts and the house feels relaxed. Children over 12 welcome.

Rooms: 1 twin with own shower & wc, 1 twin/double with own bath & wc, 1 double with own shower, bath & wc.

Price: £29-£31 p.p. twin/doubles, £37 single.

Breakfast: Included – full English.

Meals: Dinner £16 p.p., available on request.

Closed: December & January.

I wish there were more like them, retired but brimming with enthusiasm and humour and fired by ideas. She and her husband are passionate about organic gardening and all things related. The house is a sweet and unspoiled old manse, from 1869, but 'Georgianised'. Nothing modern, oak and mahogany furniture, Victorian-style bedrooms (no water), patchwork quilts (hers, of course) and fresh flowers. An aged Aga in the kitchen, views across the bay and a mild climate. Small children in off-season only.

Rooms: 2 doubles/singles, 1 family with child's bed, all sharing 2 bathrooms.

Price: £14 p.p.

Breakfast: Included – full English/continental.

Meals: Dinner £8 p.p.

Closed: Never!

From Dalbeattie go south on B793. Auchenskeoch is 7 miles down this road on right. Turn right and after 30 yards left through gate posts.

Map Ref No: 18

Christopher & Mary Broom-Smith
Auchenskeoch Lodge
By Dalbeattie
Kirkcudbrightshire
DG5 4PG
Tel: 01387-780277
Fax: 01387-780277

Take A711 to Auchencairn from Dalbeattie. Drive on right opposite 'Welcome to Auchencairn' sign.

Map Ref No: 18

Mr & Mrs Bardsley
The Rossan
Auchencairn
Castle Douglas
Kirkcudbrightshire DG7 1QR
Tel: 01556-640269

A chunk of Scottish history lies here: built in 1625 for the shipping merchants Clark, Quirk & Crane, the house was used for alcohol smuggling. Its position is indeed secluded with peaceful countryside behind and the everchanging seascape before. Half the rooms have staggering views over the sea and the distant hills. Inside it is unremarkable but bathrooms and bedrooms have been recently refurbished, the reception area is tartan, the lounge in green and pink velvet. Mrs Lamb is most sociable.

Rooms: 7 twins, 7 doubles, 3 singles – all en suite.

Price: £46-£52 p.p. doubles, £52 singles.

Breakfast: Included – full Scottish/continental.

Meals: Dinner £21 p.p., lunch available.

Closed: Mid-November – 28 February.

From the A711 Dalbeattie to Kirkcudbright road turn off towards Auchencairn. From Auchencairn hotel is 2 miles along the road on the left up a single-track road.

Map Ref No: 18

The Lamb Family
Balcary Bay Hotel
Auchencairn
Nr. Castle Douglas
Dumfries & Galloway DG7 1QZ
Tel: 01556-640217
Fax: 01556-640272

Galloway is one of the most unspoilt and unexplored parts of Scotland. Here, in a superb setting four miles from the market town of Castle Douglas, you will find Chipperkyle, an 18th-century Scottish Georgian house in its 200 acres of grazing land – a laird's house. The Dicksons have redecorated without making any structural alterations to the fine Georgian proportions. The good-sized bedrooms are traditional in style, the bathrooms white. Expect to be welcomed, well fed and put at your ease here.

Rooms: 1 twin, with separate private bathroom, shower & wc; 1 single with shared bathroom.

Price: £30 p.p. doubles, £36 single.

Breakfast: Included – full English/continental.

Meals: Dinner £20 p.p. Available on request.

Closed: 15 – 28 December.

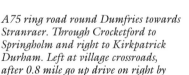

A75 ring road round Dumfries towards Stranraer. Through Crocketford to Springholm and right to Kirkpatrick Durham. Left at village crossroads, after 0.8 mile go up drive on right by white lodge to Chipperkyle.

Map Ref No: 18

Willie & Catriona Dickson
Chipperkyle
Kirkpatrick Durham
Castle Douglas
Kirkcudbrightshire DG7 3EY
Tel: 01556-650223
Fax: 01556-650223

Culzean Castle is awe-inspiring by any castle standards. The top floor, including 6 double bedrooms, is probably the most interesting hotel address in Scotland, especially loved by Americans because it was presented to General Eisenhower for his lifetime use. The rooms are exquisitely decorated in elegant 'country house' rather than 'castle' style with inimitable views of the wild coast to the Isle of Arran and Ailsa Craig. Fresh flowers everywhere and Cordon Bleu cooking from Susan Cardale. A show piece of the National Trust for Scotland.

Rooms: 5 twins, 3 en suite, 2 with shared bathroom; 1 double en suite.

Price: £75-£150 p.p. doubles, £100-£210 single.

Breakfast: Included – full Scottish/continental.

Meals: Dinner £35 p.p. Packed lunch also available.

Closed: 1 November – 15 April.

Alloway, fans will know, is Robert Burns's birthplace – a good excuse for another scotch. Doonbrae has breathtaking views over the River Doon flowing through the garden to the Carrick Hill beyond. John Pollock-Morris's grandfather's rise-and-fall electric lights are still here but the guestrooms – all on the ground floor – are being completely redecorated as we go to press. Convenient pantry with toaster, fridge and microwave, an informal family sitting room, a posher drawing room and dining room for candlelit dinner complete with views.

Rooms: 2 twins, 1 en suite, 1 with shared bathroom; 1 double with shared bathroom.

Price: £28 p.p. doubles, £30 single.

Breakfast: Included – full Scottish/continental.

Meals: Dinner £20 p.p. Available on request as is a packed lunch.

Closed: Never!

From A77 in Maybole take A719 for 4 miles following signs for Culzean Castle.

Map Ref No: 18

Mr Jonathan Cardale
The National Trust for Scotland
Culzean Castle
Maybole
Ayrshire KA19 8LE
Tel: 01655-760274
Fax: 01655-760615

A719 into Alloway on south side of Ayr. Follow Tam O'Shanter signs. Doonbrae opposite Burns Monument by Alloway church.

Map Ref No: 18

John Pollock-Morris & Moira Johnston
Doonbrae
40 Alloway
Ayr
Ayrshire KA7 4PQ
Tel: 01292-442511
Fax: 01292-442511

The house was built in the 1950s but has a very pretty garden overlooked by the ancient ruins of Dundonald Castle. Reception and guest rooms are classically, comfortably furnished (second room only let to members of same group) and you dine in style with silver, candles and linen – your hosts like to share their enthusiasm for good food and wine and their knowledge of Scotland. On a clear day you can see Arran, the Firth of Clyde and beyond and there are 20 golf courses within 20 minutes.

Rooms: 2 twins: 1 with private adjacent bathroom; further twin available for members of same party willing to share bathroom.

Price: £22.50 p.p. doubles, £27 single.

Breakfast: Included – full English/continental.

Meals: Dinner £12-£17 p.p. Available by arrangement. Packed lunch also available.

Closed: Mid-December – mid-January.

From A77 take B730 to Dundonald, right in village at War Memorial and on for 0.25 mile. Turn right up farm road. House 50m on left-hand side.

Map Ref No: 18

Robin & Elizabeth Black
The Mount
Newfield
Dundonald
Ayrshire KA2 9BH
Tel: 01563-851047
Fax: 01563-850981

The Yair is a Grade A listed 18th-century country house set in 700 acres of hill farm and woodland garden on the banks of the River Tweed. Is this not mighty evocative? The drawing room is magnificent, the dining room elegant, the library/games room snug. Open fires bring light and life, the family enjoy welcoming guests to their home and pointing them towards trout-fishing, deer-stalking, superb walks (the Southern Upland Way is here), stately homes or cashmere shops. A grand place.

Rooms: 3 twins, 1 double, sharing 2 bathrooms.

Price: £35 p.p. B&B, £55 p.p. dinner and B&B.

Breakfast: Included – full English/continental.

Meals: Dinner included.

Closed: B&B only during school term-time and closed 11th Dec – April 20th.

From Galashiels A72 to Clovenfords. Left on A707 to Caddonfoot and left at junction along river to stone bridge. Cross bridge and turn right immediately.

Map Ref No: 19

Willie & Didi Thyne
The Yair
Nr. Galashiels
Selkirkshire
TD1 3PW
Tel: 01896-850212
Fax: 01896-850212

The Thomsons will give you a genuine welcome to their Victorian manse and show you to a wonderful big bedroom with a view over either the distant hills or over the pond and the walled garden with its pool. You will find traditional furnishings, big bath towels, a black-and-white bathroom just across the landing and a fluffy bathrobe for your journeys there. They pay attention to details here. In the morning, enjoy your 'free-range breakfast'. Children over 12 welcome.

Rooms: 1 twin, 1 double with private bathroom.

Price: £20-£25 p.p.

Breakfast: Included – full English.

Meals: Not available.

Closed: October – 30 April.

'The porridge is delicious' – as is fitting in the Border Country. Birkhill is an elegant house and the style is suitably formal in the finely-furnished light-filled reception rooms to which the dogs bring a touch of controlled spontaneity. The surroundings are green woods and paddocks (the Sillars' daughter trains horses), the vegetables are homegrown organic and Sue is a trained cook. Businessman David enjoys music and shooting. Children over 12 welcome.

Rooms: 1 twin en suite, 1 twin with private bathroom, 1 double en suite shower.

Price: £30 p.p. doubles, £35 single.

Breakfast: Included – full English/continental.

Meals: £20 p.p. 1 day's notice required.

Closed: Christmas & New Year.

Towards Duns on B6438 for 5.5 miles. Left at church noticeboard. On for 0.25 miles. After Bonkyl church second right through black gate into gravel driveway.

Map Ref No: 19

Michael & Caroline Thomson
Kirkside House
Bonkyl
Nr. Duns
Berwickshire TD11 3RJ
Tel: 01361-882825
Fax: 01361-882157

2.5 miles north of Earlston A68, turn east for Birkenside. 150m after narrow bridge, at right-hand bend, keep straight on and then immediately left through stone archway.

Map Ref No: 19

Sue & David Sillar
Birkhill
Earlston
Berwickshire
TD4 6AR
Tel: 01896-849307
Fax: 01896-848206

SCOTLAND

A good-looking house with style and solid character filled with the relics of over 200 years of family history. The garden is famous, much-visited, and quite rightly so. Lady Marioth is a wonderful lady who tends her house and garden with loving care (this includes a shotgun for treatment of the grey squirrel problem), enjoys music and is very happy to welcome you into her home and introduce you to her antiques. One bedroom is particularly imposing with matching bathroom.

Rooms: 1 twin with private bathroom, 1 double with private bathroom, 2 singles sharing a bathroom.

Price: £40 p.p.

Breakfast: Included – full English/continental.

Meals: Dinner £18 p.p. Available on request.

Closed: Christmas & New Year.

Another Georgian farmhouse in the Garden of Scotland, this one with a remarkable view across the Firth of Forth. The arable farm is fully operational, the house genuinely old (1812), the tennis court playable, the pine stripped. Your wonderfully friendly jolly hostess provides beautiful rooms and superb food (more Italian and French than Scottish) and invites you to join her happy, noisy, even chaotic family – lots of lovely children – for as long as you care to stay.

Rooms: 1 twin en suite, 1 double en suite.

Price: £30 p.p.

Breakfast: Included – full English/continental.

Meals: Dinner £25 p.p. Available on request as is a packed lunch.

Closed: Christmas & New Year.

Take B6369 south from Haddington to Gifford. On leaving Gifford, Forbes Lodge is just on right through large wooden gates.

Map Ref No: 19

Lady Marioth Hay
Forbes Lodge
Gifford
East Lothian
EH41 4JE
Tel: 01620-810212

From Edinburgh take A1 towards Haddington. Turn left onto B6363. The drive to house 0.5 mile further down on left. Ignore sign to Southfield Farm, continue to concealed entrance on left.

Map Ref No: 19

Angus & Sophie Tulloch
Southfield House
Longniddry
East Lothian
EH32 0PL
Tel: 01875-853497

353 / 354

SCOTLAND

Three Georgian houses in one, nine guestrooms, a dining room to seat a house party of twenty and a warm friendly private-home feel. Despite the numbers the scale remains human, the antiques breathe family history, the private garden over the road is yours to wander in. You are a guest of this lovely lady. No 17, which once belonged to William Playfair, Edinburgh's famous Georgian architect, is a sophisticated city launching pad for forays into Edinburgh.

Rooms: 2 triples, 2 twins, 4 doubles, 1 single, all en suite.

Price: £40-£45 p.p.

Breakfast: Included – full Scottish/continental.

Meals: Dinner £25 p.p. Available on request as is a packed lunch.

Closed: Never!

Abercromby Place lies parallel to Queen Street just north of the city centre in what is known as 'New Town'.

Map Ref No: 19

Eirlys Lloyd
17 Abercromby Place
Edinburgh
Lothian
EH3 6LB
Tel: 0131-5578036

A spacious, gracious townhouse in gentle pastel colours. Nothing is overstated, it is all in sober good taste and is a most restful place in the city centre. There is lots of light, lots of wood – polished floorboards, original internal shutters, old furniture – and good textiles. You breakfast heartily, Scottishly, in the country-style kitchen. Gillian's wish is that you should be happy and comfortable – and she's good fun. Also, her teenage son is a piper.

Rooms: 1 twin with private bathroom, 1 twin/double en suite.

Price: £30 p.p. doubles, £32 single.

Breakfast: Included – full Scottish/continental/health foods.

Meals: Available nearby.

Closed: Never!

From central Edinburgh take Leith Walk northwards. Left at Pilrig Street. Through set of lights Bonnington Terrace on left part of Newhaven Road. Name & address on front gate.

Map Ref No: 19

Mrs Gillian McCowan Hill
2 Bonnington Terrace
Edinburgh
East Lothian
EH6 4BP
Tel: 0131-5549007
Fax: 0131-5549007

Only 30 years old, the house is the third to be built on this site in 300 years and the 'fantastic gardens' (our inspector) display generations of care with huge exotic 200-year-old trees, beautifully laid-out walks and a 'burn' of their own. The house is magnificent too with antiques galore, fine pictures and 'quite beautiful' rooms (ditto) in perfect traditional style. Your hosts are great fun; Angela's agency, "Noodles", supplies most of the Scottish estates with cooks and the food is, naturally, excellent. Pricey but special.

Rooms: 4 twin/doubles all en suite.

Price: From £90 per room.

Breakfast: Included – full English/continental.

Meals: Dinner £28 p.p. (must be booked in advance).

Closed: Christmas & New Year.

In beautiful countryside but very near Perth, Montague House is a lovely Georgian farmhouse with interesting furniture and family paintings. The main guestroom, with exposed beams and comfortable pine furniture, lies in a self-contained wing with its own staircase. The second room is on the ground floor and only let to members of the same group who can share the upstairs bathroom. Both your hosts are open, jolly people, Penny is a marvellous cook and a happy stay is guaranteed. Pets are welcome by arrangement.

Rooms: 2 twins: 1 with en suite bathroom and 1 downstairs suitable for accompanying children (sharing en suite upstairs).

Price: £25 p.p., children £15.

Breakfast: Included: full Scottish/continental/anything on request.

Meals: £18 booked in advance.

Closed: Christmas & New Year.

From Broxden interchange (A9 & M90) A93 towards Perth. After 0.75 miles right onto B9112 for Dunning, 4 miles to wrought-iron gates on right (Dupplin Estate).

Map Ref No: 23

From Perth A94 north towards Coupar Angus. After Perth airport 2nd right signed Rait/Kilspindie. House drive on left after 1 mile, over cattlegrid & 200m up farm drive.

Map Ref No: 23

Derek & Angela Straker
Dupplin Castle
By Perth
Perthshire
PH2 0PY
Tel: 01738-623224
Fax: 01738-444140

Roddy & Penny I'Anson
Montague House
Balbeggie
Perth
Perthshire PH2 7PR
Tel: 01821-640656

A hive of delicious antitheses. Looking out over the lush, green 'Braes O'Balquidder', this 17th-century farmhouse is blissfully tranquil by day and bursting with clamourous, merry noise by night. The brilliant mix of innovative textiles, modern art and family antiques in every room is typical of the spirited Lewis family. After an exceptional dinner continue drinking in the tiny, oak-furnished bar. Some of the best bedrooms are in the hay-loft, byre and coach house in the courtyard behind. Fishing and walking all over the 2000-acre farm; boating in the loch below.

Rooms: 3 suites, 2 twins en suite, 8 doubles en suite.

Price: £27.50-£35 p.p.

Breakfast: Included – full English.

Meals: Dinner £19-£24 p.p.

Closed: Never!

'I would love to stay here myself,' wrote our inspector. Deep in the countryside you have complete peace and old-fashioned Scottish hospitality. The gardens, somewhat wild, ramble over 20 acres and there are fine lawns with some magnificent trees. Inside: big comfortable bedrooms with very good beds, wonderfully ornate and high-ceilinged drawing room and similarly fine dining room where you eat *en famille*. Silla does traditional country cooking (lots of game).

Rooms: 2 twins en suite.

Price: £33 p.p., single £36.

Breakfast: Included – full English/continental.

Meals: Dinner £20 p.p. Packed lunch available.

Closed: Never!

Turn off A84 at Kings House Hotel following signs to Balquidder. Continue beyond Balquidder to end of Loch Voil. Monachyle is up drive on the right. The pink house.

Map Ref No: 23

Rob, Jean & Tom Lewis
Monachyle Mhor
Balquidder
Lochearnhead
Perthshire FK19 8PQ
Tel: 01877-384622
Fax: 01877-384305

From Perth A94 to Coupar Angus. In town right to Dundee, 100m right signed Enverdale Hotel; continue past hotel for 0.25 mile, round sharp bend. House 100m on right.

Map Ref No: 23

Peter & Silla Keyser
Balgersho House
Coupar Angus
Perthshire
PH13 9JE
Tel: 01828-627397

A 170-acre private loch where birds can be watched and pike fished; a great organ halfway up the main stairs with air pumped from a separate building in the grounds; a 16th-century central building with wings added in 1780 to a design filched from Adam. 'One of the prettiest houses in Scotland'? It is a very historic, very traditional country house run by delightful people. The bedrooms are big and utterly charming. Self-catering and/or B&B. Children over 12 welcome.

Rooms: 1 twin en suite, 1 double en suite. Self-catering: 1 twin with private bathroom, 1 double en suite, 1 single with private shower.

Price: £25 p.p. B&B. Self-catering: prices on application.

Breakfast: Included – full English/continental.

Meals: Available locally.

Closed: Christmas & New Year. Self-catering: 30 September – 31 March.

Rattrays have lived here for five centuries. A forebear escaped death in 1747 – the judges were reluctant to hang the world's best golfer. The gorge view (unique to Craighall) is dramatic. The 300 acres of 'Sublime-Style designed natural' woodland provide fabulous walks. A houseful of character and antiques awaits you. The North room is yellow; the French room is pink and has a four-poster. Meals may be exotic-eastern – Lachie is enthusiastic, Nicky practical about cooking. A fun and easy-going young couple.

Rooms: one 4-poster en suite; 1 triple with private adjacent bathroom.

Price: £30 p.p. doubles, £40 single.

Breakfast: Included – full English/continental.

Meals: Dinner £20 p.p. Available on request.

Closed: 22 December – 5 January.

From Blairgowrie turn onto B923 signed to Dunkeld. Just before Kinloch turn left through entrance gate posts opposite beige-coloured cottage.

Map Ref No: 23

Kenneth & Nicolette Lumsden
Marlee House
Kinloch
Blairgowrie
Perthshire PH10 6SD
Tel: 01250-884216

Take A93 towards Braemar for 2 miles. Just before end of 30mph limit there is a sharp right-hand bend and drive (also on right). Follow drive for 1 mile.

Map Ref No: 23

Nicky & Lachie Rattray
Craighall-Rattray
Blairgowrie
Perthshire
PH10 7JB
Tel: 01250-875080
Fax: 01250-875931

SCOTLAND

The estate has been in the family since 1232, the house was built in 1585 and added to – mock fortifications, etc – until Victorian times. It is unsmart and deliciously old-fashioned. The rooms are huge, there are open fires and old furniture. Paul is a Gaelic-speaking, pipe-playing historian and ecologist, Louise is highly cultivated and wonderful company and both love welcoming guests and sharing Bamff history with them. They have four children and a large farm too.

Rooms: One 4-poster with private bathroom, 1 double & 1 single with shared bathroom.

Price: £30 p.p. doubles, £35 single.

Breakfast: Included – full Scottish/continental.

Meals: Dinner sometimes available. Please check. Packed lunch available on request.

Closed: Christmas & New Year.

From Blairgowrie, A926 to Kirriemuir. After 5 miles left to Alyth. Straight through town on Airlie St. After 2.5 miles round sharp left bend. Bamff drive on right.

Map Ref No: 23

Paul & Louise Ramsay
Bamff House
Alyth
Blairgowrie
Perthshire PH11 8LF
Tel: 01828-632992
Fax: 01828-632347

Watch out for peacocks as you drive up – they strut and fret as if owners of the house. Birdlife is rife in this lovely garden where the hives hum, fruit and vegetables are produced and the chickens range free. A taste of Scotland is the theme; breakfast is Scottish and dinners may include venison or whisky-and-honey ice cream. The bedrooms are in cosy country style and the smallest distillery in Scotland is within walking distance, as is a beautiful waterfall. Lovely place, delightful people.

Rooms: 3 twins all en suite.

Price: £35 p.p. Reductions for longer stays.

Breakfast: Included – full Scottish.

Meals: Dinner £20 p.p. BYO wine. Packed lunch available.

Closed: Mid-October – 31 March.

In Pitlochry turn into E Moulin Road. Take 4th turning on the right into Tomcroy Terrace to the end. Turn right up the drive.

Map Ref No: 23

Alastair & Penny Howman
Auchnahyle
Pitlochry
Perthshire
PH16 5JA
Tel: 01796-472318
Fax: 01796-473657

The castle was built in 1583, modernised once in Georgian times (to let in more light?) and again in 1969 but it still has quirks such as gun ports and a fine arched entrance hall. Outside, the 3000-acre rolling hill farm carries sheep, deer and pheasant (the game served at dinner will be home-grown and shot); you can walk for miles, watch ospreys fishing for trout on the loch – or fish them yourself; inside is a festival of antiques and sporting prints. A fine welcoming house.

Rooms: 2 twins with private bathrooms, 1 single also with private bathroom.

Price: £33 p.p.

Breakfast: Included – full English/continental.

Meals: Dinner £20 p.p. Available on request as is a packed lunch.

Closed: Christmas & New Year.

'Dolly is wonderful!' they all say. A well-known Gaelic singer and story-teller, she loves her old house too much to vandalise it by putting in 'enn sweets'. No telly or plastic trays in bedrooms either (fresh tea or coffee in the sitting room), just nice old furniture, brass beds, creaking floorboards and somewhat excitable plumbing. Her food is superb, all local, all Scottish. How about jugged kippers, smoked haddock & home-baked bread for breakfast? No wonder people are entranced and come back again and again.

Rooms: 1 double with en suite shower; 1 twin sharing bathroom with another double.

Price: £20 p.p. doubles, £25 single.

Breakfast: Included – full Scottish/continental.

Meals: Dinner £15-£18 p.p. Packed lunch available on request.

Closed: Occasionally – please check.

From Blairgowrie take A93 north. After Bridge of Cally turn left onto B950. After about 1 mile entrance is on the right next to the lodge/cottage.

Map Ref No: 23

John & Carol Steel
Ashintully Castle
Kirkmichael
Blairgowrie
Perthshire PH10 7LT
Tel: 01250-881237

Turn off A9 at Blair Atholl and head for the castle. St. Andrews Crescent is on left as you enter the village.

Map Ref No: 23

Dolina Maclennan
Woodlands
St. Andrews Crescent
Blair Atholl
Perthshire PH18 5SX
Tel: 01796-481403

Colin (a qualified trilingual tour guide) and Fiona (a wine buff and keen cook) are passionately Scottish. Here you are in the very centre of Scotland and the peace is perfect. Fiona cooks shortbread, makes her own ice-cream and jams, bakes bread and avoids packaged foods. The handsome organic garden gushes fruit, the river yields its salmon and the countryside provides game in winter. A lovely old and traditionally-furnished farmhouse with large luxurious bedrooms and gigantic double beds run by two likeable and energetic people ... but you come here to slow down.

Rooms: 1 twin with private bath & shower; 1 double & 2 double/twins with en suite bath & shower.

Price: £30 p.p. doubles; £40 single.

Breakfast: Included – full Scottish/continental.

Meals: Dinner £17.50.

Closed: Never!

Come and meet one of our rarer moths. It lives along the stream that runs through the garden and passionate lepidopterists compete with skiers and walkers to stay at this supremely welcoming B&B. The large 1930s country house has four lovely rooms but only takes six guests at a time so you have plenty of individual attention. The vast gardens provide virtually all the fruit and vegetables used in Marjory's cooking; she makes a memorable loaf of bread while Alan talks most entertainingly.

Rooms: 1 twin/double en suite, 2 doubles en suite, 1 single with private bathroom.

Price: £35 p.p.

Breakfast: Included – full English/continental.

Meals: Dinner £25 p.p. Packed lunch available on request.

Closed: 1 November – 28 December.

From Doune A84 towards Stirling. In less than a mile, right onto B826 towards Thornhill. Mackeanston on left after 2.2 miles.

Map Ref No: 23

From A9 Perth to Inverness road take Lynwilg road opposite the southern Aviemore junction. House is the large white house facing the Cairngorms (visible from end of road).

Map Ref No: 23

Fiona Graham
Mackeanston House
Doune
Perthshire
FK16 6AX
Tel: 01786 850213
Fax: 01786 850414

Alan & Marjory Cleary
Lynwilg House
Lynwilg by Aviemore
Inverness-shire
PH22 1PZ
Tel: 01479-811685
Fax: 01479-811685

Log fires on cool evenings, al fresco breakfasts on warm mornings with homemade marmalade, porridge and haggis – red squirrels running across the bird table. There is an amazing music room with a period-piece juke-box and a piano. Elma is warm, smiling and enthusiastic about her rambling 200-year-old farmhouse and large garden, serving great quantities of 'farmhouse fayre' with homegrown veg. The big bedrooms are all fitted out on a different theme – Bamboo, Arizona, French, Hollywood – and offer the great luxury of pure Irish linen.

Rooms: 1 king/double en suite, 1 family room with private bathroom, 1 family suite with bathroom.

Price: £18-£25 p.p.

Breakfast: Included – full Scottish/continental.

Meals: Dinner £10-£15 p.p. Lunch or packed lunch also available.

Closed: Never!

The Cross is really an outstanding restaurant (stacks of awards for excellent ingredients beautifully prepared) with some equally special guestrooms. The former tweed mill has kept its original rough stone walls and beams but is furnished with modern coordinates – a perfect match. The emphasis is on natural peace: the mountains loom protectively, otters fish in the burn, red squirrels twitch and leap through the trees... and NO television. You will be treated like kings. (Not really for children or pets.)

Rooms: 9 twin/doubles, all en suite. Dinner comes with the rooms.

Price: From £85 p.p. doubles including dinner, from £105 single including dinner.

Breakfast: Included – continental/health food.

Meals: Dinner £35 for 5 courses (closed on Tuesdays). Packed lunch available.

Closed: 1 December-26 December & 8 January-28 February.

Just off A9 north of Kingussie, clearly signed.

Map Ref No: 23

Elma Gray
Mains of Balavil
By Kingussie
Inverness-shire
PH21 1LU
Tel: 01540-661932

From traffic lights in centre of village, travel uphill for 300m, then left. Down Tweed Mill Brae.

Map Ref No: 23

Tony & Ruth Hadley
The Cross
Tweed Mill Brae
Kingussie
Inverness-shire PH21 1TC
Tel: 01540-661166
Fax: 01540-661080

The former ferryman's cottage is small, simple, homely, comfortable, welcoming... and only 50 yards from the River Spey where you may see otter, osprey and dozens of other birds (see also the many nature reserves around). Elizabeth Matthews is a well-travelled, intelligent and chatty hostess. Her emphasis is on friendly attention and simple healthy fare. A superb base for walkers and she will dry your walking clothes if need be. Very good value.

Rooms: 1 twin, 1 double, 2 singles, all with shared bathroom.

Price: £17-£17.50 p.p.

Breakfast: Included – full English/health foods.

Meals: Dinner £11-£11.50 p.p. Packed lunch also available.

Closed: Occasionally when owner absent. Please check.

Not grand but very much a farmhouse, with pine and old oak furniture and attractively decorated by people who enjoy collecting watercolours by local artists. The sitting room is chintzy, the carpets plain with rugs on them... as in the bedrooms. Sally (easy-going and fun) and Malcolm farm sheep and cattle on 350 acres of gentle lush green country sloping up to the hills behind. Swim bravely in the sea 4 miles away, or drive 1.5 hours to ski at Aviemore.

Rooms: 1 twin downstairs with bath/shower en suite; 1 triple and 1 double share a bathroom upstairs.

Price: £15 p.p. Singles £17

Breakfast: Full Scottish breakfast.

Meals: Available locally.

Closed: Mid-September – 6 May.

From B970 take the road to Boat of Garten. House on left before river Spey. From A9 follow main road markings through village. Pass golf club and cross river.

Map Ref No: 23

Elizabeth Matthews
The Old Ferryman's House
Boat of Garten
Inverness-shire
PH24 3BN
Tel: 01479-831370
Fax: 01479-831370

4.5 miles north of Golspie on A9. LH side of road. Signed 'Farmhouse B&B'. 100yds off road.

Map Ref No: 27

Malcolm & Sally McCall
Inverbrora Farm
Brora
Sutherland
KW9 6NL
Tel: 01408-621208

'At peace with yourself and the world': this is Shetland. A former laird's house with its own little harbour and views across Busta Voe to the sea, this hotel says "let go here". It has elegance and high-class service but is not too grand, a superbly strong, simple exterior – thick white walls, slate roof, stone doorways – that fits the ruggedness of the land, Laura Ashley and antique decor with polished floors and oriental rugs inside. Superb Scottish food and very caring owners complete the picture.

Rooms: 6 twins, 10 doubles (one 4-poster), 1 family room, 2 singles: all en suite.

Price: £38.60 p.p. doubles, £51 single.

Breakfast: Included – full Scottish.

Meals: Dinner £22.50 p.p. Lunch & packed lunches also available.

Closed: 22 December – 2 January.

The most idyllic dwelling. The sea loch ripples beyond the garden gate; herbs flourish by the front porch; fruit ripens in the unruly walled garden. Clambering from the road down a steep, muddy field prepares you well for this slightly shambolic, utterly charming crofthouse. Honeymooners have an exclusive suite in the old boathouse. Help yourself to any boats lying around but beware of the 'dodgy dinghy'. Tony and Jackie are very informal, funny and imaginative, cooking purely vegan food that leaves even meat-eaters in raptures.

Rooms: 1 double en suite, 2 doubles sharing bathroom.

Price: £33 p.p. including dinner.

Breakfast: Included- vegetarian.

Meals: DInner included.

Closed: Never!

A970 north from Lerwick for 27 miles, through Brae and round inlet. Left turn signed to Muckle Roe and Busta House Hotel.

Map Ref No: 28

Turn off A835, 9 miles south of Ullapool. Follow road to Ardindrean. Park car by phone box & walk down steep muddy path through field to cottage on shore.

Map Ref No: 26

Peter & Judith Jones
Busta House Hotel
Busta
Brae
Shetland ZE2 9QN
Tel: 01806-522506
Fax: 01806-522588

Tony & Jackie Weston & Redding
Taighnamara Vegetarian Guesthouse
The Shore
Andindrean, Lochbroom
Nr. Ullapool IV23 2SE
Tel: 01854-655282
Fax: 01854-655292

"We made a Coffee Shop in the boat shed to play music and hang pictures but it stretched into rooms and bathrooms until up jumped the Clubhouse with its family accommodation and gallery and auditorium. ... The catchers catch, the farmers farm and the furred, the feathered and the fish arrive, wistful at our kitchen door. The boat trips trip, the climbers tell tall tales to the hill walkers and the cook provides vegetarian perfection." It is a smart hotel now but all the fun is still there ... poetry, plays, music, conversation. This book would not be the same without it.

Rooms: 3 singles: 1 en suite, 2 with shared bath; 4 twins, all en suite; 6 doubles: 5 en suite, 1 with shared bath. Also 10 bunkhouses sleeping 1/2/3/4.

Price: £40-£60 p.p., bunkhouse £10-£16 p.p.

Breakfast: Full Scottish/continental/vegetarian. Bunkhouse – not incl. but available., £1.20-£8.

Meals: Coffee shop open all day. Dinner £20-£30 p.p.

Closed: Never!

60 miles N of Inverness. From Ullapool along seafront, 1st right after pier onto West Lane. House at top of road.

Map Ref No: 26

Mrs Jean Urquart
The Ceilidh Place
14 West Argyle St
Ullapool
Wester Ross IV26 2TY
Tel: 01854-612103
Fax: 01854-612866

The ocean laps on every side; the curlew's cry echoes across the bay. Utterly solitary, this house could not be more exposed, nor more romantic. Warm and enjoyably quirky with a crackling log fire, art-deco lamps and snaking, S-shaped bookshelves. Pop art hangs above the beds; huge bath and magnificent shower in a spacious bathroom. Roger and Mairi will fill you with delicious, British food, peculiar details of local history and a desire to revisit their beguiling home. House parties of 6 or 8 people staying for 2 or more nights possible.

Rooms: 2 doubles, 2 twins all sharing bath, shower & wc; 1 separate wc.

Price: £25p.p. £5 single supplement, reduced rates for children

Breakfast: Included – full Scottish/continental.

Meals: Dinner £15 p.p. Packed lunches are £5 p.p.

Closed: 1 November – 28 February

Turn off A832 at Laide post office. Follow the road to Mellon Udrigle. Turn left at bottom of hill as entering village and continue until track reaches house, at the very end of the road.

Map Ref No: 26

Roger & Mairi Beeson
Obinan Croft
Opinan
Laide
Wester Ross IV22 2NU
Tel: 01445-731548
Fax: 01455-731635

Rural simplicity and elegance are in remarkable harmony here. Di and Inge are delightful and deeply committed to the place. They stripped the sitting-room to its original stone and pine-clad walls, put in a log-burning stove, brought in sheep, goats and chickens and resolved to serve the finest of local and home-grown food. Dine (part of the package) with white cotton, silver and china; sleep in small but pretty bedrooms. A caring, warm and cheerful haven and hauntingly beautiful views.

Rooms: 1 twin with en suite shower & wc.; 2 doubles with en suite shower & wc.

Price: £40.50-£45 p.p. inc. dinner. Minimum 2-night stay.

Breakfast: Included – full Scottish.

Meals: Dinner included in price.

Closed: November – March.

A truly Scottish farm – 200 acres on one of the Orkney islands (where the clear skies are of another world) with Aberdeen Angus cattle in the fields and open peat fires in the living room. Louise's passions are cooking (she specialises in home bakes) and gardening – there is a lovely south-facing garden and a sunroom where 'it's summer all year round'. The house is old with a modern extension, the ground floor fairly open-plan, the family delighted to meet and entertain guests from all over the world.

Rooms: 1 twin, 1 double, both en suite.

Price: £16 p.p. doubles, £18 single.

Breakfast: Included – full Scottish/Dutch/health food.

Meals: Dinner £8 p.p.

Closed: Christmas & New Year.

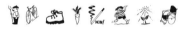

Little Lodge is just off B8021 Gairloch to Melvaig road, shortly after turning to North Erradale.

Map Ref No: 26

Di Johnson & Inge Ford
Little Lodge
North Erradale
Gairloch
Wester Ross IV21 2DS
Tel: 01445-771237

From Lyness, 3 miles to Stoneyquoy. If you pass a white kirk on your left you have missed end of drive. Farm on small hill and overlooks Longhope Bay.

Map Ref No: 25

Arthur & Louise Budge
Stoneyquoy Farm
Lyness
Hoy
Orkney KW16 3NY
Tel: 01856-791234
Fax: 01856-791234

SCOTLAND

Way off Scotland's northernmost shores lies the Hebridean Isle of Berneray; next stop St. Kilda. People come here if they love bird life – Berneray is out of the way if you haven't wings! The MacKillops describe themselves as 'a rustic couple' – Gloria is from Australia and an entertaining hostess, Don is an islander born and bred. The rooms are neat and pleasant ("people's eyes light up when they see them" says Gloria) and there are lots of vegetables from their garden served at meals.

Rooms: 1 twin with en suite shower; 2 doubles: 1 with en suite shower, 1 with separate private bathroom.

Price: £20-£24 p.p. With dinner: £26-£32 p.p.

Breakfast: Included – full Scottish/health foods.

Meals: Dinner £6-£8 p.p. Lunch & packed lunch available.

Closed: 23 December – 5 January.

A fabulous legacy of the mix of Scottish aristocracy with high colonialism. From the hall to the tiny, turret bedroom this breathtaking Victorian mansion is stuffed with hunting trophies, eastern ornaments, family portraits and antiques. Even the dining-room wall-paper is 100 years old! The MacDonalds are unassuming, informal and unphased by the magnificence of their family home. Upstairs is a warren of bedrooms of all sizes but each traditional in style. 20 acres of inviting woodland call for a gentle stroll. Be sure to visit the 'Gents' and the antique loo.

Rooms: 4 twins, all en suite; 5 doubles: 4 en suite, 1 with shared bathroom; 2 singles: 1 en suite, 1 with shared bathroom.

Price: £55 p.p. with dinner, £40 p.p. without.

Breakfast: Included – full Scottish.

Meals: Dinner £15 p.p.

Closed: Mid October – mid April.

Last house by village hall in Borve. Flights daily from Glasgow and Inverness. Car ferry from Skye. Call for advice.

Map Ref No: 25

Gloria & Donald Alick MacKillop
Burnside Croft
Isle of Berneray
North Uist
HS6 5BJ
Tel: 01876-540235
Fax: 01876-540235

On A850, coming from south, drive entrance is on left just before Portree, opposite BP garage.

Map Ref No: 21

Hugh & Linda MacDonald
Viewfield House
Portree
Isle of Skye
Highlands IV51 9EU
Tel: 01478-612217
Fax: 01478-613517

You can only reach Skiary by boat or by foot. Enveloped in the wilds of Loch Hourn it is lost to the outside world. No electricity, no roads, no neighbours; just mountains, waterfalls, otters in the loch, deer feeding along the shoreline. The tiny, pine-lined, unmodernized croft stands alone among the ruins of a 19th-century village. The Everetts brim with hospitality: hot water bottles, boats for exploring the loch and hearty dinners carried steaming from the kitchen to the damask tablecloth in the greenhouse.

Rooms: 3 twins, all with shared bathroom.

Price: £55 p.p. full board.

Breakfast: Included – full Scottish.

Meals: Light/packed lunch, dinner included in price.

Closed: Mid-October – 30 April.

This is pure heaven. No road, but come by train to Mallaig, where you are collected by boat. Once a row of cottages and now three stone lodges with views to Skye and breathtaking sunsets, there is also a self-contained Lodge for twelve. Two superb boats for charter: diving, exploring...and a Tall Ship too. Packed lunches, wonderful dinners (not just fish), a stillness that you cannot forget and delightful hosts. Is it a hotel, a B&B or a guesthouse? Who cares...go there and wallow in it all.

Rooms: 3 lodges: 1 twin, 2 doubles, all with en suite wc, shower. Also Doune Bay Lodge sleeps 12 (self-catering)

Price: From £35 – £45 p.p. per day full board. Lower prices for children.

Breakfast: English/continental £5.

Meals: Packed lunches £2.50 p.p., dinner £13 p.p.

Closed: October – April.

From Invergarry A87 N; left after 5 miles towards Kinloch Hourn. Stop at phone box near Tomdoun Hotel to warn Everetts of your arrival. Continue about 15 miles to Kinloch Hourn, at end of road where hosts will meet you.

Map Ref No: 22

John & Christina Everett
Skiary
Loch Hourn,
By Invergarry
Inverness-shire PH35 4HD
Tel: 01809-511214

No road access! They will collect you bu boat, but you must arrange in advance.

Map Ref No: 22

Mrs Mary Robinson & Mrs Liz Tibbetts
Doune
Knoydart by Mallaig
Inverness-shire PH41 4PU
Tel: 01687-462667
Fax: 01687-462667

Pine's the word. Pine-log walls, pine furniture, pine forest... and you'll pine to return. The long low cabin effortlessly houses the vast Barber family and their guests in unexpected tranquillity and smallish airy rooms. Homemade scones on arrival announce serious, characterful food to come (e.g. home-smoked fish and cheese). Guests dine in the conservatory where flowers frame Ben Nevis. Guests' children eat and play with the Barber children. Any problem, any query, Sukie and Bill will sort it out. 5 rooms even have good wheelchair access.

Rooms: 2 family, 2 double, 1 single – all en suite; 1 single with private bathroom.

Price: £50-£65 p.p. with dinner. Children free when sharing with parents.

Breakfast: Included – full Scottish.

Meals: Dinner included, but also open to non-residents. BYO wine.   Lunch always available.

Closed: Never!

The Glencoe massacre was ordered here; the Jacobites later burned down the house at the foot of the glen where history still broods. Rebuilt in 1764, it now has big rooms and antiques but nothing overly grand. After dinner, relax with a game of billiards, your skills sharpened by any of the several whiskies, then retire to your attractive room and its vast view over Loch Linnhe. Fine old walled garden where raspberries ramble and a stream tumbles on its way to the Loch. Children over 3 welcome.

Rooms: 4 twin/double, 1 double, all en suite.

Price: £36.50-£39.50 p.p. Children under 12: £20.

Breakfast: Included – full Scottish.

Meals: Dinner £23.50 p.p., children £3.50.

Closed: Christmas & New Year.

On A82, 1 mile north of Spean Bridge turn left just after Commando Memorial on to B8004 to Gairlochy. Old Pines is 300 yards down road on right.

Map Ref No: 22

Bill & Sukie Barber
Old Pines Restaurant with Rooms
Spean Bridge
Inverness-shire
PH34 4EG
Tel: 01397-712324
Fax: 01397-712433

House is just south of Ballachulish Bridge, 50 metres off A828 Oban to Fort William road. If approaching from north, 40 metres beyond Ballachulish Hotel on left.

Map Ref No: 22

John & Liz Grey
Ballachulish House
Ballachulish
Argyll
PA39 4JX
Tel: 01855-811266
Fax: 01855-811498

The most westerly manse on the Scottish mainland, the name means 'little hill of my heart'. It is so remote that the Smiths grow everything possible, bake their bread, fish in the bay and eat game from the mountains. Their much-loved house is filled with silk flowers and Janet's colourful cushions, curtains and patchwork quilts. The only traces of an austere ecclesiastical past are the tumbling graveyard and a licence prohibition (bring your own wine). Dinner is served by candlelight at a long antique table. Children over 12 welcome.

Rooms: 1 twin en suite, 2 doubles: 1 with en suite bath & shower, and 1 with private bathroom.

Price: £56-£69 p.p.

Breakfast: Included.

Meals: Dinner included. £28.95 p.p. non-residents. BYO wine.

Closed: 1 November – 31 March.

Does it matter where you sleep when you can see Rhum, Skye, Canna, otter, eagles, seals? This secluded hill sheep farm with self-catering cottages or B&B is captivating. Snow geese, rare-breed chickens and a woodland garden contrast with the rugged clifftops, Iron-Age fort and medieval burial ground. Traditional homely rooms have unexpected oriental touches that add charm and hint at the Charringtons' travels. Carolyne is a marvellous hostess – interesting, easy-going and indefatigable.

Rooms: 1 double, 1 family/double, each with washbasin and sharing bathroom.

Price: £14-£21 p.p. Family room £39.

Breakfast: Included – full Scottish/continental.

Meals: Light suppers sometimes available. Otherwise available locally.

Closed: November – February.

Enter Kilchoan on B8007 from east. House is on right just before turning to lighthouse.

Map Ref No: 22

Take B8073 from Dervaig. 2 miles past Calgary look for sign on right to Treshnish Farm – about 1 mile along farm track.

Map Ref No: 21

Roy & Janet Smith
Meall Mo Chridhe Country House
Kilchoan
West Ardnamuchan
Argyll PH36 4LH
Tel: 01972-510238
Fax: 01972-510238

Carolyne & Somerset Charrington
Treshnish Farm
Calgary
Dervaig
Isle of Mull, Argyll PA75 6QX
Tel: 01688-400249
Fax: 01688-400249

Exhilarating... the sort of wild, wacky yet beautiful place that we all long to discover. It is remote, silent... and very special. The main house, a Victorian pile, is divided into flats... some of them vast. If you are clever you can rent a couple of flats and all eat in splendour in one of them. The cottages and houses are all engagingly different, devoid of hotel-type luxury but rich in human interest and with as many comforts as any civilised person should need. Swim, walk, sail, dive, read and just lap it all up. Grand but modest, low-key and glorious.

Rooms: A variety of self-catering flats sleeping 5-11 in mansion house & 4-12 in cottages.

Price: £165-£850 per week.

Breakfast: Self-catering.

Meals: Self-catering, but also available locally.

Closed: Mansion house November – Easter, some cottages never.

Alone in a sheltered cove, this enchanting, unruly little homestead tumbles down to the shore. Goats, geese and oriental ducks roam the rocky garden. Let John regale you with his life story as he leads you to his Iona viewing spot. His cooking is so renowned that people sail to Red Bay ('Deagphort') just for dinner. Eleanor keeps to her silver-smithing workshop. Bedrooms are small and cabin-like with skylights onto the bay. A cheerful, cosy and eccentric enclave on a wild rugged coast. Not really for children.

Rooms: 2 twins, 1 double, all sharing 2 bathrooms.

Price: £15.50 p.p.

Breakfast: Included – full Scottish.

Meals: À la carte dinner always available.

Closed: Rarely! Please check.

Take Corran Ferry (01855-5243) from A82 to A861 or drive round Loch Linnhe. Left before Strontian onto A884 signed to Lochaline. Ardtornish is signed on left 2 miles before Lochaline village.

Map Ref No: 22

Angus Robertson
Ardtornish
Morvern
By Oban
Argyll PA34 5XA
Tel: 01967-421288
Fax: 01967-421211

4 miles beyond Bunessan on road to Iona ferry, take right to Kintra. After 1.5 miles turn left down track and through iron gate. Cottage is on shore.

Map Ref No: 21

John & Eleanor Wagstaff
Red Bay Cottage
Deargphort
Fionnphort
Isle of Mull, Argyll PA66 6BP
Tel: 01681-700396

The first inkling of this splendid Victorian mansion is the tips of its turrets over the trees. A phenomenal place with carved staircase, turret bathroom, vast sunny bedrooms and an exuberance of fresh flowers. The walled garden and the greenhouse (peaches in Scotland) would make any cook green with envy. There are over 100 sorts of rhododendron-rare flowers and more. The Babers are less lordly than their house, working ceaselessly to care for their land, home and guests. Children over 10 welcome.

The ebb tide rushes under the Bridge over the Atlantic in full view of this small country house, swirling down to a myriad of green-mantled islands. What better perch for a home for enthusiastic sailors? If you're lucky, Colin will take you out on his boat for the day. Nothing is too much for the Tindals, a genial, considerate couple who love their delightful home and garden. Breakfast and dinner are excellent but your attention is ever diverted by the magical views beyond. Afternoon tea in huge cups. Children over 8 welcome.

Rooms: 3 doubles, all en suite. (1 with bathroom in turret)

Rooms: 1 twin, 2 doubles, all with private bathrooms.

Price: £70 p.p.

Price: £30 p.p.

Breakfast: Included – full Scottish.

Breakfast: Included – full Scottish.

Meals: Dinner £35 p.p.

Meals: Dinner from £20 p.p.

Closed: November – April.

Closed: Christmas, New Year & some winter dates. Please check.

House is 5 miles south of Oban on A816. Turn left just after bridge beyond Kilmore and go about 0.75 miles up drive.

This white house is on right, 12 miles S.W. of Oban on B844 to Easdale, just before "The Bridge over the Atlantic" to Seil Island.

Map Ref No: 22

Map Ref No: 22

Patricia & David Baber & James Petley
Glenfeochan House
Kilmore
By Oban
Argyll PA34 4QR
Tel: 01631-770273
Fax: 01631-770624

Colin & Jane Tindal
Clachan-Beag
By Oban
Argyll
PA34 4RH
Tel: 01852-300381
Fax: 01852-300381

Farm or manor? On land or on water? The house is elegantly white, the farm definitely working; and while the site is green and earthy, the eye rests on the waters and boats of Loch Craignish. A place of stupendous views where the drawing room is the original 16th-century bothy with its coved ceiling, 4ft-thick walls and log fire. The Services have 400 acres of hill but find time for real hospitality and delicious food, including shellfish from the Ardfern landings. Excellent rooms too.

Rooms: 1 twin, 1 double, 3 singles, all with shared bathrooms.

Price: £30 p.p. doubles, £35 single.

Breakfast: Included – full English/continental.

Meals: Dinner £20-£35 p.p. Lunch available on request.

Closed: 22 December – 3 January & third week of August.

Whatever you want from outdoor life and sports, you can get it all here. Walks and climbing, fishing and sailing and golf. Plus fabulous gardens, National Trust properties and special archaeological sites. Perhaps you should book for a week? Whatever you come to do elsewhere, Knock Cottage is a comforting place to come home to; not in the least bit grand or sophisticated but welcoming and cottagey. Views over Lochgair from the drawing room, in particular, are sensational; oh...the great, still beauty of it all.

Rooms: 1 twin – 1 double, both with private adjacent bathroom.

Price: £28 p.p. doubles.

Breakfast: Included – full Scottish/continental.

Meals: Dinner £18 p.p. Available on request as is a packed lunch.

Closed: Christmas & New Year.

From A816 take B8002 to Ardfern. Go through village. 0.75 miles beyond church right by Heron's Cottage and up drive to Corranmor.

Map Ref No: 22

Hew & Barbara Service
Corranmor House
Ardfern
By Lochgilphead
Argyll PA31 8QN
Tel: 01852-500609F
Fax: 01852-500609

A83 Inverary to Lochgilphead. 0.25 mile south of the Lochgair Hotel, road bends sharply to right. Entrance 50m on right.

Map Ref No: 22

Mark & Nisa Reynolds
Knock Cottage
Lochgair
Lochgilphead
Argyll PA31 8RZ
Tel: 01546-886331

Built in 1793, this was a school in the 19th century so is on the road (which is now fairly busy), but windows are double-glazed. There are views of Loch Lomond from the lovely rooms and Judy is the most welcoming of hostesses. Her house is spotless with a slightly small-hotel air to it (John apparently likes to 'do a Basil Fawlty' and delights in banging a gong for dinner). The bedrooms are pastel-decorated except for one which is tartan – Ecosse oblige. Children over 12 welcome.

Rooms: 1 twin, 2 doubles, 1 single, all en suite.

Price: £25 p.p. Single supp. £10.

Breakfast: Included – full Scottish/continental.

Meals: Dinner £17.50 p.p. Available on request as is a packed lunch.

Closed: Never!

A fine, honest-looking, harmonious house built in the year of the French Revolution, Gartinstarry is utterly peaceful, has beautiful gardens and great views of the Campsie Range including Ben Lomond. The loch of 'bonny bank' fame is nearby too. Janey and Leslie are welcoming, warm-hearted and happy to give one end of their antique-furnished house to their guests. The bedroom is big and attractive (second room only let to members of same group). Children over 10 welcome.

Rooms: 2 twins forming self-contained suite: 1 en suite, 1 with shared bathroom when part of family group.

Price: £20 p.p. doubles, £17.50 in second bedroom.

Breakfast: Included – full Scottish/continental.

Meals: Dinner available locally. Packed lunch available on request.

Closed: Christmas.

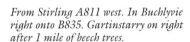

From Stirling take A811 west to Loch Lomond. House is on the right just before Gartocharn.

Map Ref No: 22

John & Judy Harbour
The Old School House
Gartocharn
By Loch Lomond
Strathclyde G83 8SB
Tel: 01389-830373
Fax: 01389-830373

From Stirling A811 west. In Buchlyvie right onto B835. Gartinstarry on right after 1 mile of beech trees.

Map Ref No: 23

Leslie & Janey Fleming
Gartinstarry
Buchlyvie
Stirlingshire
FK8 3PD
Tel: 01360-850252
Fax: 01360-850252

Kilmichael is possibly the oldest house on the Isle of Arran but its noble history is belied by its intimate character and scale. How could you resist the romance of staying in Grizel's Room, named after the 17th-century declaration of love carved on the wall, or the Forest Room with sylvan views, a 4-poster and corner bath for two? Silver, linen and crystal, water from the spring, the finest malt whiskies (naturally), glorious walks from the doorstep – and home-made ice cream.

Rooms: One 4-poster, 5 doubles – all en suite.

Price: £38-£59 doubles, £60 singles.

Breakfast: Included – full Scottish.

Meals: Dinner £27.50 p.p. or à la carte.

Closed: Christmas.

From ferry right towards Lochranza on Shore Road. To sports field opposite golf course and left at hotel sign by bungalow. Inland past Brodick church and to end of public road to long hotel drive.

Map Ref No: 17

Geoffrey Botterill & Antony Butterworth
Kilmichael Country House Hotel
Glen Cloy, By Brodick
Isle of Arran KA27 8BY
Tel: 01770-302219
Fax: 01770-302068

On Arran, a converted flax mill, beside a salmon burn, in a 'lagg' (natural wooded hollow), 10 minutes walk from the sea, with all your catering done for you and board games for rainy days – what better place for a family holiday? There are birds and wild animals of many sorts for avid watchers, terrains of many kinds for walkers, crags for climbers, tougher sports for tougher sportsmen, and log fires in the wood-lined main room. It is not smart, the welcome is genuine, you are here to let go.

Rooms: 1 twin/double, 1 double, 1 single, all sharing 2 bathrooms.

Price: £14-£16 p.p.

Breakfast: Included – full English.

Meals: Dinner £10 p.p. available on request.

Closed: Never!

On the coastal road go through Lamlash and Whiting Bay until you reach Lagg. House is 16 miles on, opposite village shop and post office.

Map Ref No: 17

Mrs Anne Caldwell
Kilmory House
Lagg
Isle of Arran
KA27 8PQ
Tel: 01770-870342

A magical and mysterious house, Golden Grove is pure Elizabethan (with Queen Anne 'improvements') in its oak panelling and heavy furniture, myriad maze-like passages, rich jewel colour scheme (the dining room is red) and formal garden; but surely the gables are straight from Bruges? Yes, a fashionable fantasy of 1580. The 'conveniences' are conveniently modern and the family foursome run a farm as well as their excellent B&B. Friendly, fascinating, worth the trip. Children over 12 welcome.

Rooms: 1 twin, 1 double, each with private bath & wc; 1 double en suite.

Price: £34 p.p. doubles, £39 single.

Breakfast: Included – full English.

Meals: £19.50 p.p., and good food available locally.

Closed: 24 December – 2 January.

Wales

Turn off A55 onto A5151 for Prestatyn. At Spar shop before Trelawnydd, turn right. Branch left immediately. Over first cross roads and turn right at T-junction. Gates are 170 metres on left.

Map Ref No: 14

Ann & Mervyn & Ann & Nigel Steele-Mortimer
Golden Grove
Llanasa, Nr. Holywell
Flintshire CH8 9NE
Tel: 01745-854452
Fax: 01745-854547

The breakfast, as you sit in the conservatory looking out over the incomparable Vale of Clwyd, is Welsh. The tiny hamlet of Llangynhafal with its ancient church is unquestionably Welsh as is the Saturday evening singing in the local pub. The absolute newness of the Houstons' 1980s house is no hindrance to their complete belonging to their adopted land. They are straightforward and helpful and their airy bedrooms are peacefully pastel. A gentle place to rest and walk.

Rooms: 2 twins, 1 double, 1 family room, all en suite.

Price: £20 p.p. doubles, with £2.50 discount per night for 2/3 night stays. Single: £25 or £20 for 2/3 night stay.

Breakfast: Included – full Welsh/continental.

Meals: Dinner £15 p.p. on request. Packed lunch for walkers.

Closed: 24-26 December.

Haven't you always dreamed of sleeping in a shippon? This typical black and white former cow byre opposite the 15th-century wattle-and-daub house has been sensitively converted for guests, keeping its low sloping ceilings, beams and small windows; you can still see the outlines of the original thick stone walls. The easy furniture adds to the relaxed atmosphere, the staircase creaks, the sitting room looks over the Vale of Clwyd and your jolly hosts will drop and collect you from Offa's Dyke walks.

Rooms: 1 double, 1 triple, both with en suite shower & wc.

Price: £16 -£20 p.p.

Breakfast: Included – full English.

Meals: Dinner £9 p.p. Also nearby inn.

Closed: Never!

From Ruthin head east on A494 to LLanbedr. Turn left by Griffin Hotel & follow sign to LLangynhafal. Take first left after Golden Lion Inn.

Map Ref No: 8

Take A494 east from Ruthin. Turn left opposite Griffin Hotel onto B5429. After 0.5 mile turn right to Llangynhafal. After 2 miles Esgairlygain is signed on right, about 50m past Plas Draw.

Map Ref No: 8

Gwilym & Margaret Houston & Sandra Edwards
Cygnet
Llangynhafal, Nr. Denbigh
North Wales LL16 4LN
Tel: 01824-790322
Fax: 01824-790322

Mrs Irene Henderson
The Old Barn (Esgairlygain)
Llangynhafal
Ruthin
Denbighshire LL15 1RT
Tel: 01824-704047

Dee Farmhouse is perched high on a hill in the hamlet of Rhewl and looks down to the River Dee. It was once a slateminers' inn – the ground floor has slate slabs underfoot – and is now a working farm. Comfortable antique furniture, old beams, welcoming spaniels and Welsh air will soothe the weary traveller. The food is simple but delicious and most vegetables come from the well-tended garden. Tranquillity is the best word to describe the atmosphere.

Rooms: 1 twin en suite, 1 twin with private bathroom which 1 single can also share if 3 in same party.

Price: £18-£20 p.p.

Breakfast: Included – full British.

Meals: Dinner £7 -£10 p.p. By prior arrangement. Local inn nearby.

Closed: November – February.

From A5 Shrewsbury turn right at traffic lights in Llangollen. Over bridge and left onto A542. After 1.5 miles left again onto B5108. Continue for 2.5 miles. Do not cross river. Red brick chapel on right, Dee Farm on left.

Map Ref No: 8

Mrs Mary Harman
Dee Farm
Rhewl
Llangollen
Denbighshire LL20 7YT
Tel: 01978-861598
Fax: 01978-861187

The Ty-Gwyn prides itself on its exotic menu – in this remote part of north Wales you can eat kangaroo, alligator, bison and venison as well as local lamb. The house was originally a coaching inn (and therefore on the road) and rambles in proper 17th-century fashion. The stone walls are bare, the staircase winds, there are antiques, old mirrors, cushions and rugs everywhere and the rooms have a delicious atticky feel. The whole family works here, the atmosphere is warm and friendly.

Rooms: 3 four poster rooms en suite; 1 four-poster suite with spa tub; 5 twin/doubles en suite; 1 twin with shared bathroom; 5 doubles: 3 en suite, 2 sharing bathroom.

Price: £17.50-£40 p.p.

Breakfast: Included – full English/continental.

Meals: Dinner, lunch & packed lunches available.

Closed: Never!

On the A5 about 0.25 mile from the centre of Betws-y-Coed.

Map Ref No: 8

Sheila & Jim Ratcliffe
Ty Gwyn Hotel
Betws-y-Coed
Conwy

Tel: 01690-710383
Fax: 01690-710383

In this superbly-preserved example of Neo-Gothic architecture (1861), the hall dominated by the oak staircase winding to the galleried landing full of period pictures, the decor painstakingly restored in Victorian style (plus modernities such as beautiful shower rooms) by Karon and Ken who know what guests want. The bright sunny bedrooms give lovely views over the bracken-gilt Berwyn Mountains. The weeping ash is 135 years old and Pistyll Rhaeadr, Wales' highest waterfall, is just up the lane.

Rooms: 1 twin, 1 double, 1 family, all en suite.

Price: £18-£20 p.p. £2 sing. supp.

Breakfast: Included – full English.

Meals: Dinner £10 p.p. By prior arrangement. Packed lunch available on request. (Restaurant available locally).

Closed: Never!

I would not care if the house were a wood shed so long as this staggering view was mine for the contemplation. Across the Mawdach tidal estuary and up to Cader Idris (Arthur's Seat), almost down to the sea, the landscape is a gift of powerful, moody, wild beauty. And the house is not a shed! Creeper-clad stone elegance outside, it is warmly traditional inside with log fires, deep armchairs, handmade patchwork bedcovers and welcoming hosts. Over 15's welcome.

Rooms: 1 twin, 3 doubles, 1 single, all with en suite bath or shower.

Price: £28.50-£35 p.p. doubles, £28-£35 single.

Breakfast: Included – full English/continental/health food.

Meals: Dinner £15.50 p.p.

Closed: Never!

We are situated 12m west of Oswestry on the B4396. In village right after Midland bank into Waterfall. Road.

Map Ref No: 8

Karon & Ken Raines
Bron Heulog
Waterfall Road
Llanrhaeadr YM Mochnant
Powys SY10 0JX
Tel: 01691-780521

West on A496. Turn right 2.4 miles beyond Esso garage in Bontddu. As come out of obvious double bend, 2 grey/green wheelie bins mark arrival at Plas Bach.

Map Ref No: 8

Hazel & Barrie Michael
Plas Bach
Glandwr, Nr. Bontddu
Barmouth
Gwynedd LL42 1TG
Tel: 01341-281234
Fax: 01341-281234

Where the Snowdonian mountains come down to the crystal sea, you will hear only the waves on the shore and the sheep on the hill. Pentre Bach promises some of the best sunsets you'll ever see. The Smyths grow their own organic veg. and Margaret was Welsh Cook of the Year 1994 – try potato cakes with laverbread for breakfast. The old stone farmhouse sheltered by wind-shaped trees has simple, functional rooms with easy chairs and great views. Self-catering cottages too.

Rooms: 1 twin, 2 doubles, all en suite; 3 self-catering cottages for 4,6+7 people.

Price: £19-£25 p.p. doubles, £6 single supplement.

Breakfast: Included – full Welsh/continental/vegetarian/health food.

Meals: Dinner £13.95 p.p. Packed lunch available on request.

Closed: Christmas & New Year. Cottages open all year.

Tim and Nancy Morrow know their business and have pulled out all the stops to do it perfectly. This handsome Victorian mansion zings with new life thanks to the Morrows' decorative pizzazz . The 'art' room is, surprise surprise, a gallery of various artworks, the library is truly 'snug', the bedrooms are decked out in a mix of French, English and contemporary furniture and styles. Great breakfasts, their own vegetables and a restaurant licence. Five acres include a Beatrix Potter-type walled garden. Lovely Montgomery is nearby.

Rooms: 2 twin/doubles en suite, 4 doubles en suite, 1 single en suite with shower.

Price: £25-£45 p.p. doubles, £35-£60 single.

Breakfast: Included – full English/continental.

Meals: Dinner £15 p.p. Hampers also available.

Closed: Ring to check

Off A493 Dolgellau-Tywyn coast road, 12 miles from Dolgellau. Entrance 40m south of old stone bridge in Llwyngwril.

Map Ref No: 8

Nick & Margaret Smyth
Pentre Bach
Llwyngwril
Nr. Dolgellau
Gwynedd LL37 2JU
Tel: 01341-250294
Fax: 01341-250885

6 miles south of Welshpool on A483. Driveway is on the right 50m after The Nags Head Hotel.

Map Ref No: 9

Tim & Nancy Morrow
Garthmyl Hall
Garthmyl
Montgomery
Powys SY15 6RS
Tel: 01686-640550
Fax: 01686-640550

Fancy a long walk through a deer park? Dysserth Hall used to be an estate of 2,000 acres surrounded by Powis Castle estate. The house now belongs to the retired castle estate agent but still has the park through which you can walk to Welshpool. The house has well-loved antiques, lovely landscape paintings, a glass collection and big, bright rooms in a variety of decorative styles, creaking oak floorboards and a very grand oak staircase. Maureen Marriott loves to meet new people of all nationalities. Children over 7 welcome.

Rooms: 1 twin with en suite shower; 1 double with separate private shower/bath; 1 single with private separate bathroom.

Price: £18-£20 p.p.

Breakfast: Included – full English.

Meals: Dinner £15 p.p. Available on request.

Closed: December, January & February (except for shooting parties).

Not obligatory, but bring children if you have them or can borrow! There are goats, ducks, chickens and dogs to be walked, watched or fed; a pianola and dressing-up box, a doll's house and loads of games. Hilary offers free babysitting and paid day-time child care if you want to walk the hills child-free. The house is spectacularly isolated in glorious country with views from every window. Hilary runs 'special events' – Fungus Feasts, Women's Wilderness Courses – and provides generous, delicious meals round the huge circular dining table.

Rooms: 1 double en suite, 1 twin/single with shared bathroom, 2 singles with shared bathroom.

Price: £15-£20 p.p. doubles, £13-£15 single. Discounts for children sharing.

Breakfast: Included – full English/health food/vegetarian.

Meals: Available.

Closed: Christmas.

Follow all Powis Castle signs. Turn off the main road and go up the lane. Dysserth Hall is first left off the lane.

Map Ref No: 9

Paul & Maureen Marriott
Dysserth Hall
Nr. Powis Castle
Welshpool
Powys SY21 8RQ
Tel: 01938-552153
Fax: 01938-552153

Leaving Machynlleth on A489, first right signed Forge. In Forge bear right to Uwchygarreg up 'dead end'. 3 miles past phone box on left, up steep hill. House on left at top.

Map Ref No: 8

Hilary Matthews
Talbontdrain
Uwchygarreg
Machynlleth
Powys SY20 8RR
Tel: 01654-702192

An upland hill farm, working hard but with time for guests... perfect; and far from roads and noise among lush low hills. The rooms are in a 17th-century converted barn that housed the Jones's cows just five years ago, all hard to believe as you luxuriate in the peace and the sounds of the brook babbling, the ducks quacking and the birds warbling. Pine furniture, beams, white walls, plain carpets. Sue was AA landlady of the year in 1995, a real pro. but with an amateur's enthusiasm.

Rooms: 1 twin, 2 doubles, all with en suite bathrooms.

Price: £22 p.p. double, £24 single. Babies up to 4 years free.

Breakfast: Included – full English/health food.

Meals: Dinner £13 p.p.

Closed: Never!

From Newtown take B4568 through Aberhafesp, right to Bwlch-y- ffridd. Bear left at next junction, left twice, then right at crossroads. Farm is down hill on right.

Map Ref No: 8

Dave & Sue Jones
Dyffryn
Aberhafesp
Newtown
Powys SY16 3JD
Tel: 01686-688817
Fax: 01686-688324

Here are secret doors and passageways, a hidden bathroom where cider was once made and a massive fireplace decorated with hops and peacock feathers. Meals are taken around a large communal table in a cheery blue and red dining room where the magnificent food and good company encourage guests to linger late, making friends and enjoying the atmosphere. Outside there are carp pools, horses, peacocks, livestock of every sort raised organically.

Rooms: 1 twin, 1 double/honeymoon suite, 1 twin/double, all en suite. Stable block: 1 twin/double, 2 doubles, 1 family room, all en suite.

Price: £40-£46 p.p. doubles, £25-£28 single occupancy.

Breakfast: Included – full English.

Meals: Lunch available on request. Dinner £12 p.p. available on request.

Closed: Never!

From A483 north of Newtown, A489 to Kerry. Through village, second right, B4368. House is 1.25 miles along.

Map Ref No: 8

Gary & Margaret Barbee
Cilthriew
Kerry
Nr. Newtown
Powys SY16 4PF
Tel: 01686-670667

WALES

Eight years of restoration and conversion work on the Legges' Grade II listed mill has had spectacular results. They have honoured the original building, even leaving corn milling machinery in the dining room. Lots of wood, flagstone and terracotta with wood-burning stoves and deeply comfortable chairs. One of the bedrooms has a wooden terrace with table and chairs and there is a separate bunkhouse and camping facilities. Food is vegetarian (except for breakfast sausages): the whole approach has a planet-friendly bias. Walking and biking is, of course, wonderful.

Rooms: 1 twin en suite, 2 doubles en suite.

Price: £18.50 p.p.

Breakfast: Included – cooked vegetarian/continental.

Meals: Dinner £9 p.p. Available on request.

Closed: Christmas.

12 miles north of Brecon on A470. The mill is set back on the left between the villages of Llyswen and Erwood.

Map Ref No: 8

Alistair & Nicky Legge
Trericket Mill Vegetarian Guesthouse
Erwood,
Builth Wells
Powys LD2 3TQ
Tel: 01982-560312

Penpont is magnificent in its grounds on the River Usk and folded into the gentle Brecon hills. It has not a whiff of pretension yet a relaxed stateliness of its own: great panelled dining room, snug book-lined log-fired library, sweeping creaking wooden staircase, vast bedrooms (one with tapestried walls) and atmosphere to dream of. Fish with flies, overflow into tents (£2.50), borrow wellies and stroll the forest garden labyrinth – wonderful! Come not to be cosseted but to be welcomed into an easy-going family home of unexpected beauty.

Rooms: 1 twin, 1 double, 1 triple, all en suite; 1 family room with 5 singles sharing 2 bathrooms. 1 flat sleeping 12.

Price: £22.50-£25 p.p. Children half price. Babies £5 (free with own bedding).

Breakfast: Included – full English.

Meals: Evening meals for groups – but book ahead.

Closed: Christmas.

From Brecon go west on A40 through Llanspyddid. Pass telephone kiosk on left. Entrance to house is on right with green hanging sign.

Map Ref No: 8

Davina & Gavin Hogg
Penpont
Brecon
Powys
LD3 8EU
Tel: 01874-636202

"Mor hyfryd a'r byd yn bell, I'r enaid yw Glanrannell." It is Welsh for 'So pleasant with the world at bay, Glanrannell in my soul will stay'. It's by the Welsh bard Elis Aethwy about this magnificent bit of Wales. Sure enough, you can hide from the world in this haven, an 'Edwardian Gentleman's Residence' overlooking serene lake, stream and parkland. The people here provide warm Welsh hospitality. Comfy, quiet rooms with fabulous views of the lawns and paddocks; menus include fish from their own river and good things from neighbouring farms. Well-known for its clever wine list. Superlative for walkers, cyclists, nature lovers.

Rooms: 2 twins, 4 doubles, 2 triples, all en suite except one with washbasin & separate bathroom.

Price: £36 p.p. doubles, £41 single.

Breakfast: Included – full English.

Meals: Lunch & dinner available.

Closed: 1 November – 19 March.

Between them the Winstones have 5 generations connected with the hotel business, so 'wine runs in the blood,' Mrs. W. admits. She greets you, puts flowers everywhere and carries luggage. He cooks with a Belgian bias (French without the portion control). The rooms are cottagey, with limed oak panelling in the drawing room. Sociability is encouraged with no bedroom TV so guests stay late, comparing notes and gossip. To help things along, Mrs. W., an expert on the subject being Belgian herself, will serve Belgian beer of all sorts.

Rooms: 3 twins, 4 doubles, all en suite.

Price: £32.50 p.p. doubles, from £40-£55 single.

Breakfast: Included – full English.

Meals: Dinner £25 p.p. Lunch available on request.

Closed: December, January, 1-14 February.

North up the A482 for 6 miles; hotel signed on left. Follow hotel signs for 1 mile.

Map Ref No: 8

David & Bronwen Davies
Glanrannell Park Country House Hotel
Crugybar
Llanwrda
Carmarthenshire SA19 8SA
Tel: 01558-685230
Fax: 01558-685784

On A438 Brecon – Hereford Road. 27m from Hereford, 11m from Brecon, 4m from Hay-on-Wye, signed.

Map Ref No: 8

Mr & Mrs Winstone
Three Cocks Hotel
Three Cocks
Nr. Brecon
Powys LD3 0SL
Tel: 01497-847215
Fax: 01497-847215

A place steeped in history (Charles I slept here) and stonework (the lions deserve close scrutiny), this Elizabethan manor stands on a Druid sanctuary, has some (purloined?) Norman bits, a minstrels' gallery in a panelled banqueting hall and possibly the only renaissance gardens left intact, but underground, in Britain. It is great but as yet not grand, a home not a hotel; there are no modern gadgets and the Beethams' enthusiasm for their estate and their country is contagious. Come and be enchanted.

Rooms: 3 twins, two 4-posters, 4 doubles, 2 singles: 9 en suite, 2 with shared bathroom.

Price: £35-£44 p.p. doubles, £36-£41 p.p. single.

Breakfast: Included – full English/continental.

Meals: Dinner £19.50 p.p.

Closed: Christmas & New Year.

The Black Mountains are an indulgent extra with such a fine house... 500 years old. The Cracrofts are the original landowners of the valley but have always travelled further afield: Willow guides people on trips overseas and Peter has worked abroad too. Lovely people... and they have generated a warmth unexpected with such an elegant house. You are greeted by a a very pretty hall and fine Georgian staircase yielding to Jacobean on the landing. Lots of Welsh oak and views of the castle.

Rooms: 1 twin with private bathroom, 1 twin/double en suite shower.

Price: £23-£25 p.p.

Breakfast: Included – full English.

Meals: Not available.

Closed: Christmas.

Three Cocks is 12 miles NE of Brecon on A438 in Hereford direction. At Three Cocks Hotel turn right then first right again to Felindre. Right at junction, past Three Horseshoes pub. Manor is on right.

Map Ref No: 9

Roger & Dawn Beetham
Old Gwernyfed Country Manor
Felindre
Three Cocks, Brecon
Powys LD3 0SU
Tel: 01497-847376

From Abergavenny A40 through Crickhowell. Soon after village, bear right on A479. Watch for unsigned driveway on left about 40 metres past turning to Tretower Castle.

Map Ref No: 8

Mr & Mrs P.K. Cracroft
Tretower House
Tretower
Crickhowell
Powys NP8 1RF
Tel: 01874-730225

A Grade 11 Star Tudor manor of staggeringly ancient beauty. Under-floor heating warms the flagstones (once Julia found a lamb settling in), the dining room is lit by many candles (even at the Welsh breakfast) and the inevitable 'modern necessities' are unobtrusive. All the bedrooms have dramatic mountain views and there is a fascinating herb and knot garden plus a newly planted yew maze. Conservation and commitment to the environment is evident everywhere. Enjoy its patina and sense of history. Sumptuous, healthy dinner on request; bring booze.

Rooms: 3 doubles all en suite.

Price: £35 p.p. doubles, £45 single.

Breakfast: Included – full Welsh.

Meals: Dinner available on request. 4 courses & coffee £20 p.p.

Closed: Never!

Come to this part of Wales; Aberaeron is a Georgian gem built around a fishing harbour, brightly painted in Mediterranean colours. Lisa, too, is a gem, enthusiastic, committed and knowledgeable about the area. She makes her own jams and serves local food for memorable breakfasts. (Make your own tea and coffee at any time; there is a fridge, too. The family lives next door.) The conservatory is filled with exotic plants and light and the walled garden is a sun trap. Traditional paint techniques, fine fabrics and very good value.

Rooms: 2 doubles both en suite; 2 twins with shared bath & shower.

Price: £20 p.p. doubles, £18 p.p. twins.

Breakfast: Included.

Meals: Lunch and dinner not available, packed lunch available on request.

Closed: Never!

North from Abergavenny on A465. 5 miles later left to Pantygelli. After 0.25 mile right up stone track between house and bungalow.

Map Ref No: 9

Julia Horton Evans & Ken Peacock
Penyclawdd Court
Llanfihangel Crucorney
Nr. Abergavenny
Monmouthshire NP7 7LB
Tel: 01873-890719
Fax: 01873-890848

In Aberaeron on the A487 from Cardigan or Aberystwyth, turn into Bellevue Terrace (one way). Halfway down on left, overlooking the harbour, is the pink house.

Map Ref No: 8

Lisa Raw-Rees
7/8 Bellevue Terrace
Aberaeron
Ceredigion
Dyfed SA46 0BB
Tel: 01545-570107
Fax: 01545-570107

Jenny, the Ayrshire dairy cow, and the dogs are as welcoming as Carole and her husband Allen. They are organic farmers so you will eat well. This is a simple farmhouse with bow windows and wonderful views of the Preseli hills. The colours are warm and natural, the decor traditional (with paintings and woollen tapestries) and there is a pretty garden for relaxing. Birds abound: buzzards, tree-creepers, wrens, redstarts. Foreign guests can take English language courses. Allen teaches, on the spot.

Rooms: 1 twin en suite with shower, 1 double private bath.

Price: £17.50 p.p. Reduced weekly rate.

Breakfast: Included – full English/continental.

Meals: Packed lunch on request, dinner £9.50, light supper £5.00.

Closed: Never!

A Regency gem reached via a winding parkland drive, with magical glimpses of the mansion on the way. No disappointment close up. Encounter peace, tranquillity and perhaps the reputedly friendly ghost inside. The house is dripping with elegant style and spoiling comfort everywhere you go including a sumptuous dinner, if requested, in the lovely dining room. This is a sporting outfit with riding and fishing arranged in season. Or, even better, woodland walks in totally unspoilt countryside.

Rooms: 1 twin with shared bathroom, 1 double with own bathroom, 1 single with shared bathroom.

Price: £35 p.p.

Breakfast: Included – full English/continental.

Meals: Dinner £25-£30 p.p. Available on request.

Closed: 10 December – 15 March.

From Aberaeron A487 south for 6 miles towards Brynhoffnant. Left at B4334 to Rhydlewis; left at red-painted Post Office and shop, first lane on right, then first track on right.

Map Ref No: 8

Carole & Allen Jacobs
Broniwan
Rhydlewis
Llandysul
SA44 5PF
Tel: 01239-851261
Fax: 01239-851261

West towards Aberaeron on A482. After 9 miles at phone box on right and Cilidu Aeron turn right to Pennant. 2 miles down hill, over bridge, on left.

Map Ref No: 8

Nigel & Wendy Symons Jones
Monachty Mansion
Pennant
Llanon
Dyfed SY23 5JP
Tel: 01545-570215
Fax: 01545-571707

The dramatic course of the River Cych is a wonderful prelude. With trout fishing at the bottom of the garden and the Pembrokeshire coastal path only 7 miles away, this is a beautiful, easy-going haven for lovers of the outdoors. Very much a family home with comfortable, traditionally decorated bedrooms, a cosy book-lined library and a more formal drawing room with grand piano. Breakfast at a sunlit table in the window of the great dining room, order a hearty packed lunch and set off to explore – Wales awaits. Tony and Sarah are friendly, easy and unstuffy.

Rooms: 1 twin en suite, 1 double en suite, 1 double with shared bathroom, 1 single with shared bathroom.

Price: £30 p.p. doubles, £35 single.

Breakfast: Included – full English/continental.

Meals: Dinner available locally.

Closed: 1 November – 1 March

M4 to Carmarthen, A484 Cardigan road, until Cenarth, left onto B4332. Continue for 1.5 miles to yellow Nags Head pub. Turn left. Llancych is 1 mile on left-hand side.

Map Ref No: 7

Antony & Sarah Jones-Lloyd
Llancych
Boncath
Pembrokeshire
SA37 0LJ
Tel: 01239-698378
Fax: 01239-698686

Cresswell House – the old Quaymaster's house – sits on the bank of the River Cleddau which will literally lap against the garden wall. Boldly decorated in sympathy with its Georgian interior. Philip and Rhian, an interesting young couple, relish producing good food, so energise for the day with a breakfast choice of house smoked salmon or homemade sausages or fish cakes. Then go and walk off the guilt along the miles of river footpaths to watch kingfishers, herons and cormorants looking for their own breakfast. Phillip, by the way, has built his own coracle. There's a fine old-fashioned pub/hostelry just a minute's walk away.

Rooms: 1 twin, 1 double and a 4-poster – all with 2 shared bathrooms.

Price: £18.50-£20 p.p. doubles, £23.50 single.

Breakfast: Included – full English/vegetarian.

Meals: Dinner (£8-£17.50 p.p.) and packed lunches available on request.

Closed: Christmas.

From A477 take A4075. Turn left at the 4x4 garage. House is on the left after 1.5 miles, just before bridge.

Map Ref No: 2

Philip Wight
Cresswell House
Cresswell Quay
Kilgetty
Pembrokeshire SA68 0TE
Tel: 01646-651435

WALES

The Quinns' house is somewhat deceptive. It looks like a neat two-up, two-down from the front, but once inside the front door you need a map! The original early 19th-century cottage has been constantly enlarged and is now delightfully higgledy-piggledy. Guests usually forget about lunch after one of Jennifer's breakfasts, sometimes served in the little garden: Welsh Rarebit, fried laverbread and bacon, eggs any way you like. Only 100 yards from the harbour and near the beach. Careful dogs are welcome to bring well-trained owner.

Rooms: 1 twin/triple with shared bathroom, 1 double with en suite shower & wc.

Price: £15-£16 p.p. Under 3s free, 3-12s half price.

Breakfast: Included – full traditional.

Meals: Dinner available locally.

Closed: Occasionally. Please check.

From Carmarthen A477. At Kilgetty roundabout right onto A478. 1.5 miles after railway bridge left into Sandyhill Road (becomes Stammers Road). House on left.

Map Ref No: 7

Malcolm & Jennifer Quinn
Primrose Cottage
Stammers Road
Saundersfoot
Pembrokeshire SA69 9HH
Tel: 01834-811080

How comforting to find an old house saved, like an old horse, from years of neglect and brought back to life! 'Freddie' has done a tremendous job and restored her 'Church of David Higher' in traditional country style – brass beds, chintz and patchwork, terracotta and beams (only the modern bar in the corner of the 'baronial' dining hall is unexpected) – while grazing a modern herd of breeding deer on her lush acres. On fine days guests can ride out in a horse and carriage for picnics.

Rooms: 1 twin with private bathroom; 3 doubles: 2 en suite, 1 sharing bathroom with 1 single.

Price: £23.50 p.p. double, £35.25 single.

Breakfast: Included – full English/continental.

Meals: Dinner £17 p.p.

Closed: Christmas.

Take B4300 from Carmarthen for about 5 miles to Capel Dewi. Leaving village follow sign on left and go down the drive off the main road.

Map Ref No: 8

Fredena Burns
Capel Dewi Uchaf Farm
Capel Dewi Road
Capel Dewi
Carmarthen SA32 8AY
Tel: 01267-290799
Fax: 01267-290003

Be the Dents' house guest, share their house, their garden, their activities if you wish. Go for the annual cricket match on the lawn with a marquee to recreate a 1890s photograph. From your window you look beyond the ha-ha and the sheep up to a Norman hill fort, down to the salmon-rich River Cothi. Merlin was born near here too. The big porticoed Georgian house has an air of faded elegance, the bedcovers are lace, the basins old-fashioned, the welcome utterly genuine.

Rooms: 2 twins with shared bathroom.

Price: £20 p.p.

Breakfast: Included – full English/continental.

Meals: Dinner available locally.

Closed: Christmas.

From Carmarthen A40 towards Llandeilo. 7 miles to Pontargothi. Before bridge in village follow 'Stoves' sign for 2 miles. Pass Cothi Vale Stoves on right. House is 180m along on right.

Map Ref No: 8

Charlotte & Gerard Dent
Plas Alltyferin
Pont-ar-gothi
Nantgaredig
Carmarthenshire SA32 7PF
Tel: 01267-290662
Fax: 01267-290662

Navigating with Place Names
or
Why so many River Avons?

Navigating your way around Britain can be much easier and more interesting if you can interpret the map. Maps contain amazing amounts of information for those who can learn the 'language'. The place names are themselves 'signposts'. For instance there is no point in looking for that B&B in Wales at Pontdulus (bridge over the river Dulus) halfway up a mountainside! Similarly, you are more likely to get appropriate directions from a local if you can pronounce the place name.

England

Celtic Origin
porth	a harbour or gateway
withiel	a wooded upland

Old English (Anglo-Saxon) Origin
bourne	a stream
bury	a fort or town
burgh, borough	a Roman fort
by	a village, homestead
chipping	a market place
combe, coombe	a narrow valley
cot, cote	cottage or sheep shelter (Middle English)
croft	smallholding
den, dean, dene	a valley
ham, hom	river meadow
ing	the people of....
ley, legh, leigh	woodland clearing
minster	a monastery
stead	place, site of, farm (in north)
stoke, stow	a holy place
thorpe	a hamlet
ton, tun	homestead, village
wold, weald	forest, woodland
worth, worthy, wardine	enclosure (round a homestead)

Old Scandinavian or Norse (Viking) Origin
hurst	a wooded hill (Berks, Sussex), a vineyard (Hants).
thwaite	a meadow, a piece of land

Wales
aber	mouth or confluence of a river
afon	river (hence all those River Avons!)
bach, fach (vach)	small
blaen	source of a river
bron	hillside
bryn	hill
bwlch	mountain pass
cae (kai)	field
caer	camp or fortified place
castell	castle
cerrig, carreg, craig, graig	stone, rock
cefn (kevn)	ridge
coed	wood
croes, groes	cross
cwn	narrow valley
dinas, ddinas	fort, camp
dôl	meadow
du, ddu (dee, thee)	black

eglwys	church
esgair	ridge
glan	riverbank
gwern, wern	marsh
gwyn, wyn, wen (gwin, win)	white
hafod	summer dwelling
hen	old
llan	church of
llyn	lake
isaf (eesav)	lower
maen	rock
maes, faes	field
mawr, fawr (vawr)	big
melin, felin (velin)	mill
mynydd, fynydd (muneeth, vuneeth)	mountain
nant	stream
pant	hollow
pen, ben	head of, top
pentref, pentre	village
plas	mansion
pistyll	spring
pont, bont	bridge
rhyd (reed)	a ford
tref, tre, dref, dre (trev)	town
ty (tee)	house
tyn	farm
uchav (eechav)	higher
ystrad	broad valley
Cymru	Wales

Scotland

Scots Gaelic Origin

aber	mouth or confluence of river
aird, ard	a promontory
alt	stream
auch	a field
ben	mountain
blair	a plain
brae	the upper part of...
cairn	a heap of stones
corrie	a hollow
dal	a field
drum	a ridge
dun	a hill fort
eilean	island
glass	grey
inch, innis	island
inver	mouth of a river
kil	church
knock	a knoll
kyle	strait
loch	lake
macha	sandy grassland
mor	great or extensive
strath	broad valley
tarbet	isthmus

Lowland Scots Origin

burn	stream
brae	a hill
ilk	the same
law	a conical hill

Alastair Sawday's Special Places to Stay in Spain

At last, the guide that takes the risk – but not the fun – out of staying in Spain.

Beautiful Spain draws you again. But how many times have you been forced to stay in one of those concrete banalities that so often pass as hotels in that fascinating country? How often have you yearned for just a little more character instead of concrete, human warmth instead of the blaring television?

This guide puts an end to your misery. It describes over 200 personally-inspected hostelries throughout Spain from grand old country mansions in Galicia to mountain hotels and little-known B&Bs in Catalonia to elegant farmsteads in Andalucia. They are mostly small, family-owned and attractive. Many are newly-converted and delectably rural. All have one thing in common: a human touch.

You will find authenticity and charm in every corner of Spain and wonderful value for all budgets.

Available from all major bookshops. Price £10.95.

Alastair Sawday's Guide to Special Paris Hotels

Alastair Sawday's
GUIDE TO
Special Paris Hotels

Some of the best hotels in Paris, selected for their authenticity, character, charm.....and superb value.

A night in Paris is far too precious to be spent in the wrong hotel.

You are off to Paris, full of hope, but there is a nagging doubt: where to stay? So you ask friends who went last year, or before... and cross your fingers. The risk of ending up in a touristy monster, or recently-spoiled favourite, is ever-present.

This book is like an up-to-date and ultra-reliable friend who knows *all* the Paris hotels and makes choices for you... whether you are rich or poor, artistic or not.

Written with wit and style by an Englishwoman living in Paris, this highly personal selection of 70 of Paris's nicest, most attractive and welcoming hotels is all you need to make your visit a complete success. You can easily save the cost in just one night's sleep in the right hotel.

Colour photographs and lots of detail. A delightful book and the only one of its kind. Price: £8.95

Alastair Sawday's
French Bed & Breakfast

3rd Edition
– Spring 1997 –
Completely updated

This guide leads you through 'deepest' France to encounters with the French in all the Frenchness and warmth of their beautiful homes.

Friendly descriptions of over 500 hosts and homes; details of rooms, prices and meals; the whole of France in 16 regions, with clear maps, directions and reference systems.

Each B&B is illustrated with a colour photograph. The guide is available in all major bookshops. Price: £12.95

REPORT FORM

If you have any comments on entries in this guide, please let us have them.

If you have a favourite house, hotel or inn or a new discovery in Britain, please let us know about it.

Please send reports to: Alastair Sawday Publishing, 44 Ambra Vale East, Bristol BS8 4RE, UK.

Report on:

Entry No _____ New Recommendation ☐ Date _____

Name of owners or hotel/B&B _____

Address _____

_____

_____

_____ Tel No _____

My reasons for writing are :

_____

_____

_____

_____

_____

_____

_____

_____

_____

_____

_____

_____

_____

_____

My name and address :

Name

Address

Tel:

ORDER FORM for the UK. See over for USA.

All these books are available in the major bookshops but we can send them to you quickly and without effort on your part. Post and packaging is FREE if you order 2 or more books.

	No. of copies	Price each	Total value
French Bed & Breakfast – 3rd Edition (To be published in February 1997)		£12.95	
Special Paris Hotels		£8.95	
Special Places to Stay in Spain		£10.95	
Special Places to Stay in Britain		£10.95	
Add Post & Packaging: £1 for Paris book, £2 for any other, **FREE** if ordering 2 or more books.			
TOTAL ORDER VALUE *Please make cheques payable to Alastair Sawday Publishing*			

All orders to: Alastair Sawday Publishing, 44 Ambra Vale East, Bristol BS8 4RE
Tel: 0117 9299921. (Sorry, no credit card payments).

Name _____

Address _____

_____

_____ Postcode _____

Tel _____ Fax _____

If you do not wish to receive mail from other companies, please tick the box ☐   BR1

ORDER FORM for USA.

These books are available at your local bookstore, or you may order
direct. Allow two to three weeks for delivery.

	No. of copies	Price each	Total value
French Bed & Breakfast		**$19.95**	
Special Paris Hotels		**$14.95**	
Special Places to Stay in Spain		**$19.95**	
Special Places to Stay in Britain		**$19.95**	
Add Post & Packaging: $4 for Paris book, $4.50 for any other.			
TOTAL ORDER VALUE *Please make cheques payable to Publishers Book & Audio*			

All orders to: Publishers Book & Audio, P.O. Box 070059, 5446 Arthur Kill
Road, Staten Island, NY 10307, phone (800) 288-2131. For information on bulk
orders, address Special Markets, St. Martin's Press, 175 Fifth Avenue, Suite 500,
New York, NY 10010, phone (212) 674-5151, ext. 724, 693, or 628.

Name _____

Address _____

_____

_____ Zip code _____

Tel _____ Fax _____

INDEX OF NAMES

INDEX OF PLACES